HELMET FOR
MY PILLOW

Robert Leckie, 1942

HELMET FOR MY PILLOW

ROBERT LECKIE

**EBURY
PRESS**

9 10 8

Published in 2010 by Ebury Press, an imprint of Ebury Publishing
A Random House Group company

This edition published 2011

First published in the USA by Bantam, an imprint of
Random House Group Inc.

Copyright © Robert Leckie

The Random House Group Limited Reg. No. 954009

Addresses for companies within the Random House Group can be found at
www.randomhouse.co.uk

A CIP catalogue record for this book is available from the British Library

ISBN 9780091937515

To buy books by your favourite authors and register for offers visit
www.randomhouse.co.uk

The Random House Group Limited supports The Forest Stewardship
Council (FSC®), the leading international forest certification organisation.
Our books carrying the FSC label are printed on FSC® certified paper.
FSC is the only forest certification scheme endorsed by the leading
environmental organisations, including Greenpeace. Our
paper procurement policy can be found at
www.randomhouse.co.uk/environment

Printed and bound in Great Britain by Clays Ltd, St Ives PLC

To Those Who Fell

The Battle of the Tenaru, August 21, 1942
by Robert Leckie

A helmet for my pillow,
A poncho for my bed,
My rifle rests across my chest—
The stars swing overhead.

The whisper of the kunai,
The murmur of the sea,
The sighing palm and night so calm
Betray no enemy.

Hear!, river bank so silent
You men who sleep around
That foreign scream across the stream—
Up! Fire at the sound!

Sweeping over the sandspit
That blocks the Tenaru
With Banzai-boast a mushroomed host
Vows to destroy our few.

Into your holes and gunpits!
Kill them with rifles and knives!
Feed them with lead until they are dead—
And widowed are their wives.

Sons of the mothers who gave you
Honor and gift of birth,
Strike with the knife till blood and life
Run out upon the earth.

Marines, keep faith with your glory
Keep to your trembling hole.
Intruder feel of Nippon steel
Can't penetrate your soul.

Closing, they charge all howling
Their breasts all targets large.
The gun must shake, the bullets make
A slaughter of their charge.

Red are the flashing tracers,
Yellow the bursting shells.
Hoarse is the cry of men who die
Shrill are the woundeds' yells.

God, how the night reels stricken!
She shrieks with orange spark.
The mortar's lash and cannon's crash
Have crucified the dark.

Falling, the faltering foemen
Beneath our guns lie heaped.
By greenish glare of rocket's flare
We see the harvest reaped.

Now has the first fierce onslaught
Been broken and hurled back.
Hammered and hit, from hole and pit—
We rise up to attack!

Day bursts pale from a gun tube,
The gibbering night has fled.
By light of dawn the foe has drawn
A line behind his dead.

Our tanks clank in behind him,
Our riflemen move out.
Their hearts have met our bayonet—
It's ended with a shout.

"Cease fire!"—the words go ringing,
Over the heaps of the slain.
The battle's won, the Rising Sun
Lies riddled on the plain.

St. Michael, angel of battle,
We praise you to God on high.
The foe you gave was strong and brave
And unafraid to die.

Speak to The Lord for our comrades,
Killed when the battle seemed lost.
They went to meet a bright defeat—
The hero's holocaust.

False is the vaunt of the victor,
Empty our living pride.
For those who fell there is no hell—
Not for the brave who died.

HELMET FOR
MY PILLOW

ONE
BOOT

1

A cutting wind slanted up Church Street in the cheerless dawn of January 5, 1942. That day I departed for the United States Marines.

The war with Japan was not yet four weeks old, Wake Island had fallen. Pearl Harbor was a real tragedy, a burning bitter humiliation. Hastily composed war songs were on the lips of everyone, their heavy patriotism failing to compensate for what they lacked in tune and spirit. Hysteria seemed to crouch behind all eyes.

But none of this meant much to me. I was aware of my father beside me, bending into the wind with me. I could feel the wound in my lower regions, still fresh, still sore. The sutures had been removed a few days earlier.

I had sought to enlist the day after Pearl Harbor, but the Marines had insisted that I be circumcised. It cost me a hundred dollars, although I am not sure to this day whether I paid the doctor or not. But I am certain that few young men went off to war in that fateful time so marked.

We had come across the Jersey meadows, riding the Erie commuter line, and then on the ferry over the Hudson River to downtown New York. Breakfast at home had been subdued. My mother was up and about; she did not cry. It was not a heart-rending leave-taking, nor was it brave, resolute—any of those words that fail to describe the thing.

It was like so much else in this war that was to produce unbounded heroism, yet not a single stirring song: it was resigned. She followed me to the door with sad eyes and said, "God keep you."

It had been a silent trip across the meadows and it was a wordless good-by in front of the bronze revolving doors at Ninety, Church Street. My father embraced me quickly, and just as quickly averted his face and left. The Irish doorman measured me and smiled.

I went inside and joined the United States Marines.

The captain who swore us in reduced the ceremony to a jumble. We all held up our hands. We put them down when he lowered his. That way we guessed we were marines.

The master gunnery sergeant who became our momentary shepherd made the fact plainer to us. Those rich mellow blasphemous oaths that were to become so familiar to me flowed from his lips with the consummate ease of one who had spent a lifetime in vituperation. I would meet his masters later. Presently, as he herded us across the river to Hoboken and a waiting train, he seemed to be beyond comparison. But he was gentle and kind enough when he said good-by to the thirty or forty of us who boarded the train.

He stood at the head of our railroad car—a man of middle age, slender, and of a grace that was on the verge of being ruined by a pot belly. He wore the Marine dress blues. Over this was the regulation tight-fitting overcoat of forest green. Green and blue has always seemed to me an odd combination of colors, and it seemed especially so then; the gaudy dark and light blue of the Marine dress sheathed in sedate and soothing green.

"Where you are going it will not be easy," the gunnery sergeant said. "When you get to Parris Island, you'll find things plenty differ-ent from civilian life. You won't like it! You'll think they're overdo-ing things. You'll think they're stupid! You'll think they're the cruelest, rottenest bunch of men you ever ran into! I'm going to tell you one thing. You'll be wrong! If you want to save yourself plenty of heartache you'll listen to me right now: you'll do everything they tell you and you'll keep your big mouths shut!"

He could not help grinning at the end. No group of men ever had a saner counselor, and he knew it; but he could not help grinning. He knew we would ignore his every word.

"Okay, Sarge," somebody yelled. "Thanks, Sarge."

He turned and left us.

We called him "Sarge." Within another twenty-four hours we would not dare address a lowly Pfc. without the cringing "sir." But today the civilian shine was still upon us. We wore civvies; Hoboken howled around us in the throes of trade; we each had the citizen's polite deprecation of the soldier, and who among us was not certain that he was not long for the ranks?

Our ride to Washington was silent and uneventful. But once we had arrived in the capital and had changed trains the atmosphere seemed to lift. Other Marine recruits were arriving from all over the east. Our contingent was the last to arrive, the last to be crammed aboard the ancient wooden train that waited, puffing, dirty-in-the-dark, smelling of coal—waited to take us down the coast to South Carolina. Perhaps it was because of the dilapidated old train that we brightened and became gay. Such a dingy, tired old relic could not help but provoke mirth. Someone pretended to have found a brass plate beneath one of the seats, and our car rocked with laughter as he read, "This car is the property of the Philadelphia Museum of American History." We had light from kerosene lamps and heat from a potbellied stove. Draughts seemed to stream from every angle and there was a constant creaking and wailing of wood and wheels that sounded like an endless keening. Strange old train that it was, I loved it.

Comfort had been left behind in Washington. Some of us already were beginning to revel in the hardship of the train ride. That intangible mystique of the marine was somehow, even then, at work. We were having it rough, which is exactly what we expected and what we had signed up for. That is the thing: having it rough. The man who has had it roughest is the man to be most admired. Conversely, he who has had it the easiest is the least praiseworthy.

Those who wished to sleep could cat-nap on the floor while the train lurched down through Virginia and North Carolina. But these were few. The singing and the talk were too exciting.

The boy sitting next to me—a handsome blond-haired youth from south Jersey—turned out to have a fine high voice. He sang several songs alone. There being a liberal leavening of New York Irish among us, he was soon singing Irish ballads.

Across the aisle there was another boy, whom I shall call Armadillo because of his lean and pointed face. He was from New York and had attended college there. Being one of the few college men present, he had already established a sort of literary clique.

The Armadillo's coterie could not equal another circle farther down the car. This had at its center a stocky, smiling redhead. Red had been a catcher for the St. Louis Cardinals and had once hit a home run at the Polo Grounds off the great Carl Hubbell.

There was no measuring the impact of such a celebrity on our group, composed otherwise of mediocrities like myself. Red had been in the big time. He had held daily converse with men who were nothing less than the idols of his newfound comrades. It was quite natural they should ring him round; consult him on everything from pitching form to the Japanese General Staff.

"Whaddya think it'll be like at Parris Island, Red?"

"Hey, Red—you think the Japs are as tough as the newspapers say they are?"

It is an American weakness. The success becomes the sage. Scientists counsel on civil liberty; comedians and actresses lead political rallies; athletes tell us what brand of cigarette to smoke. But the redhead was equal to it. It was plain in his case what travel and headlines can do. He was easily the most poised of us all.

But I suspect even Red's savoir-faire got a rude jolt when we arrived in Parris Island. We had been taken from the railroad station by truck. When we had dismounted and had formed a motley rank in front of the red brick mess hall, we were subjected to the classic greeting.

"Boys," said the sergeant who would be our drill instructor. "Boys—Ah want to tell yawl something. Give youah hearts to Jesus, boys—'cause youah ass belongs to me!"

Then he fell us in after our clumsy civilian fashion and marched us into the mess hall.

There were baloney and lima beans. I had never eaten lima beans before, but I did this time; they were cold.

The group that had made the trip from New York did not survive the first day in Parris Island. I never saw the blond singer again, nor most of the others. Somehow sixty of us, among the hundreds who had been aboard that ancient train, became a training platoon, were assigned a number and placed under the charge of the drill sergeant who had delivered the welcoming address.

Sergeant Bellow was a southerner with a fine contempt for northerners. It was not that he favored the southerners; he merely treated them less sarcastically. He was big. I would say six feet four inches, two hundred thirty pounds.

But above all he had a voice.

It pulsed with power as he counted the cadence, marching us from the administration building to the quartermaster's. It whipped us, this ragged remnant, and stiffened our slouching civilian backs. Nowhere else but in the Marine Corps do you hear that peculiar lilting cadence of command.

"Thrip-faw-ya-leahft, thrip-faw-ya-leahft."

It sounds like an incantation; but it is merely the traditional "three-four-your-left" elongated by the southern drawl, made sprightly by being sung. I never heard it done better than by our sergeant. Because of this, and because of his inordinate love of drill, I have but one image of him: striding stiff-backed a few feet apart from us, arms thrust out, hands clenched, head canted back, with the whole body following and the great voice ceaselessly bellowing, "Thrip-faw-ya-leahft, thrip-faw-ya-leahft."

Sergeant Bellow marched us to the quartermaster's. It was there we were stripped of all vestiges of personality. It is the quartermasters who make soldiers, sailors and marines. In their presence, one strips down. With each divestment, a trait is lost; the discard of a garment marks the quiet death of an idiosyncrasy. I take off my socks; gone is a propensity for stripes, or clocks, or checks, or even solids; ended is a tendency to combine purple socks with brown tie. My socks henceforth will be tan. They will neither be soiled, nor rolled, nor gaudy, nor restrained, nor holey. They will be tan. The only other thing they may be is clean.

So it is with it all, until one stands naked, struggling with an embarrassment that is entirely lost on the laconic shades who work in quartermaster sheds.

Within—in the depths the psychiatrists call subliminal—a human spark still sputters. It will never go quite out. Its vigor or its desuetude is in exact proportion to the number of miles a man may put between himself and his camp.

Thus naked, thus quivering, a man is defenseless before the quartermaster. Character clings to clothes that have gone into the discard, as skin and hair stick to adhesive tape. It is torn from you. Then the quartermaster shades swarm over you with measuring tape. A cascade of clothes falls upon you, washing you clean of personality. It is as though some monstrous cornucopia poised in the air above has been tilted; and a rain of caps, gloves, socks, shoes, underwear, shirts, belts, pants, coats falls upon your unfortunate head. When you have emerged from this, you are but a number: 351391 USMCR. Twenty minutes before, there had stood in your place a human being, surrounded by some sixty other human beings. But now there stood one number among some sixty others: the sum of all to be a training platoon, but the parts to have no meaning except in the context of the whole.

We looked alike, as Chinese seem to Westerners and, I suppose, vice versa. The color and cut of our hair still saved us. But in a minute these too would fall.

The cry rose as we marched to the barbers: "You'll be sorree!" Before the last syllable of the taunt had died away, the barber had sheared me. I think he needed four, perhaps five, strokes with his electric clipper. The last stroke completed the circle. I was now a number encased in khaki and encompassed by chaos.

And it was the second of these twin denominators of Parris Island that was the real operative thing. In six weeks of training there seemed not to exist a single pattern—apart from meals. All seemed chaos: marching, drilling in the manual of arms; listening to lectures on military courtesy—"In saluting, the right hand will strike the head at a forty-five-degree angle midway of the right eye"; listening to lectures on marine jargon—"From now on everything, floor, street, ground, everything is 'the deck' "; cleaning and polishing one's rifle until it shone like an ornament; shaving daily whether hairy or beardless. It was all a jumble.

"Whadda we gonna do—salute the Japs to death?"

"No, we're gonna blind them with spit and polish."

"Yeah—or barber the bastards."

All the logic seemed to be on our side. The Marine Corps seemed a madness.

————

They had quartered us on the second floor of a wooden barracks and they kept us there. Save for a week or so on the rifle range and Sunday Masses, I never stirred from that barracks but at the beck of Sergeant Bellow. We had no privileges. We were half-baked; no longer civilians, just becoming marines. We were like St. Augustine's definition of time: "Out of the future that is not yet, into the present that is just becoming, back to the past that no longer is."

And always the marching.

March to the mess hall, march to the sick bay, march to draw rifles slimy with cosmoline, march to the water racks to scrub them clean, march to the marching ground. Feet slapping cement, treading the packed earth, grinding to a halt with rifle butts clashing. "To the rear, march!...Forrr-ward, march!...Left oblique, march!... Platoon, halt!"...*clash, clash*... "Right shouldeh, ahms!"... *slap, slap...my finger! my red and white finger*... "Goddammit, men! Strike youah pieces! Hear me? Strike youah pieces, y'hear? Ah want noise! Ah want blood! Noise! Blood! Pre-sent, ahms!"...*my finger!*... "Forrr-ward, march!"...*now again...march, march, march...*

It was a madness.

But it was discipline.

Apart from us recruits, no one in Parris Island seemed to care for anything but discipline. There was absolutely no talk of the war; we heard no fiery lectures about killing Japs, such as we were to hear later on in New River. Everything but discipline, Marine Corps discipline, was steadfastly mocked and ridiculed, be it holiness or high finance. These drill instructors were dedicated martinets. Like the sensualist who feels that if a thing cannot be eaten, drunk, or taken to bed, it does not exist, so were these martinets in their outlook. All was discipline.

It is not an attitude to be carried over into pursuits civilian; but it cannot be beaten for straightening civilian backs.

Sergeant Bellow was as strict as most. He would discipline us in the ordinary way: command a man to clean out the head with a toothbrush, or sleep with one's rifle because it had been dropped, or worse, called "a gun." But above all he insisted on precision in marching.

Once he grabbed me by the ear when I had fallen out of step. I am short, but no lightweight; yet he all but lifted me off my feet.

"Lucky," he said with a grim smile, seeming to delight in mispronouncing my name. "Lucky—if you don't stay in step they'll be two of us in the hospital—so's they can get mah foot out of youah ass!"

Bellow boasted that though he might drill his men into exhaustion beneath that semitropical South Carolina sun, he would never march them in the rain. Magnificent concession! Yet there were other instructors who not only drilled their charges in the downpour, but seemed to delight in whatever discomfiture they could inflict upon them.

One, especially, would march his platoon toward the ocean. His chanted cadence never faltered. If they hesitated, breaking ranks at the water's edge, he would fly into a rage. "Who do you think you are? You're nothing but a bunch of damned boots! Who told you to halt? I give the orders here and nobody halts until I tell them to."

But if the platoon would march on resolutely into the water, he would permit his cadence to subside unnoticed until they had gone knee-deep, or at least to the point where the salt water could not reach their precious rifles. Then he would grin and simulate anger. "Come back here, you mothers' mistakes! Get your stupid behinds out of that ocean!"

Turning, fuming, he would address Parris Island in general: "Who's got the most stupid platoon on this whole damned island? That's right, me! I got it!"

On the whole, the sergeants were not cruel. They were not sadists. They believed in making it tough on us, but they believed this for the purpose of making us turn out tough. Only once did I see something approaching cruelty. A certain recruit could not march without downcast eyes. Sergeant Bellow roared and roared at him until even his iron voice seemed in danger of breaking. At last he hit upon a remedy. The hilt of a bayonet was tucked beneath the belt of the recruit, and the point beneath his throat. Before our round and fearful eyes, he was commanded to march.

He did. But when his step faltered, when his eye became fixed and his breathing constricted, the sergeant put an end to it. Something like fear had communicated itself from recruit to sergeant, and Bellow hastened to remove the bayonet. I am sure the sergeant has had more cause to remember this incident than has his victim.

2

It was difficult to form a lasting friendship then. Everyone realized that our unit would be broken up once the "boot" period ended. Some would go to sea, most would fill the ranks of the Fleet Marine force at New River, others would stay on at Parris Island. Nor was there much chance of camaraderie, confined as we were to those high-ceiled barracks. Warmth there was, yes, but no intimacy.

Many friendships were mine in the Marine Corps, but of these I will write in another place. Here the tale concerns a method, the making of marines.

It is a process of surrender. At every turn, at every hour, it seemed, a habit or a preference had to be given up, an adjustment had to be made. Even in the mess hall we learned that nothing mattered so little as a man's own likes or dislikes.

I had always suspected I would not like hominy grits. I found that I did not; I still do not. But on some mornings I ate hominy or went hungry. Often my belly rumbled, ravenously empty, until the noon meal.

Most of us had established ideas of what passes for good table manners. These did not include the thick sweating arm of a neighbor thrust suddenly across our lips, or the trickle-down-from-the-top method of feeding, whereby the men at the head of the table, receiving the metal serving dishes from the messmen, always dined to repletion, greedily impervious of the indignant shouts of the famished ones in the middle or at the end.

Some of us might be disquieted at the sight of knives laden with peas or the wolfish eating noises that some of the men made, but we were becoming less and less sensitive in more and more places. Soon my taste buds served only as intestinal radar—to warn me that food was coming—and my sense of propriety deserted for the duration.

Worst in all this process of surrender was the ruthless refusal to permit a man the slightest privacy. Everything was done in the open. Rising, waking, writing letters, receiving mail, making beds, washing, shaving, combing one's hair, emptying one's bowels—all was done in public and shaped to the style and stricture of the sergeant.

Even food packages from home were seized by the drill instructor. We were informed of their arrival; that the drill instructor had sampled them; that he had found them tasty.

What! Now you are aroused! This is too much. This is tampering with the United States Mails! Ah, my friend, let me ask you this. Between the United States Mails and the United States Marines, who do you say would win?

If you are undone in Parris Island, taken apart in those first few weeks, it is at the rifle range that they start to put you together again.

Bellow marched us most of the way to the rifle range—about five miles—in close order drill. (There is close order drill and there is route march, and the first is to the last as standing is to slouching.) We had our packs on our backs. Our sea bags would be at the tents when we arrived. We would complain of living out of packs and sea bags, blissfully unaware of the day when either would be a luxury.

Then more than ever Bellow seemed a thing of stone: still lance-straight, iron voice tireless. Only at the end of the march did it sound a trifle cracked; a heartening sign, as though to assure us there was an impure alloy of us in him, too.

We lived in tents at the rifle range, six men to a tent. Mine had wooden flooring, which most of the tents did not, and my tentmates and I counted this a great blessing. Nor did we fail to perceive the hand of Providence in keeping us six New Yorkers and Bostonians together; northern wheat separated from southern chaff. But the morning, the cold coastal morning, brought an end to that flattering notion. Yankee sangfroid was shattered by those rebel yells of glee which greeted the sound of our chattering teeth and the sight of our blue and quivering lips.

"Hey, Yank—Ah thought it was cold up Nawth. Thought you was used to it. Haw! Lookit them, lookit them big Yanks' lips chatterin'."

Bellow was so tickled he lost his customary reserve.

"Ah guess youah right," Bellow said. "Ever time Ah come out heah Ah hear teeth chatterin'. And evra time it's nawth'n teeth. Ah dunno." He shook his head. "Ah dunno. Ah still cain't see how we lost."

In another half hour, the sun would be shining intensely, and we would learn what an alternating hell of hot and cold the rifle range could be.

After washing, a surprise awaited us new arrivals in the head. Here was a sort of hurdle on which the men sat, with their rear ends poised above a stained metal trough inclined at an angle down which fresh water coursed. A group had gathered at the front of this trough, where the water was pumped in. Fortunately I was not among those engaged on the hurdle at the time. I could watch the surprise. One of the crowd had a handful of loosely balled newspapers. He placed them in the water. He lighted them. They caught the current and were off.

Howls of bitter surprise and anguish greeted the passing of the fire ship beneath the serried white rears of my buddies. Many a behind was singed that morning, and not for as long as we were at the rifle range did any of us approach the trough without misgivings. Of course, we saw the foul trick perpetrated on other newcomers, which was hilarious.

We got our inoculations at the rifle range. Sergeant Bellow marched us up to the dispensary, in front of which a half dozen men from another platoon were strewn about in various stages of nausea, as though to warn us what to expect.

Getting inoculated is inhuman. It is as though men were being fed into a machine. Two lines of Navy corpsmen stood opposite each other, but staggered so that no one man directly confronted another. We walked through this avenue. As we did, each corpsman would swab the bared arm of the marine in front of him, reach a hand behind him to take a loaded hypodermic needle from an assistant, then plunge the needle into the marine's flesh.

Thus was created a machine of turning bodies and proffering, plunging arms, punctuated by the wickedly glinting arc of the needle, through which we moved, halted, moved on again. It had the efficiency of the assembly line, and also something of the assembly line's inability to cope with human nature.

One of my tentmates, called the Wrestler because of his huge strength and a brief career in the ring, had no idea of what was happening. He stood in front of me, in position to receive the needle; but he was so big he seemed to be in front of both corpsmen at the same time.

While the corpsman on his right was swabbing, jabbing, so was the corpsman on his left.

The Wrestler took both volleys without a shiver. But then—before my horrified gaze, so quickly that I could not prevent it—the corpsmen went through their arm-waving, grasping motions again, and fired two more bursts into the Wrestler's muscular arms.

This was too much, even for the Wrestler.

"Hey, how many of these do I get?"

"One, stupid. Move on."

"One, hell! I've had four already!"

"Yeah, I know. You're the base commander, too. Get going, I told you—you're holding up the line."

I broke in, "He isn't kidding. He did get four. You both gave him two shots."

The corpsmen gaped in dismay. They saw unmistakable chagrin on the Wrestler's blunt features and something like mirth on mine. They grabbed him and propelled him to one of the dispensary doctors. But the doctor showed no alarm. He made his diagnosis in the context of the Wrestler's muscles and iron nerve.

"How do you feel?"

"Okay. Just burned up."

"Good. You're probably all right. If you feel sick or nauseous, let me know."

It is the nature of anticlimax to report that the Wrestler did not feel sick. As for nausea, this engulfed the oversensitive among us who witnessed his cavalry charge upon the meat loaf some fifteen minutes later.

The rifle range also gave me my first full audition of the marine cursing facility. There had been slight samplings of it in the barracks, but never anything like the utter blasphemy and obscenity of the rifle range. There were noncommissioned officers there who could not put two sentences together without bridging them with a curse, an oath, an imprecation. To hear them made our flesh creep, made those with any depth of religious feeling flush with anger and wish to be at the weather-beaten throats of the blasphemers.

We would become inured to it, in time, have it even on our own lips. We would come to recognize it as meaning no offense. But then it shocked us.

How could they develop such facility with mere imprecation? This was no vituperation. It was only cursing, obscenity, blasphemy, profanity—none of which is ever profuse or original—yet it came spouting out in an amazing variety.

Always there was the word. Always there was that four-letter ugly sound that men in uniform have expanded into the single substance of the linguistic world. It was a handle, a hyphen, a hyperbole; verb, noun, modifier; yes, even conjunction. It described food, fatigue, metaphysics. It stood for everything and meant nothing; an insulting word, it was never used to insult; crudely descriptive of the sexual act, it was never used to describe it; base, it meant the best; ugly, it modified beauty; it was the name and the nomenclature of the voice of emptiness, but one heard it from chaplains and captains, from Pfc.'s and Ph.D.'s—until, finally, one could only surmise that if a visitor unacquainted with English were to overhear our conversations he would, in the way of the Higher Criticism, demonstrate by measurement and numerical incidence that this little word must assuredly be the thing for which we were fighting.

On the firing line, angry sergeants filled the air with their cursing, while striving to make riflemen of us in what had become an abbreviated training course. Marines must learn to fire standing, prone and sitting. Perhaps because the sitting position is the hardest to learn, that posture had some sort of vogue at the Parris Island rifle range.

They impressed the fashion upon us for two whole days on that miserable island's blasted blistering sand dunes. We sat in the sun with sand in our hair, our ears, our eyes, our mouths. The sergeants didn't care where the sand was, as long as it was not on the oiled metal parts of our precious rifles. There was no mercy for the unfortunate man who permitted this to happen. Punishment came swiftly:

a hard kick and a horrible oath screamed directly into the miscreant's ear.

To assume the sitting position, as the sergeant instructor would say, was to inflict upon yourself the stretching torture of the rack.

The rifle was held in the left hand, at the center or "balance of the piece." But the left arm had been inserted through a loop of the rifle sling, which was run up the arm to the bicep, where it was drawn unbelievably tight. Thus held, while sitting with the legs crossed, Buddha-style, the butt of the rifle was some few inches away from the right shoulder. The trick was to fit that butt snugly against the right shoulder, so that you could lay the cheek alongside the right hand, sight along the barrel, and fire.

The first time I tried it I concluded it to be impossible, unless my back would part down the middle permitting each side of my torso to swing around and to the front as though hinged. Otherwise, no. Otherwise, the sling would cut my left arm in two, or my head would snap off from the strain of turning my neck, or I would have to risk it and aim the rifle single-handed, as a pistol. Fortunately, if I may use the word, the decision was not mine. Sergeant Bellow came over.

"Trouble?" he inquired sweetly.

His manner should have warned me, but I mistook it for an unsuspected human streak.

"Yes, sir."

"My gracious."

It was too late. I was caught. I looked up at him with dumb, pleading eyes.

"Okay, lad, you jes get that rifle firmly in the left hand. Fine. Now the right. My, my. That is hard, ain't it?"

Whereupon Sergeant Bellow sat on my right shoulder. I swear I heard it crack. I thought I was done. But I suppose it did nothing more than stretch a few ligaments. It worked. My right shoulder met

HELMET FOR MY PILLOW | 19

the rifle butt and my left arm remained unsevered, and that was how I learned the unprofitable sitting position of shooting.

I saw but one Jap killed by a shot fired from the sitting position, and this only when no fire was coming from the enemy.

Still it was amazing how the marines could teach us to shoot within the few days they had us on the range; that is, teach the remarkable few among us who needed instruction. Most of us knew how to shoot; even, surprisingly, the big-city boys. I have no idea of how or where, in the steel-and-concrete wilderness of our modern cities, these boys had developed prowess in what seems a countrified pastime. But shoot they could, and well.

All the southerners could shoot. Those from Georgia and the border state of Kentucky seemed the best. They suffered the indignity of the rifle sling while "snapping in" on the sand dunes. But when live ammunition was issued and the shooting butts were run up, they scorned such effete support, cuddled the rifle butts under their chins and blazed away. The drill instructors let them get away with it. After all, there is no arguing with a bull's-eye.

I was one of those unacquainted with powder. I had never fired a rifle before, except an occasional twenty-two in a carnival shooting gallery or the gaudy arcades of midtown New York. A thirty-caliber Springfield seemed to me a veritable cannon.

The first time I sat on the firing line, with two five-round clips beside me, and the warning "Load and lock!" floating up from the gunnery sergeant, I felt as a small animal must feel upon the approach of an automobile. Then came the feared commands.

"All ready on the firing line!"

"Fire!"

BA-ROOM!

It was the fellow on my right. The sound seemed to split my eardrums. I jumped. Then the entire line became a splitting, roaring cauldron of sound; and I got my Springfield working with the rest of them, firing, ejecting, reloading. The ten rounds were gone in seconds. Silence came, and with it a ringing in my ears. They still ring.

It was not long before I overcame my timidity and began to enjoy shooting. Of course, I made the mistakes all neophytes make—shooting at the wrong target, shooting under the bull's-eye, getting my windage wrong. But I progressed and when the day came to fire for record I had the monumental conceit to expect I would qualify as an expert. An Expert Rifleman's badge is to shooting what the Medal of Honor is to bravery. It even brought five dollars a month extra pay, a not inconsiderable sum to one earning twenty-one.

The day when we shot for record—that is, when our scores would be official and determine whether we qualified or not—dawned windy and brutally cold. I remember it as dismal, and that I longed to be near the fires around which the sergeants clustered, smoking cigarettes and forcing a gaiety I am sure no one could feel. My eyes ran water all day. When we fired from the six-hundred-yard range, I think I could just about make out the target.

I failed miserably. I qualified for nothing. A handful qualified as marksmen, two or three as sharpshooters, none as experts. Once we had shot for "record" we were marines. There were a few other skills to be learned—the block-parry-thrust of bayonet drill or pistol shooting—but these had no high place in the marine scale of values. The rifle is the marine's weapon. So it was that we marched back to the barracks, with our chests swelling with pride and our feet slapping the pavement, with the proud precision of men who had mastered the Springfield, or at least pretended that they had.

We were veterans. When we arrived at the barracks, our path crossed that of a group of incoming recruits, still in civilian clothes, seeming to us unkempt, bedraggled as birds caught in the rain. As though by instinct we shouted with one voice: "You'll be sorree!" Bellow grinned with delight.

3

In five weeks they had made us over. Another week of training remained, but the desired change already had taken place. Most important in this transformation was not the hardening of my flesh or the sharpening of my eyes, but the new attitude of mind.

I was a marine. Automatically this seemed to raise me above the plodding herd of servicemen. I would speak disparagingly of soldiers as "dog-faces" and sailors as "swab-jockeys." I would guffaw when the sergeant referred scathingly to West Point as "that boys' school on the Hudson." I would accept as gospel truth those unverifiable accounts of army or navy officers resigning their commissions to sign up as marine privates. I would acquire a store of knowledge covering the history of the Corps and would delight in relating anecdotes pointing up the invincibility of the embattled marine. To anyone but another marine, I would become insufferable.

For the next week or so we merely went through the motions while awaiting assignment. We talked easily of "sea duty" or "guard duty." In these waking dreams we all wore dress blue uniforms, drank copiously, danced, copulated, and generally played the gallant. Occasionally, as the name of a family miscreant haunts the conversation of reunions, the name of "New River" popped up. This is the base where the First Marine Division was forming. At New River there were no dress blues, no girls, no dance bands; there was only beer and that marshland called the boondocks. To mention New River was to produce painful pauses in the talk, until it would be forgotten in the next onrush of happy speculation.

The day for departure came.

We swung our sea bags onto supply trucks. We donned our packs. We fell out gaily on the sidewalk before the barracks. We stood in the shadow of the balcony, a place made odious to us one day, when, to punish a butterfingers who had dropped his rifle, Bellow had commanded him to stand there, erect, rifle at port arms, chanting from sunup to sundown: "I'm a bad boy, I dropped my rifle."

There we stood, awaiting orders. Bellow fell us in. He ran us through the manual of arms. Our hands, slapping the rifle slings, made sure sounds.

"At ease. Fall out. Get on those trucks."

We scrambled aboard. Someone at last mustered the courage to inquire: "Where we goin', Sergeant?"

"New River."

The trucks drove off in silence. I remember Bellow watching as we pulled away, and how astonished I was to see the sadness in his eyes.

We arrived at New River in darkest night. We had come from South Carolina by rail. There had been a good meal in the diner, as there always was in train travel. We had slept in our seats; packs on the racks above us, rifles by our sides.

They fell us out of the train with much shouting and flashing of lights, and we formed ranks on the siding. All was shadowy. None of these yelling rushing figures—the N.C.O.'s and officers who received us—seemed related to reality, except in those moments when a flashlight might pin one of them against the darkness. Black as it was, I was still able to gain the impression of vastness; the dome of heaven arching darkly overhead and stretching away from us—a limitless flatness broken only by silent huts.

They marched us quickly to a lighted oblong hut, with a door at either end. We stood at one end, while an N.C.O. called our names.

"Leckie."

I detached myself from my platoon, ending, in that motion, my association with the majority of the men who had been my comrades for six weeks.

I walked quickly into the lighted hut. An enlisted man bade me sit down opposite his desk. There were three or four others like him in the hut, similarly "interviewing" new arrivals. He asked questions rapidly, interested only in my answers, ignoring me. Name, serial number, rifle number, etc.—all the dry detail that tells nothing of a man.

"What'd you do in civilian life?"

"Newspaper, sports writer."

"Okay, First Marines. Go out front and tell the sergeant."

That was how the Marines classified us. The questions were perfunctory. The answers were ignored. Schoolboy, farmer, scientist-of-the-future—all were grist to the reception mill and all came forth neatly labeled: First Marines. There were no "aptitude tests," no "job analyses." In the First Marine Division the presumption was that a man had enlisted to fight. No one troubled about civilian competence.

It may have been an affront to those vestiges of civilian self-esteem which Parris Island had not had time to destroy, but New River soon would take care of that. Here, the only talent was that of the foot soldier, the only tool the hand gun; here the cultivated, the oblique, the delicate soon perished, like gardenias in the desert.

I felt the power of that attitude, and I felt, for the first time in my life, an utter submission to authority as I emerged from the lighted hut and mumbled "First Marines" to a cluster of sergeants standing there expectantly. One of them pointed with his flashlight to a group of men; I took my place among them. About a half dozen other groups were being formed in the same way.

Then, at a command, I swung up on a truck with my new comrades. The driver started the motor and we rolled off, bumping over pitted muddy roads, past row upon row of silent darkened huts, rolling, ever rolling, until suddenly we stopped with a lurch and were home.

Home was H Company, Second Battalion, First Marine Regiment.

Home was a company of machine guns and heavy mortars. Someone in that cheerless hut had decided that I should be a machine gunner.

The process of enrollment in H Company hardly differed from the method of our "assignment" the night before, except that we were run through a hut occupied by Captain High-Hips. He fixed us with his gloriously militant glass eye, he fingered his military mustache, and he questioned us in his clipped British manner of speech. Then, with an air of skepticism, he assigned us to our squad huts and into the keeping of the N.C.O.'s now arriving from other regiments.

These men came from the Fifth and the Seventh, the veteran line units in whose ranks were almost all of the First Division's trained troops. My regiment, the First, had been disbanded, but now, after Pearl Harbor it was being reactivated. The First needed N.C.O.'s, and many of those who came to us betrayed, by a certain nervousness of voice, a newness of rank. Their chevrons were shiny. A few had not found time to set them onto their sleeves; they were pinned on.

A few weeks before these corporals and Pfc.'s had been privates. Some predated us as marines by that margin only. But in such an urgent time, experience, however slight, is preferred to none at all. The table organization had to be filled. So up they went.

But the First also received a vital leavening of veteran N.C.O.'s. They would teach us, they would train us, they would turn us into fighting troops. From them we would learn our weapons. From them we would take our character and temper. They were the Old Breed.

And we were the new, the volunteer youths who had come from the comfort of home to the hardship of war.

For the next three years, all of these would be my comrades—the men of the First Marine Division.

Robert Leckie, 1942

TWO

MARINE

1

Huts, oil, beer.

Around these three, as around a sacramental triad, revolved our early life at New River. Huts to keep us dry; oil to keep us warm; beer to keep us happy. It is no unholy jest to call them sacramental; they had about them the sanctity of earth. When I remember New River, I remember the oblong huts with the low roofs; I remember the oil stoves and how we slipped out at night, buckets in hand, to pilfer oil from the other companies' drums, passing the men from the other companies, thieves in the night like ourselves; I remember the cases of canned beer in the middle of the hut and how we had pooled our every penny to go down to the slop chute to buy them, carrying them back boisterously on our shoulders, shouting and cheerful, because the warm dry huts awaited us, and soon the beer would be in our bellies and the world would be ours.

We were privates, and who is more carefree?

Like the huts, oil and beer, I had a trinity of friends: Hoosier, the Chuckler and the Runner.

I met Hoosier the second day at New River. He had arrived two days before us, and Captain High-Hips had made him his runner. In that first unorganized week, his clothes were always spattered with mud from his countless trips through the mire between the captain's office and the other huts.

I disliked him at first. He seemed inclined to look down on us from his high position in Captain High-Hips' office. He seemed surly, too, with his square strong figure, tow hair and blue eyes—his curt intelligences from on high: "Cap'n wants two men bring in the lieutenant's box."

But I was too inexperienced to see that the surliness was but a front for his being scared, like all of us. The immobile face was a façade; the forced downward curve of the mouth a hastily erected defense against the unknown. With time and friendship, that mouth would curve in a different direction, upward in a grin that was pure joy.

Chuckler was easier to know. We became friends the first day of gun drill, our introduction into the mysteries of the heavy, water-cooled, thirty-caliber machine gun. Corporal Smoothface, our instructor, a soft-voiced, sad-eyed youth from Georgia, made the drill a competition between squads to see which one could get its gun into action sooner. As gunner, Chuckler carried the tripod. As assistant gunner, I lugged the gun, a metal incubus of some twenty pounds. At a command, Chuckler raced off to a given point, spun the tripod over his head and set it up, while I panted off after him to slip the gun's spindle into the tripod socket. We beat the other squad and the Chuckler growled with satisfaction.

"Attaboy, Jersey," he chuckled, as I slid alongside him and placed the machine gun box in feeding position. "Let's show them bastards."

That was his way. He was fiercely competitive. He was profane.

He had a way of chuckling, a sort of perpetual good humor, that stopped his aggressiveness short of push, and which softened the impact of his rough language. Like Hoosier and me, he was stocky, and like Hoosier, he was fair; but he had a rugged handsomeness that the Hoosier's blunt features could not match.

The three of us, and later, the Runner, who joined us on Onslow Beach, were all stocky and somewhere under five feet ten inches tall—a good build for carrying guns or tripods or the tubes and base plates which the men of our Mortar Section had to lug. And flinging these heavy pieces about seemed to constitute all of our training.

Gun drill and nomenclature. Know your weapon, know it intimately, know it with almost the insight of its inventor; be able to take it apart blindfolded or in the dark, to put it together; be able to recite mechanically a detailed description of the gun's operation; know the part played by every member of the squad, from gunner down to the unfortunates who carried the water can or the machine gun boxes, as well as their own rifles.

It was dull and it was depressing, and the war seemed very far away. It was always difficult to remain attentive, to keep from falling asleep under that warm Carolina sun, while the voice of the gunnery sergeant droned on—"Enemy approaching at six hundred yards... up two, right three... fire..."

But for every hour there was a ten-minute break, in which we might talk and smoke and clown around. Hoosier and I were the clowns. He loved to mimic the Battalion Executive Officer, the Major, who had a mincing walk and a prim manner that was almost a caricature in itself.

"All right, men," said the Hoosier, sashaying back and forth before us like the Major, "let's get this straight. There'll be no thinking. No enlisted man is permitted to think. The moment you think, you weaken this outfit. Anyone caught thinking will be subject to a general court-martial. Anyone in H Company having brains will immediately return them to the Quartermaster. They're running short of them up in Officer's Country."

In these times also we would sing. Neither the Hoosier nor I could carry a tune, our idea of a scale being to raise or lower our voices. But we liked to bellow out the words. Unfortunately for us—for all of us—we had no songs to sing except those tuneless pointless "war songs" then arriving in a sticky flood.

Refrains like "Just to show all those Japs, the Yanks are no saps" or "I threw a kiss in the ocean" hardly fill a man with an urge to kill or conquer. After a few days of singing these, we came to scorn them, and turned to singing the bawdies, which are at least rollicking.

It is sad to have to go off to war without a song of your own to sing. Something like a rousing war song—something like the "Minstrel Boy" or something jolly and sardonic like the Englishman's "Sixpence"—might have made the war a bit more worth fighting. But we got none. Ours was an Advanced Age, too sophisticated for such outdated frippery. War cries or war songs seemed rather naïve and embarrassing in our rational time. We were fed food for thought; abstractions like the Four Freedoms were given us. Sing a marching song about that, if you can.

If a man must live in mud and go hungry and risk his flesh you must give him a reason for it, you must give him a cause. A conclusion is not a cause.

Without a cause, we became sardonic. One need only examine the drawings of Bill Mauldin to see how sardonic the men of World War Two became. We had to laugh at ourselves; else, in the midst of all this mindless, mechanical slaughter, we would have gone mad.

Perhaps we of the Marines were more fortunate than those of the other services, because in addition to our saving laughter we had the cult of the Marine.

No one could forget that he was a marine. It came out in the forest green of the uniform or the hour-long spit-polishing of the dark brown shoes. It was in the jaunty angle of the campaign hats worn by the gunnery sergeants. It was in the mark of the rifleman, the fingers of the gun hand longer than those of the other. It characterized every lecture, every drill or instruction circle. Sometimes a gunnery sergeant might interrupt rifle class to reminisce.

"China, that's the duty, lads. Give me ol' Shanghai. Nothing like this hole. Barracks, good chow—we'd even eat off plates—plenty of liberty, dress blues. And did them Chinese gals love the marines! They liked Americans best, but you couldn't get them out with a swabbie or a dog-face if they was a Gyrene around. That was the duty, lads."

And because a marine is a volunteer there is always a limit to his griping. He can complain so far, until he draws down this rebuke: "You asked for it, didn't you?"

Only once did I hear it possible that we might meet our match. At bayonet drill two lines of men faced each other. We held rifles to which were affixed bayonets sheathed in their scabbards. At a command the two lines met and clashed.

But we did not suit the sergeant. Perhaps it was our disinclination to disembowel each other. He screamed for a halt and strode over to seize someone's rifle.

"Thrust, parry, thrust!" he shouted, swinging the rifle through the exercise.

"Thrust, parry, thrust! Then the rifle butt. Hit him in the belly! Damn it, men, you're going to face the most expert bayonet fighter in the world. You're going to fight an enemy who loves cold steel! Look what they did in the Philippines! Look what they did in Hong Kong! I'm telling you, men, you'd better learn to use this thing if you don't want some little yellow Jap slashing your belly wide open!"

It was embarrassing.

Even the other sergeants were a bit red-faced. I could not help comparing this sergeant and his simulated rage to the methods of those other sergeants in Parris Island, who used to taunt us to come at them with drawn bayonet, and laughingly disarm us.

Poor fellow; he thought to frighten was to instruct. I see him now as he was on Guadalcanal: eyes sunken in sockets round with fear, unfleshed face a thing of bone and sinew stretched over quivering nerve. Mercifully they evacuated him, and I never heard of him again.

Nor did we ever have another unseemly suggestion of inferiority.

When we were done drilling we would form ranks and march home. Until a quarter mile from the huts, we walked in "route march." Our rifles were slung; a man might slouch as he pleased. There was no step to be kept. Talking, joking, crying out to each other in the gathering dusk, it was a pleasant way to come home.

But at the quarter-mile point, the company commander's voice roared out. "Commm-panee!" Our backs straightened. "Tennn-shun!" The rifles snapped straight, spring came back to our step, the familiar cadence began. That was how we came home to the huts of H Company when the shadows were lengthening over the coastal marsh. Thirsty and dirty, we swung into the company street with the snap and precision of garrison troops on parade.

Within another hour we would have revived with a wash and a hot meal. Someone would check the oil supply.

"Hey, Lucky—we're running low on oil."

I would take the bucket and slip out into the night, bound for the oil dump.

Chuckler and Hoosier would head for the slop chute. They would be back soon with the beer. The Gentleman, or someone, would sweep out the hut. Perhaps Oakstump would help—Oakstump, that short, bull-like farm lad from Pennsylvania, who didn't drink or smoke (at least not then) but loved to squat on the floor, throwing his dice, shuffling his cards, plastering his hair with scented oil. To Oakstump, this was living: dice, cards, hair oil.

Then, with the fire alight, the beer case set in the middle of the floor, we would lie back on our cots, heads propped against the wall, swilling the beer and talking.

What did we talk about those nights?

There would have been much shop talk—gossip about our outfit and our destination, endless criticism of the food, the N.C.O.'s, the officers. There certainly would have been much talk of sex. Of course everyone would exaggerate his prowess with women, particularly the younger ones, as they would stretch the size of their income as civilians.

I suppose much of our conversation was dull. It would seem so, now, I am sure. It was dull, but it was homey. We were becoming a family.

H Company was like a clan, or a tribe of which the squad was the important unit, the family group. Like families, each squad differed from the other, because its members were different. They resembled in no way those "squads" peculiar to many war books—those beloved "cross sections" composed of Catholic, Protestant and Jew, rich boy, middle boy and poor boy, goof and genius—those impossible confections which are so pleasing to the national palate, like an All-American football team.

Nor was my squad troubled by racial or religious bigotry. We had no "inner conflict," as the phrase goes. These things happen most often in the imagination of men who never fought. Only rear echelons with plenty of fat on them can afford such rich diseases, like an epicure with his gout.

We could not stand dissension, and we sank all differences in a common dislike for officers and for discipline; and later on, for the twin enemies of the Pacific, the jungle and the Jap.

The squad, as the sociological sample, squirming under the modern novelist's microscope or pinioned on his pencil, is unreal. It is cold. It is without spirit. It has no relation to the squads I knew, each as gloriously different from the other as the men themselves were separate and alone.

Lew Juergens ("Chuckler")

2

Sergeant Thinface took over our platoon. Lieutenant Ivy-League, our platoon leader, would join us a few days later. But, for the present, Thinface was in charge. He could not have been much older than I—perhaps a few months—but he had been in the Marines for three years. That made him ages my senior.

"All right, here it is," he told us. He brushed back his lank blond hair quickly. His thin boy's face was screwed up earnestly, as it always was when he was giving the troops the straight. "Here it is. We're moving out to the boondocks. Enlisted men"—how N.C.O.'s love that phrase—"enlisted men will fall out tomorrow morning in full marching gear. Sea bags will be locked and left in the huts. Check your mess gear. Be sure your shelter half is okay. You better have the right amount of tent pegs or it'll be your ass.

"All liberty is canceled."

We grumbled and returned to our huts. We fell to assembling our packs. And then, for the first time, the officers began to amuse themselves at playing-with-soldiers. Every hour, it seemed, Sergeant Thinface burst in on us with a new order, now confirming, now contradicting his earlier marching instructions. ·

"C.O. says no tent pegs."

"Battalion says to take your sea bags."

"Belay that—get those tent pegs in your shelter halves."

Only the Hoosier, who had the born private's calm contempt for officers, refused to join the general confusion. Each time the harried Thinface came panting in with a fresh order, Hoosier arose from his cot and listened to him with grave concern. But when Thinface disappeared, he shrugged and returned to his cot to sit there, smoking, surveying us with a superior look.

"Hoosier," I said. "Aren't you going to pack?"

"I got my stuff out," he said, pointing to an array of socks, shorts, shaving cream and other impedimenta.

"Aren't you going to pack it?"

"Hell, no, Lucky! I'll pack it in the morning—soon's they make their silly minds up."

Chuckler's husky voice cut it, that quality of mirth softening the rebuke.

"You'd better. They'll have an inspection and it'll be your ass. They'll throw you so far back in the brig, they'll have to feed you with a slingshot."

Hoosier snorted derisively, lapsing into a wide-mouthed grin. All afternoon he watched us, smoking, pulling away at two cans of warm beer he had secreted the night before, certain all the while he would be proven right.

He was. We put and took incessantly, veering like weather vanes in the shifting wind of orders blowing down from officer's country. But Hoosier was right. In the morning the final order came from the battalion commander. He had abstained from playing soldier. But when his order came through it was like none of the others, because it was official.

We tore our packs down, reassembled them, and then swung the whole bulky business onto our backs.

I do not recall how much the marching order weighed. Maybe twenty pounds. Even in this, men are so different. I carried the barest minimum, exactly what the colonel prescribed. But a man concerned for cleanliness might slip in a few extra bars of soap or carry a bottle of hair oil; another might cache two cans of beans in the bottom of his pack; a third could not bear to come away without a bundle of letters from home.

A soldier's pack is like a woman's purse: it is filled with his personality. I have saddened to see the mementos in the packs of dead Japanese. They had strong family ties, these smooth-faced men, and their packs were full of their families.

We fell in in front of the huts. The packs had a warm comfortable heavy feeling.

"Forrr-ward—harch! Route step—harch!"

Off we went to the boondocks.

Perhaps we walked ten miles; not much by the standards of veterans, but it was a great distance then. The route was through the pine woods, over a dirt road barely wide enough to admit a jeep. A whole battalion was on the march, and my poor squad was tucked away somewhere at center or center rear. Clouds of red dust settled upon us. My helmet banged irritably against the machine gun that was boring into my shoulder, or else it was bumped forward maddeningly over my eyes by the movement of my pack. A mile or so out, I dared not drink any more from my canteen. I had no idea how far we had to go. My dungarees were saturated with sweat, their light green darkened by perspiration. There had been joking and even some singing the first mile out. Now, only the birds sang; but from us there was just the thud of feet, the clank of canteens, the creak of leather rifle slings, the occasional hoarse cracking of a voice raised and breath wasted in a curse.

Every hour we got a ten-minute break. We lay propped against the road bank, resting against our packs. Each time, I reached under my pack straps to massage the soreness of my shoulders where the straps had cut. We would smoke. My mouth was dusty dry, my tongue swollen. I would moisten them with a swig of precious water, and then, stupidly, dry the whole thing out again, instantly, with a mouthful of smoke. But it was blissful lying there against the road bank, with all the pain and strain and soreness gone—or at least suspended—and our nostrils filled with the mistaken pleasures of tobacco.

Then came the command: "Off and on!"

It means off your behind and on your feet. Cursing, hating both command and commandant, straining, we rose to our feet and began again the dull plodding rhythm of the march.

This was how we came to where the Higgins Boats were waiting for us. It was where the road arrived at one of those canals which interlace this part of North Carolina and are part of the Inland Waterway System. It was like a live thing, this watery labyrinth, curving and darting through the pine wood, seeming to cavort on its way to the sea.

We climbed stiffly into the boats, sitting with our heads just above the gunwales, our helmets between our knees.

Hardly had our boat begun to move than the man on my left threw up. He was Junior, a slender, timid kid, much too shy for the Marines. Junior was from Upstate New York and was no sailor: leeward or windward were all one to him. He vomited to windward. It came back upon us in a stringy spray, unclean, stinking. Curses beat upon Junior's head unmatched in volume even by the thin cry of the gulls wheeling overhead.

"Cain't you use your helmet," Hoosier growled. "Cripes, Junior. What do you think it's fer?"

By this time others were sick and were making full use of their helmets. Poor Junior smiled his timid smile of appeal, obviously glad that he was not the only culprit. By the time we had reached the sea and were wallowing offshore in the deep troughs of the surf, half of the boat had become sick, to the immense glee of the boatswain.

Endlessly, with the finality of judgment, the boat lifted and dropped; the desolate ocean swelled and subsided; and above it all stood the boatswain behind his wheel, compassionate as a snake, obviously rehearsing the gleeful tale with which he would regale his swab-jockey buddies—of how the stuck-up marines survived their first ordeal with the great salt sea.

We were circling, I know now, while awaiting word to head shoreward in what was to be our first amphibious maneuver. When it came, our boat's motor roared into full voice. The prow seemed to dig into the water and the boat to flatten out. Mercifully, the rocking motion was abated.

"Down!"

The boats fanned out into assault line. We roared shoreward. The spray settled coolly on my face. There was nothing but the sound of the motors. There came a rough jolt, followed by the crunching sound of the keel beneath us plowing into the sand. We had landed.

"Up and over!"

I held my rifle high, grasped the gunwale with the other hand, and vaulted into the surf. I landed in cold water just above my calves. But the weight of my pack and weapons brought me almost to my knees. I was soaked. Weighted now by water as well as gear, we pelted up the beach.

"Hit the deck!"

We did. When we arose, after working our weapons against an imaginary defender, the sand clung to us like flour to a fillet.

The sweat of the march already had enflamed the moving parts of the flesh; the salt of the sea was into it, burning, boring; now to this was added the ubiquitous sand. The order came to fall in and to march off to our new camp, about a mile farther on, and as we did, the pain was excruciating. Each step, each thoughtless swing of the arm, seemed to draw a ragged blade across crotch and armpits.

When we had hobbled the distance, we came to a thick pine wood. On one side of the road the secondary growth had been cleaned out, and there the wood was more of a glade. In it were erected three pyramidal tents—one for the galley, another for sick bay, a third for the company commander. They fell us out here and told us this was our camp.

A cold rain had begun to fall as the compound began to be divided and subdivided into platoon and squad areas. Pup tents began to appear—not in careful, precise rows as in the old days, but carefully staggered à la the new passion for camouflage.

Exhausted as we might have been, suffering from the irritations of the march and the sea, hungry, shivering now in this cold rain— the business of setting up camp should have been a grim and cheerless affair. But it was not. We did not even curse the officers. Suddenly the thing became exciting, and the heat of the excitement was far too much for cold rain or empty stomachs or aching bones.

Soon we were limping about in search of pine needles to place beneath our blankets.

What a bed! Dark green blanket above, another below, and beneath it all the pliant pungent earth and fragrant pine needles.

As I say, we hurried about, and soon the glade resounded to our calls, the shouting back and forth and the good-natured swearing at the clumsy ones who could not then, or ever, erect a pup tent. And the rain—that baleful, wet intruder—perhaps confused at being the only mournful one among our carefree company, alternated between a drizzle, a drip and a downpour.

When we had ditched our tents—that is, dug a trough around them so that the ground within the tent would remain dry—we heard the call for chow. The food was hot, as was the coffee, and men living in the open demand no more. It had grown late, and it was in darkness that we finished our meal and washed our metal mess gear.

Returning to our company, we came through F Company's area, tripping over pegs, lurching against tents and provoking howls of wrath from the riflemen within.

Penetrating references were made to machine gunners, and there were lucid descriptions of the lineage from which all gunners sprang. But such maledictions, though there is about them a certain grand vulgarity, are unprintable.

So ended—in rain, in darkness, in a volley of oaths—our first day in the field. We had qualified for the ranks of the gloriously raggedy-assed.

Next day I met Runner. He had been in Hoosier's squad for the past few days, a late arrival, but I had not encountered him. He was coming away from Chuckler's tent, laughing, tossing a wisecrack over his shoulder, and we bumped into each other. He almost knocked me over, moving with that brisk powerful walk. That was the thing about Runner: those strong, phenomenally developed legs. He had been a sprint man in prep school—a good one, as I learned later—and the practice had left its mark in those bulging calves.

Runner fitted us like a glove. His admiration for Chuckler was akin to hero worship. But Chuckler had the strength to prevent that without offending the Runner, and I suspect that he took a human delight in the adulation of the dark-haired boy from Buffalo, who spoke so knowingly of formal dances and automobiles, a world quite apart from Chuckler's Louisville rough-and-tumble.

As friendship became firmer among us four, it became clear that Chuckler's word was going to carry the most weight, simply because he could rely on Runner's support.

So Chuckler became the leader, a fact which neither Hoosier nor I ever admitted and which Runner indicated only by his deference to him.

It is odd, is it not, that there should have been need of a leader? But there was. Two men do not need a leader, I suppose; but three do, and four most certainly, else who will settle arguments, plan forays, suggest the place or form of amusement, and generally keep the peace?

This was the beginning of our good times here in the boondocks. We slept on the ground and had but a length of canvas for a home, but we had begun to pride ourselves on being able to take it. Under such conditions, it was natural that the good times should be uproarious and, often, violent.

A day's training could not tire such young spirits or bodies. If there were no night exercises, or company guard, we were free from after chow until reveille. Sometimes we would gather around a fire,

Wilber "Bud" Conley ("Runner")

burning pine knots and drinking from a bottle of corn liquor bought from local moonshiners. The pine knots burned with a fragrant brilliance, as did the white lightning in our bellies.

We would sing or wrestle around the fire. There would be other fires; and sometimes rival singing contests, which soon degenerated into shouting matches, developed. Occasionally a luckless possum would blunder into the circle, and there would arise a floundering and a yelling followed by a frantic shucking of shoes, with which life was pounded out of the poor little animal. Then the men who loved to sharpen their blades would whip out these razor bayonets and skin the beast. Its tiny, greasy carcass would be consigned to the flames, and a pitiful few mouths it was that ever got to taste of the poor thing.

At other times, Hoosier and Chuckler and Runner and I would gather after chow and walk the two miles from camp to the highway, the sound of our going muffled by the thick dust underfoot; sometimes silent in that violet night with the soft pine wood at either side; sometimes boisterous, dancing in the dust, leaping upon one another, shouting for the sake of hearing our voices flung back by the hollow darkness; sometimes sober, smoking, talking in low voices of things at home and of when or where we would ever get into action.

The highway was a midway. It was lined with honky-tonks. To reach it was to sight a new world: one moment the soft dark and the smell of the wood, our shoes padding in the dust; in the next, cars and military vehicles hurtling down the cement strip, the crude shacks with their bare electric bulbs shining unashamed, their rough joints plastered with Coca-Cola and cigarette ads.

There were no girls, though. Sex was farther up the road, in Morehead City and New Bern. Here it was drinking and fighting. There was a U.S.O. at Greenville, but marines from the boondocks, clad in their dungarees, rarely went there except at the risk of being picked up by the M.P.'s for being out of uniform. Chuckler and I chanced it, once, and were rewarded with delicious hamburgers.

The Green Lantern became my battalion's hangout, probably because it stood closest to us on that garish highway, on the corner where the dirt road met the concrete and seemed to slip beneath it. It had the attraction that banks advertise, conveniently located.

Fights were common in The Green Lantern. They were always just ending or just beginning or just brewing no matter when you arrived. Every morning at sick call the evidence was plain: gentian violet daubed with a sort of admiring liberality over bruised cheekbones and torn knuckles.

We had our first adventure in another of the shacks. It was on a weekend and we were in full uniform, having come back to the huts and been given a rare liberty. The four of us were en route to Morehead City at night and drinking along the way. We hitchhiked because we could not afford the exorbitant taxi fares. But we tired of fruitlessly thumbing for rides and frequently crossed the road into the shacks. In one, when we had discovered our money was getting low, I proposed stealing a case of beer. The cases were stacked up at the back of the room in full view.

"You're nuts," Chuckler growled in a low voice. "You'll never make it. He can see every move you make."

I persisted. "No. We'll go to the head—it's right near the beer. The door opens inward. We'll crawl out and work one of the cases loose. He can't see over the counter. We'll push it right under his nose, and when we get near the door—we'll just jump up and run for it."

Chuckler grinned. "Okay."

It was smooth. We worked a case free, and, worming on our bellies, silently conveyed it to the door beneath the very nose of the proprietor. We were as two caterpillars connected by the case of beer, a sort of copula. Only the endurance of the boondocks enabled us to hold that bulky, heavy case a few inches from the floor, so that it would emit no telltale scraping while we squirmed doorward.

When we had arrived there, we got our knees under us, secured the case between us, came halfway erect and shot through the open door like Siamese twins.

It was exhilarating. The night air was like a buoyant tonic as we streaked for the highway, then across it impervious to the breakneck traffic streaming up and down. On the other side, we dropped the case on the shoulder of the road and rolled down the bank, laughing, whooping gleefully, half hysterical. We would all be six bottles of beer richer, and the night seemed to stretch out in time.

Chuckler crawled back up to the road, while I remained to relieve myself. When I returned I saw he was not alone. A man was with him, and he spoke to me as I approached.

"Take that damn case back," he said. It was the proprietor.

I pretended a jolly laugh. "Take it back yourself," I said. Then I saw he had a gun. He waved it at me. I could see he was angry. But I was stupid, and when he repeated: "Take it back," I thought he was going to shoot me. But he merely was tightening his grip on the pistol. My bravado departed. With Chuckler, I took hold of the case and carried it back across the road, the proprietor covering us from behind with his pistol.

Shame burned my cheeks upon our re-entry. Runner hid a grin behind his hand. We marched to the back of the shack, like men walking the plank, and restored the case to its place.

Compassion is a specialty; it is a hidden talent. The proprietor had compassion. When we turned, he was walking behind the bar toward Runner and Hoosier. His pistol must have been pocketed at the door. He had conveyed to everyone in the shack the notion that our unsuccessful robbery was a great joke. He had four bottles of beer opened when we rejoined Runner and Hoosier.

"Here, boys," he said, "have one on me."

We told him we were sorry. He grinned.

"Lucky for you Ah'm soft-hearted. When Ah saw yawl run out of heah with that case, Ah was so damn mad Ah felt like shooting yuh right in the ass. Reckon you lucky Ah changed mah mind."

We laughed and drank up. He grinned again, pleased that he had mastered us and could dispense with punishment like the gracious conqueror he was.

One could always bargain for trouble in those shacks. And one could always bargain for trouble of a different sort in the cafés of the camp towns—New Bern, Morehead City, Wilmington. I call them cafés, because that was how their proprietors styled them. They were hardly better than the shacks, except that they were on the streets of the towns rather than the highway and they had paint on the walls.

But there was also this great difference: there were girls. They came from the town and had no connection with the cafés. Probably the proprietors encouraged their presence, perhaps presented them with favors, but they did not have the official standing, to use a euphemism, as do dime-a-dance girls or the professional teasers of the big-city clip joints.

In the marine towns of New Bern and Morehead City—where the streets were thronged with green on Saturdays—there were cafés at every turn: cheap, dingy, the air banked with clouds of cigarette smoke, and the juke-box wail so piercing that one half expected to see it stir up eddies in the lazy smoke.

Always the girls.

They sat at marble-topped tables where the faded wide-ringed imprints of soda glasses were linked to one another by the newer, narrower marks of the beer bottles. This was the beer hall, superimposed on the soda parlor.

They sat at the tables, drinking slowly, smoking, giggling, their bodies seeming to strain to be free of their tight clothing—mouths working, sometimes with gum, sometimes with words, but no matter, for it was the eyes that counted, the eyes roving, raking the tables, parading the aisles, searching . . . hunting . . . hungering for the bold, answering look . . . and when it came, the deliberate crushing of the cigarette, the languid getting to the feet and straightening of the skirt, the sauntering, thin-hipped progress to the table, as though they had sat through endless showings of "Hell's Angels" and had sex down stride perfect.

When I went to New Bern and the cafés, it was usually with Corporal Smoothface. He called me "Licky." "C'mon, Licky," he'd say, "let's go to New Bern," running the syllables of the town's name together so that they sounded as one.

Corporal Smoothface married a girl he met in a café. An hour after he met her, he took off for South Carolina in a car hired with money I got from pawning my watch. He couldn't get married in New Bern on a Saturday afternoon, but he knew of a South Carolina justice of the peace who would perform the ceremony. After the wedding, he turned around and drove back, spending a one-day honeymoon in New Bern and appearing at Monday morning reveille in New River.

Smoothface never paid me back for the watch. I am sure he considered it a wedding present.

So be it.

3

Liberty became less frequent as training grew more intense. Soon we were not going back to the base at all. The days clicked off dully, all the same. Saturdays and Sundays were no different from the rest, except that we could be sure to be routed out of bed every Sunday morning by a forest fire.

No one was ever positive that the Major set them, neither did anyone doubt that he did. There was no arson in his heart, we reasoned, merely an unwillingness to contemplate the troops' resting easy in their sacks. But, as I say, there was no proof—who wants proof of fact?—except that the fires always seemed to occur Sunday morning in the same general area, and in parts of the wood where there was little danger of their spreading.

So we would be piled into trucks, heaping imprecation on the Major, beseeching heaven to fry him to a cinder in his own holocaust, and be bundled off to the burning.

We put out the fires by building backfires, digging trenches, or sometimes, merely squelching the upstarts among this red breed by flailing away at them with branches before they could blossom into flaming maturity. It was in one of these that my clothes caught fire.

I was standing in the middle of a scorched and smoking meadow, so hot that my feet felt on fire, even through the thick crepe soles of my shoes, through my heavy socks and formidable calluses. I looked down and saw with quick horror that at the inner ankle of my left leg my rolled pants cuffs were smoldering, now puffing into flame.

I ran like the wind, not in fright but in a deliberate sprint for a log fence on the other side of which lay high grass and cool earth. I knew that I could not extinguish the myriad smoldering places in my pants by slapping them; I had to roll on the ground, heap dirt on myself. This I could not do where I stood.

I ran. I raced for the fence; and my buddies, thinking me daft with fear, gave pursuit—bellowing entreaties for me to halt. I beat them to the fence and dived over it, landing on my shoulder, rolling over and over, over and over, scooping up handfuls of dirt and rubbing them on my burning pants and socks.

When they dived on top of me, as though I were liable to be up and off again, I had the fire out. It was Runner who landed on me first. Thank God I had had a head start on him, else I would never had made the fence; and I am no longer curious to know what my friends would have done, had they overtaken me in the middle of that hot and sparking meadow.

I got a nasty burn on my inner ankle where the sock had been alight. It crippled me for a few days and I still carry a faint scar.

Now the training was ending. Days, days, endless grinding days, aimless sweating complaining days, running into each other without point like the mindless tens of days of the French Revolution... days on the mock-up, clambering up and down the rough, evil-smelling cargo nets draped over the gaunt wooden structure, like the Trojan Horse, built to resemble the side of a ship... digging days, out in the field scooping out shallow holes, the depressions for which the men in the Philippines had given the name foxholes—digging, scooping, scraping; got to get below the contour of the earth, got to dig, got to flop into the earth's fresh wound, the face pressed deep into the fragrant soil while the worms squirm round in consternation as though dismayed by the hastiness of the graves and the heartiness of the bodies that filled them.... days on the march, the sun on the helmet and the sweat gathering in the eye-brows like the sea in a marsh, powdering the upper lip with water, dropping off the point of the chin, while the whole body, soft no longer, rejoices in its movement, the fluid, sweat-oiled movement—the teasing trickle down the groove of the back, and the salt savor of it when the sensuous tongue curls out to kiss the upper lip... days of all kinds, boring and brutalizing, tedious hours wallowing in the gray sea troughs... days of lectures, of shooting, of inspections, of cleaning tents and weapons, of military courtesy, of ennui in the midst of birds singing and officers wrangling over maps... of tedium... of indifference to pain... of rain dripping in forests and wet blankets... of no God but the direct assault... of eyes brightening and bones hardening... and now the last day, like the stooks rising "barbarous in beauty," we are finished.

On the last day Secretary of the Navy Knox came down from Washington to look at us. They drew us up in serried, toy-soldier ranks beside the Inland Waterway, in the shadow of our mock-up.

I do not recall how long we waited for Knox. It may have been an hour, or it may have been two. But it was not too uncomfortable, standing there in the sun, once they had given us a "parade rest."

Suddenly a bugle call pealed from the Waterway. They snapped us to attention. A gleaming launch swept up the canal, banners streaming, prow high and haughty, stern down and driving—like a spirited horse. It was the Secretary.

The company commander joined the ranks of the official party as it reached our ranks, leaving Old Gunny behind to give the salute. He stood there, square and ancient, a mandarin of marines, hash-marked and privileged—an awesome figure to any officer below the rank of colonel. The Secretary and the others passed. The unpopular Major brought up the rear. Just as he came by, Old Gunny's voice broke into a clear precise growl that could be heard by the battalion: "At ease!"

We slumped over our rifles. The Major's face colored like sunrise at sea. A silent spasm of mirth ran through the company. You could not hear it; but it could be felt. The Major hastened on, as though departing a place accursed.

When Old Gunny swung round in that deliberate about-face of his, his wrinkled visage was creased in a curve of satisfaction; like the Cheshire Cat, he was all grin.

The Secretary did not inspect us—not my company, anyway. I have always felt that he came down to New River in those despairing days only to be sure that there were actually men there, as though he might have suspected that the First Marine Division, like so many of our military then, might be composed only of paper.

The period at the boondocks ended that day. No sooner had the Secretary regained his launch than we were breaking camp. We were going back to the comparative luxury of the huts, the mess halls, the slop chutes. We were glad of it. The war was still far away from us. Even then, no one grasped the import of the Secretary's visit.

Life was easier on the base. Our officers became kinder. The sixty-two-hour liberty, from four o'clock Friday afternoon until reveille

Monday, made its appearance. Immediately the surrounding towns lost their attraction and we began going home.

The highway outside the compound was thronged with taxicabs. On Friday afternoons it was a sight to see them load up with marines and roar off, one after another, like big race cars rolling out of the pits.

Usually five of us would charter a taxicab for Washington, approximately three hundred miles distant. From there we caught the regular trains to New York. It was expensive—something like twenty dollars apiece for the driver to take us up and to wait to take us back Sunday night. Naturally, the money had to come from our parents. Twenty-one-dollar-a-month privates could not afford it, nor could twenty-six-dollar privates first class, a rank I had recently attained. Though costly, the taxicab was the fastest and surest way to travel. Train service was slow and spotty. If a man missed connections, he was sure to be A.W.O.L. at Monday morning reveille.

At times the taxicab would sway with the speed of our homeward dash up the coast, especially if one of us would take the wheel from a driver reluctant to obey our commands to "step on it." Then we would fairly fly—ninety, ninety-five, whatever speed we could reach by stamping the gas pedal down to the floor.

We usually arrived at Union Station in Washington at about midnight, never having left New River much before six o'clock. The trains to New York always were crowded. Every car seemed equipped with a Texan or a hillbilly, replete with banjo and nasal voice, or had its quota of drunks draped over the arms of the seats or stretched out on the floor like rugs. We stepped over them on our way to the parlor car, where we would drink away the night and the miles, until dawn crept dirtily, mosquito-in-the-morning-like, over the Jersey meadows.

That was the way of it: impatience burning in our bellies and only the whiskey to wet it down.

Who could eat? My father took me, on one of those flying visits, to a famous English fish and fowl house in downtown New York. I toyed with my half of a roast pheasant, able to swallow only a mouthful, impervious to savor, while eagerly gulping beer after beer. How that unfinished pheasant haunted me two months later on Guadalcanal, when hunger rumbled in my belly like the sound of cannonading over water.

We were impatient. We were wound up. We could no more relax than we could think. In those days there was not an introspective person among us. We seldom spoke of the war, except as it might relate to ourselves, and never in an abstract way. The ethics of Hitler, the extermination of the Jews, the Yellow Peril—these were matters for the gentlemen of the editorial pages to discuss.

We lived for thrills—not the thrills of the battlefield, but of the speeding auto, the dimly lighted café, the drink racing the blood, the texture of a cheek, the sheen of a silken calf.

Nothing was permitted to last. All had to be fluid; we wanted not actuality, but possibility. We could not be still; always movement, everything changing. We were like shadows fleeing, ever fleeing; the disembodied phantoms of the motion picture screen; condemned men; souls in hell.

Soon the spate of sixty-two-hour liberties was ended. Mid-May of 1942 saw me home for the last time. My family would not set eyes on me again for nearly three years.

The Fifth Marine Regiment left before we did. It departed during the night. When we awoke, their regimental area was deserted, picked clean, as though not even a shade had dwelt there, let alone thirty-five hundred exuberant young men. Not so much as a shredded cigarette butt or an empty beer can remained.

Clean.

My own First Regiment followed the Fifth within weeks. We packed our sea bags with all our excess clothing and personal gear.

Each bag was carefully stenciled with our company markings. Then all were carried off on trucks. I never saw mine again until I returned to the States. From that day forward—save for brief intervals in Australia—we lived out of our packs, the single combat pack about the size of a portable typewriter case.

We were under orders to carry only our weapons and a prescribed amount of clothing; specifically, no liquor. A day before we left I managed to get into Jacksonville, where I pawned my suitcase for enough money to buy two pints of whiskey.

The two flat bottles were in my pack, hard and warm against my back, when we clambered aboard the train. We finished them that night, when the porter had made our beds and all was dark in our Pullman car. Yes, we traveled by Pullman and we had a porter. We ate in a dining car, too, and the porter could be bribed to fetch us a turkey sandwich at night. It was a wonderful way to ride off to war, like the Russian nobleman in *War and Peace* who dashed off to the fray in a handsome carriage, watching Borodino from a hillock while his manservant brewed tea in a silver samovar.

We had a jovial porter. He loved to josh the Texan, newly arrived in our platoon. Once, he overheard the Texan making one of his tall Texas boasts.

"Hell," the porter laughed, "dat Texas so dried up a rabbit doan dare cross without he carry a box lunch and canteen."

A roar of laughter rose around the blushing Texan, and the porter retired grinning happily.

Our spirits were high and our hearts light as we rode across America. Our talk was full of the air-sea Battle of Midway, which had just been fought, and we were full of admiration for the marine and navy pilots who had stopped the Japanese.

Mostly we played poker or watched the countryside flowing past. To me, who had never been west of Pittsburgh, almost every waking moment was one of intense excitement. This was my country. I was seeing it for the first time and I drew it into me, here in its grandeur, again in the soft beauty of a mountain like the curve of a cheek, in the vastness of its plains or the bounty of the fields. I cannot recall it all and, now, I regret that I took no notes. There are only blurs and snatches...disappointment at crossing the Mississippi at night, only the impression of a great wetness and the gentle sway of the railroad barge beneath us...the beauty of the Ozarks, green woods swelling to a fragile blue sky, with the White River leaping straight and clean like a lance beneath them, and the one hill with the cross at the crest, stretching its gaunt arms like an entreaty...the Rockies (Where was the grandeur? Were we too close?) seeming like peaks of vanilla ice cream down which coursed great runnels of chocolate sauce, but no grandeur, only when we had reached the heights and could look back, gasping...ah, but here it is, now, here is the splendid West, here is the Colorado River thrusting through the Royal Gorge in one white, frothing instant...up, up, up in Nevada, the train climbing like a great dignified roller coaster, and then the sweeping ascent into California and the sun.

But we lost the sun in the San Francisco mists. We were at the waterfront and surrounded by the brown hills of Berkeley. The great curving bay, like a watery amphitheater, was before us. There were seals playing in the bay.

I was only twenty-one. I could see the Golden Gate, and out beyond lay the Thing that I would see.

Not yet, though. Not for ten days would we go out the Golden Gate. They marched us aboard the *George F. Elliott*. She became our ship. She was an African slaver. We hated her.

They let us go ashore every day.

These days were the final and the frantic hours of our flight. Except for Chinatown, I saw nothing but bars and cafés in San Francisco. My father had sent me a hundred dollars in response to my last plea for money. Because of this, I could see the best cafés as well as the lowest bars. They are all one.

I can remember nothing of them, save for a juke box playing

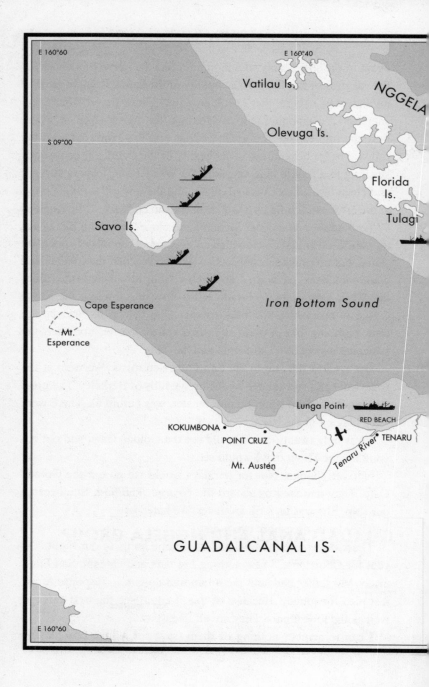

E 160°60

E 160°40

Vatilau Is.

NGGELA

Olevuga Is.

S 09°00

Florida
Is.

Savo Is.

Tulagi

Iron Bottom Sound

Cape Esperance

Mt.
Esperance

Lunga Point

RED BEACH

KOKUMBONA

POINT CRUZ

TENARU

Mt. Austen

Tenaru River

GUADALCANAL IS.

E 160°60

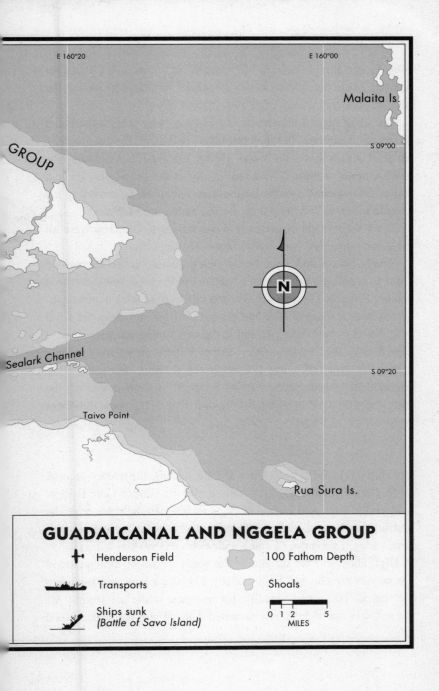

E 160°20   E 160°00

Malaita Is.

GROUP

S 09°00

N

Sealark Channel

S 09°20

Taivo Point

Rua Sura Is.

GUADALCANAL AND NGGELA GROUP

✛ Henderson Field

⚓ Transports

🚢 Ships sunk
(Battle of Savo Island)

100 Fathom Depth

Shoals

0 1 2   5
MILES

"One Dozen Roses" over and over again, and once, in a Chinatown walk-up being thrown out bodily because I had leapt in among the wearily gesturing chorus girls and shouted "Boo!"

The same night I chased two Chinamen away from a marine. I never saw the knives, but they must have had them, for the marine's tan shirt was bright with blood. He lay slumped in a doorway—a lunch counter, I think. I shouted in fury at the proprietor. He had watched the assault stonily, but now, as I shouted, he moved to his telephone and called the police. I left, fearing the M.P.'s.

There were many episodes in those ten days. But they were all the same—smeared with lust or bleared by appetite.

Finally I was sated. I was jaded. San Francisco ended for me one night as I rode in a taxicab with Jawgia, the freckled, sharp-featured cracker from the Okefenokee Swamp of Georgia, whose name suggested both his home state and his habit of jawing about the Civil War. Jawgia clambered out and the guard swung the gate open. I peered into the driver's face, dropped three pennies—the only money we had left—into his outstretched hand, and said, "Buy yourself the best damn newspaper in town!" I slipped through the gate, and with a wild yell ran for my ship. One of the coins the driver threw hit me as I ran.

Our ship left in the morning, in a drizzle, on June the twenty-second, 1942. It moved, unlovely gray hulk, under the Golden Gate Bridge. I sat on the stern and looked back, searching. In the manner of the immigrant who takes a clod of his country's soil on his voyage with him, I sought a memory to take with me.

High above, in the middle of the wetly gleaming bridge, stood a sentry in poncho and kelly helmet, his rifle a hump on his back. He waved. He waved steadily, for minutes, while all around me the snickers and the catcalls mounted. I loved him for it. He waved to me.

THREE

WARRIOR

1

Fires flickered on the shores of Guadalcanal Island when we came on deck.

They were not great flaming, leaping fires, and we were disappointed. We had expected to see the world alight when we emerged from the hatches. The bombardment had seemed fierce. Our armada, for such we judged it to be, seemed capable of blasting Guadalcanal into perdition.

But in the dirty dawn of August 7, 1942, there were only a few fires flickering, like the city dumps, to light our path to history.

We were apprehensive, not frightened. I was still angry from my encounter with the sailor messman. I had been overlong eating my breakfast of beans, and when I had finished I had perceived the sailors frantically cleaning up the galley. Perhaps this would become the ship's surgery for the shore wounded. The chief messman behind the counter was just closing a crate of oranges, distributed as a sort of eve-of-battle gift to the troops, when I had rushed up to claim mine. He refused to reopen the crate. We shouted furiously at each other. I wanted that orange more than General Vandergrift wanted Guadalcanal. The sailor would not surrender it to me and threatened— oh, inanity of inanity!—threatened to report me for insolence. Report me! Report me who am about to spill my blood among the coconuts! I wanted to skewer him on my bayonet, but I thrust him aside, tore off the lid, seized my orange and fled up the ladder to my comrades on deck, the messman's outraged cries dwindling behind me.

So I was flickering, myself, like the long curving coastline of Guadalcanal, when Old Gunny bellowed:

"First Platoon over the side! Down those cargo nets!"

The *George F. Elliott* was rolling in a gentle swell. The nets swayed out and in against her steel sides, bumping us. My rifle muzzle knocked my helmet forward over my eyes. Beneath me, the Higgins Boats wallowed in the troughs.

The bombardment was lifting; I looked to both sides of me, clinging, antlike, to the net. Sealark Channel was choked with our ships. To the left, or west of me, was hulking Savo Island. In front of me, to the north, but obscured by the side of the *Elliott,* stretched Florida Island and tiny Tulagi. The Marine Raiders and Paramarines were already at their bloody work on Tulagi. I could hear the sound of gunfire. Behind me, to the south, was Guadalcanal.

Three feet above the rolling Higgins Boats the cargo nets came to an end. One had to jump, weighted with fifty or more pounds of equipment. No time for indecision, for others on the nets above were all but treading your fingers. So there it was—jump—hoping that the Higgins Boat would not roll away and leave only the blue sea to land in. But we all made it safely.

Now I could see the assault waves forming near the other ships. Boat after boat would load up, then detach itself from the mother ship to join its mates, circling, circling, like monster water bugs on frolic.

"Everybody down!"

Now I could see the circles fan out into the attack line. Like my buddies, I was crouching below the gunwales, feeling the boat beneath me swing slowly round to point its nose shoreward. The deck vibrated in a rush of power.

The assault began.

Now I was praying again. I had prayed much the night before, carefully, deliberately, impetrating God and the Virgin to care for my family and friends should I fall. In the vanity of youth, I was positive I would die; in the same vanity, I was turning my affairs over to the Almighty, like an older brother clapping the younger on the back and saying, "John, now you're the man of the house."

But my prayers were a jumble. I could think of nothing but the shoreline where we were to land. There were other boatloads of marines ahead of us. I fancied firing from behind their prostrate bodies, building a protecting wall of torn and reddened flesh. I could envision a holocaust among the coconuts. I no longer prayed. I was like an animal: ears straining for the sound of battle, body tensing for the leap over the side.

The boat struck the shore, lurched, came to a halt. Instantly I was up and over. The blue sky seemed to swing in a giant arc. I had a glimpse of palm fronds swaying gently above, the most delicate and exquisite sight I have ever seen.

There followed a blur. It was a swiftly shifting kaleidoscope of form and color and movement. I lay panting on the sand, among the tall coconut trees, and realized I was wet up to the hips. I had gotten some twenty yards inland.

But there was no fight.

The Japanese had run. We lay there, fanned out in battle array, but there was no one to oppose us. Within moments, the tension had relaxed. We looked around our exotic surroundings. Soon there were grins and wisecracks.

"Hey, Lieutenant," the Hoosier pouted, "this is a helluva way to run a war."

Sergeant Thinface screamed shrilly at someone opening a coconut.

"You wanna get poisoned. Doncha know them things could be
full of poison?"

Everyone laughed. Thinface was so stupidly literal. He had been
briefed on Japanese propensities for booby-trapping or for poisoning water supplies; thus, the coconuts were poisoned. No one bothered to point out the obvious difficulties involved in poisoning
Guadalcanal's millions of coconuts. We just laughed—and went on
husking the nuts, cracking the shells, drinking the cool sweet coconut milk. Thinface could only glower, at which he was expert.

From somewhere came the command: "Move out!"

We formed staggered squads and slogged off.

We left our innocence on Red Beach. It would never be the same.
For ten minutes we had had something like bliss, a flood of well-
being following upon our unspeakable relief at finding our landing
unopposed. Even as we stepped from the white glare of the beach
into the sheltering shade of the coconut groves, there broke out behind us the yammer of antiaircraft guns and the whine of speeding
aircraft. The Japs had come. The war was on. It would never be the
same.

We plodded through the heat-bathed patches of kunai grass. We
crossed rivers. We recrossed them. We climbed hills. We got into the
jungle. We cut our passage with machetes or followed narrow, wind-
ing trails. We were lost every step of the way.

At intervals we would pass little knots of officers, bending anxiously over a map. That pitiful map! Here there was Red Beach,
which was right enough, and there was the Tenaru River, which it
was not, and there were the coconut groves—miles and miles of
them, neatly marked out by symbols looking more like fleurs-de-lis

than coconuts—and you would think this whole vast island was under cultivation by Lever Brothers.

It was a lying map and it got us into trouble from the outset.

The officers were apprehensive.

They knew we were lost.

"Hey, Lieutenant—where we headed?"

"Grassy Knoll."

"Where'zat?"

"Up ahead, where the Japs are."

Our very naïveté spoke. Grassy Knoll . . . up ahead . . . where the Japs are. Cowboys and Indians, cops and robbers, hide-and-seek—we were playing a game. Even the division commander had calmly announced an expectation of taking his evening meal on the summit of Grassy Knoll.

"Synchronize your watches, gentlemen—the assault has begun."

Last one up to Grassy Knoll is a rotten egg.

Ah, well, we had much to learn, and five months in which to learn it; and there would be precious few who would get to Grassy Knoll in the process.

So began, on the very first day, the frustration. So, too, began the loneliness. The sounds of battle subsiding behind us had an ominous tinge, the faces of the officers we passed had an anxious tone. The Jap was closing the ring, and we—poor gallant fools—we thought we were pursuing him!

We were drenched with sweat. Our progress through the kunai patches had nearly prostrated us. Now, in the clammy cool of the rain forest, our sweat-darkened dungarees clung to us with chill tenacity.

"Hey, Lucky," the Hoosier called. "Ah bet Ah could get a quart of Calvert off your back. Wring out your jacket, Lucky, and give ever'body a shot."

It was not whiskey we wanted, though. For the first time in my life I was experiencing real thirst. The heat, and now the dripping, enervating forest, seemed to have dehydrated me. I had water in my canteen, but I dared not touch it. Who could tell when it might be replenished? We had been walking three hours or more, and had seen no water.

Then, in that sudden way of the jungle, there was revealed to us a swift-running river.

With incautious shouts we fell upon her. She dissolved us, this river. We became a yelling, splashing, swilling, milling mass, and even Lieutenant Ivy-League shared the general retreat from discipline. Oh, what a sweet sight would we have been for Japanese eyes! What a chance for massacre they missed!

Some even lay on their backs in this shallow stream—the lyrically named Ilu—and opened their mouths, letting the water plunge into their systems as though into yawning drains. Lieutenant Ivy-League was swinging water to his lips by the helmetful, bellowing meanwhile, "Don't drink! It may be poisoned! Don't drink until you've used your purifying pills."

Everyone nodded gravely and went right ahead with the orgy, drinking, drinking, drinking—sighing like a lover as the sweet, swift little river swept the salt sweat from our bodies.

Refreshed, sated, we resumed the march.

We were sopping. But it was the clean wetness of water. It is nothing to be sopping in the jungle rain forest, and it is better if it be water than sweat.

Night came in a rush while we were still marching. We set up a hasty defense. The first day had passed without event, though we had lost one man. He had been wide on the flank of our advancing column and had simply disappeared.

It began to rain, while we set up our guns on top of a hill. The rain fell drearily as we sat hunched in our ponchos, bidden to keep silence, munching the cold rations we took from our packs—each man to himself alone, but all afloat on a dark sea of the night.

It could—it should—have been a night of purest terror. We were bewildered. We were dispirited. We were cold. We were wet. We were ignorant of our surroundings, so we were afraid of them. We knew nothing of our enemy, so we feared him. We were alone, surrounded by a jungle alive with the noise of moving things which could only seem to us the stealthy tread of the foe moving closer.

But we saw all these things dully, as a stunned boxer gaping with indifferent anticipation at the oncoming knockout blow, too paralyzed by previous punches to move, too stupefied to care. The steady drumfire of the day's events had done this to us.

Once there came a burst of gunfire. It shattered the night. We leaned over our guns, our mouths agape in the darkness. But then the night closed in again. Darkness. The trees dripping. The jungle whispering.

No one came.

At dawn we learned the import of the gunfire. A medical corpsman had been killed. He had been shot by his own men.

When the sentry had challenged him as he returned from relieving himself, he had boggled over the password "Lilliputian" and so met death: eternity at the mercy of a liquid consonant.

I shall never forget the sad faces of the friends who buried him. In that dismal dawn, the scraping of their entrenching tools was as plaintive as the scratching of a mouse.

The light was still dim. Lieutenant Ivy-League asked the company commander for permission to smoke.

"I don't know if it's light enough," said the captain. "Why don't you go over by that tree and light a match? Then I can tell if it's too dark."

The lieutenant strode off. When he had reached the tree and lighted his match, we could just make out the tiny flare of it and hear him calling softly, "How's that, Captain?"

The captain shook his head.

"No. Keep the smoking lamp out. It's too dark, yet."

I peered at the captain. Anxiety was on his face as though carved there by the night's events. It startled me. Here was no warrior, no veteran of a hundred battles. Here was only a civilian, like myself. Here was a man hardly more confident than the trigger-happy sentry who had killed the corpsman. He was much older than I, but the responsibility of his charge, the unknown face of war, had frightened him past trusting the evidence of his senses.

He thought the tiny flare of matches might bring the enemy down on us, as though we were lighting campfires at night. In another minute, it was clear daylight; everyone was smoking; soon the captain was, too.

We marched all day. Grassy Knoll was still "up ahead" and so were the Japs. We squirmed up the side of rain-bright hills, in slow sideways progress, like a land crab or a skier; we slid down the reverse slopes, the poor gunners cursing weakly while their tripods banged cruelly against the backs of their heads. The terrain of Guadalcanal seemed composed of steel, over which the demons of the jungle had spread a thin treacherous slime. Our feet were forever churning for a purchase on these undulating paths, our hands forever clawing the air, our progress constantly marked by the heavy clanking fall of a gunner in full gear.

We advanced on the enemy with all the stealth of a circus. If there had been a foeman in that dim dripping jungle he would have annihilated us. The Japanese would have done to us what our military ancestor, Washington, prevented the French from doing completely to Braddock, what our forefathers did to the British on the retreat from Lexington.

We saw none of the enemy. That day was a dull, lost witness to the cycle of the sun, of which I have neither memory nor regret.

The night I shall never forget.

I awoke in the middle of it to see the sky on fire. So it seemed. It was like the red mist of my childhood dream when I imagined Judgment to have come while I played baseball on the Castle Grounds at home. We were bathed in red light, as though fixed in the eye of Satan. Imagine a myriad of red traffic lights glowing in the rain, and you will have a replica of the world in which I awoke.

The lights were the flares of the enemy. They hung above the jungle roof, swaying gently on their parachutes, casting their red glow about. Motors throbbed above. They were those of Japanese seaplanes, we learned later. We thought they were hunting us.

But they were actually the eyes of a mighty enemy naval armada that had swept into Sealark Channel. Soon we heard the sound of cannonading, and the island trembled beneath us. There came flashes of light—white and red—and great rocking explosions.

The Japs were hammering out one of their greatest naval victories. It was the Battle of Savo Island, what we learned to call more accurately the Battle of the Four Sitting Ducks. They were sinking three American cruisers—the *Quincy, Vincennes* and *Astoria*—and one Australian cruiser—the *Canberra*—as well as damaging one other American cruiser and a U.S. destroyer.

The flares had been to illuminate the fight. At one point, the Japanese turned their searchlights on. These accounted for the eerie lights we saw, as we huddled in our slimy jungle.

It took us hardly a day to withdraw from the rain forest, although we had spent two days getting into it. But we knew the way back; we had not known the way in.

Amphibious tractors laden with food and water awaited us when we emerged and came down the slopes into the kunai fields. Chuckler was in front of me. He slipped on the last slope. As he fell, his tripod caught him wickedly behind the head.

He got up and kicked it. Then he swore. He swore with the shrill fury of exasperation.

He bent and grasped the tripod as though it were a living thing and he had it by the throat, turning his wrists to it as though he could choke the life from it—this hard cruel unbending thing in which was now concentrated the frustration, the hunger, the thirst, the wetness and the anxieties of these past two days. He flung it then. It sailed through the air and landed with an uncaring clank in the tall kunai.

Chuckler sat down and lit a cigarette, and that was where the battalion deployed as the men came spilling down from the hills in their mud-caked formless green twill, with their ugly cartridge belts and bowl helmets, their slung rifles and their stubble of beard, and the eyes that were just beginning to stare. Water and cans of C-rations came streaming off the amtracks. When we had refilled our canteens and our bellies, and sucked at blessed cigarettes, we were up again and off.

It was dusk when we reached the beach. We saw wrecked and smoking ships—a clean, unshipped expanse of water between Guadalcanal and Florida Island.

Our Navy was gone.

Gone.

We rested there. Columns of men were trudging up the beach. Their feet clapped softly against the sand. The sun had sunk behind the jungle. Night rolled toward us from the eastward-lying sea, gathering purplish over Florida as though it would come upon us in a bound.

Silhouetted against the gathering dark were the men. In the half light, they seemed to have lost the dimension of depth; they seemed shades. They moved, these weary men, as though chained to one another, with the soulless, mechanical tread of zombies. Behind them, low on the horizon, the reflected sun glowed dully. Despair seemed to walk in desolation.

I was glad when night closed in. Then my company was on its feet in turn, plodding up the silent beach in darkness.

We took up defensive positions. We scooped out shallow emplacements and turned the mouths of our machine guns toward the sea. We told off a guard and went to sleep, the last sound in our ears the pound of the surf against that long low coastline.

They bombed us the next day. But it was nothing to fear. It was not even the foretaste of how it would be.

"Condition Red!" someone shouted, and we heard the drone of their engines. They were high above, perhaps a dozen or so bombers, silvery and slender. They swept above us in a splendid V and loosed their loads over Henderson Field. We shouted and danced about in derision. We were fools. The bombs were not for us, but for our poor comrades on the airfield. We could hear the explosions and feel the earth shake, but it was not enough to make a child blink.

In that stupidity born of false security we laughed and shook our fists at the now departing bombers, as though we had taken their worst and put them to flight.

Ah, well. We had much to learn.

Not even the excitement of the bombing could match the delirium following discovery of the Japanese sake cache.

Case upon case of it was found in a log-and-thatch warehouse not far west of our beach positions. There were cases of wonderful Japanese beer, too—quart bottles clothed in little skirts of straw. Soon the dirt road paralleling the shoreline became an Oriental thoroughfare, thronged with dusty, grinning marines pushing rickshaws piled high with balloon-like half-gallon bottles of sake and cases of beer.

There was food at the warehouse, too; huge tins of flour and rice and smaller cans of fish heads, those ghastly delicacies of Nippon. But no one took the food.

Besides, each squad had set up its own mess. We had our own flour and Spam and cans of peaches and sugar and coffee—all stolen in raids on the piles of food which had been hastily unloaded by the transports, fleeing the armada that sank the cruisers. Our ship had been set aflame the day we landed when a Zero crashed amidships. So we had no battalion mess. Marvelously, these little squad messes sprang up all along the beach. The provender was of the best that could be stolen.

With these, and the sake and beer, we lived a rollicking, boisterous life for about a week, until the liquor ran out and the Major came around to commandeer the food.

What a wonderful week it was! What a delicious way to fight a war!

Chuckler, Hoosier, Runner and I had buried our sake and beer in the sands, deep down where the sea had seeped and where it was cool. It was our cache, and no one else could touch it. So it was the four of us who drank the most of it, except when the drink within us enkindled the warmth of generosity. Then we invited others into the circle.

We sat squatting. Because the huge sake bottles were difficult to pour, we had to push them to one another, and we drank by turns, as the Indians smoke the peace pipe. But our method needed the skills of a contortionist. One would grasp the huge bottle between one's thighs, and then, with one's head bent forward so that one's mouth embraced the bottleneck, one would roll backward, allowing the cool white wine to pour down the throat.

Oh, it was good!

My palate was not at all sophisticated, yet no mere refinement of taste could ever match the sheer exuberance flowing from every mouthful of that sake. It is glorious to drink the wine of the enemy.

And we were getting gloriously drunk.

After one of these nocturnal drinking bouts I retired tipsily to my sleeping quarters; that is, I rolled back a few feet from the circle and fell into the shallow depression I had scooped out of the ground. High above me sighed the palm fronds, like lovely asterisks through which filtered the soft and starlit tropic night. I fell asleep. I awoke to the tiny twanging of hordes of invisible insects winging over my chest. I realized they were bullets when I heard the sound of firing to my rear. I went back to sleep, sadly convinced that the Japanese had got behind us.

Such was the power of sake.

In the morning someone explained that the firing had been two companies of the Fifth Regiment, each mistaking the other for the enemy. "Trigger-happy," he said. I believed him. He needed no authority. He had a theory, which was the only authority required on Guadalcanal.

Morning was the best time for the beer; it was cool with the cool of night and the dark sea beneath the sands.

Oakstump did not last long with the beer. It was not that he drank so much, but that he drank it so fast—which is the same thing, perhaps. He arose unsteadily from our circle, stepped from the shade and keeled over almost the instant the sun touched his head. We adorned his body with palm fronds and stood an empty sake bottle on his chest so that he resembled a Shinto shrine.

Then Hoosier became solemnly aware that he was not properly dressed. He had no trousers on. Such a breach of decorum, even in the company of men not customarily correct in these matters, seemed to pain the Hoosier. He lurched to his feet, groped for his missing trousers and staggered down to the water.

"Hey, Hoosier—where you going with those pants? You going to wash your pants, Hoosier?"

"Ah'm gonna put mah pants on."

"In the water?"

He showed his big strong teeth in a silly grin: "Ah always put mah pants on in the ocean."

His dignity was matchless. Each time the surf receded, he would place his left foot in the trouser leg. With the exaggerated care of the inebriate, he would draw that leg up, and then, while balanced precariously on the right foot, a wave would pound up behind him and smack him on his pink behind.

He arose each time in dignity. Gravely, he would go through it once more. Merrily, the wave would roll up again and let him have it. Once or twice, he would teeter for a moment on that disloyal right foot, looking quickly behind him with a half grin, as though to see if his old friend the wave were still there. It always was.

Such was the power of Japanese beer.

Since that first day we had been bombed regularly; at least once, often several times daily. Enemy naval units began to appear in the channel. Contemptuous of our power to retaliate, they sailed in and bombarded us in broad daylight. The Japanese were returning to the battle.

To protect vital Henderson Field against an enemy who seemed determined now to fight for Guadalcanal, special nocturnal patrols were required. The first time that my company was commanded to furnish the patrol marked the end of our drinking, and our careers as beachcombers came crashing to a close in tragicomic style.

It was the day our liquor ran out I was among those who joined the other men from our company and marched away from the beach, through the coconut grove, into the kunai, and so to the point we would defend outside Henderson Field.

In front of me marched No-Behind. He was a tall, slender, noisy fellow from Michigan who was oddly capable of exasperating anyone in H Company merely by marching in front of him. It was an odd affliction in that it was no affliction: No-Behind actually seemed not to have a behind. So long and flat were his hips that his cartridge belt seemed always in danger of slipping to his ankles. No curve of bone or flare of flesh was there to arrest it. He seemed to walk without bending the knees of his long thin legs, and most maddening, where his trousers should have bulged with the familiar bulk of a behind, they seemed to sag inward! When to this was added a girlish voice that seemed forever raised in high-pitched profanity, there emerged an epicene quality which enraged those unlucky enough to march behind No-Behind. Often I quivered to draw my bayonet and skewer No-Behind where his behind was not.

This day, as we passed with fixed bayonets through the kunai toward the line of wood beyond which a round red sun had fallen, Corporal Smoothface marched behind No-Behind. Smoothface was drunk on the last of the sake. He seemed to be babbling happily enough, when, suddenly, with a crazy yell, he lowered his rifle and drove the bayonet at No-Behind.

We thought Smoothface had killed him, for No-Behind's scream had been that of a dying man. But, fortunately for No-Behind, his very insufficiency in the target area had saved him; the bayonet passed through his trousers without even breaking the flesh, and it had not been the cutting edge of the bayonet but the hard round feel of the rifle muzzle that had provoked his expiring shout.

Smoothface found it so funny he had to sit down to contain his laughter. Then, as he arose, a battery of artillery concealed in the wood gave nerve-jangling voice. They were our seventy-five-millimeter howitzers, shooting at what, we did not know, for they shot frequently and we never knew if they were merely registering terrain or actually blasting the enemy. But the sudden crash of field pieces is always a disturbing thing, even if the guns turn out to be friendly.

Smoothface bared his small, even teeth in an animal snarl. He unlimbered his rifle again, and returned the fire. That was the end of the Guadalcanal Campaign for Corporal Smoothface. He was led away under guard.

But he had one last glorious round remaining. Placed in the rear of a captain's jeep, he rose to his feet, abusing him.

"Ah'll never ride with Captain Headlines," he swore, and as he swore it, the jeep leapt forward. Smoothface was ejected in a slow somersault into the air, came down on his ankle, broke it and was taken to the hospital, where, that very night, a rare transport landed on our airfield. He was evacuated to New Zealand, was cured, given a light brig sentence, and finally turned loose to browse among the fleshpots of Auckland. His broken ankle, although perhaps not honorably suffered, was the very first of the "beer wounds," which all veterans covet so mightily—those merely superficial holes or cuts or breaks which take a man out of battle and into the admiring glances and free drinks of civilization.

It was still light over the airfield when we left it and stepped into the gloom of the jungle. It was as though one had walked from a lighted, busy street into the murk and silence of a church, except that here was no reverence or smell of candle-grease, but the beginning of dread and the odor of corruption.

We were told off at staggered intervals of about ten yards. I have no idea how many men were on the patrol, perhaps slightly more than a hundred of us, of which some thirty would have been from H Company. We never knew these things. All that we knew was that in front of us lay the dark and moving jungle and quite probably the enemy, behind us the airfield in which reposed absolutely all of Guadalcanal's military value.

Our entrenching tools made muffled noises while we scooped foxholes out of the jungle floor. It was like digging into a compost heap ten thousand years old. Beneath this perfection of corruption lay a dark rich loam. We had barely finished when night fell, abruptly, blackly, like a shade drawn swiftly down from jungle roof to jungle floor. We slipped into the foxholes. We lay down and waited.

It was a darkness without time. It was an impenetrable darkness. To the right and the left of me rose up those terrible formless things of my imagination, which I could not see because there was no light. I could not see, but I dared not close my eyes lest the darkness crawl beneath my eyelids and suffocate me. I could only hear. My ears became my being and I could hear the specks of life that crawled beneath my clothing, the rotting of the great tree which rose from its three-cornered trunk above me. I could hear the darkness gathering against me and the silences that lay between the moving things.

I could hear the enemy everywhere about me, whispering to each other and calling my name. I lay open-mouthed and half-mad beneath that giant tree. I had not looked into its foliage before the darkness and now I fancied it infested with Japanese. Everything and all the world became my enemy, and soon my very body betrayed me and became my foe. My leg became a creeping Japanese, and then the other leg. My arms, too, and then my head.

My heart was alone. It was me. I was my heart.

It lay quivering, I lay quivering, in that rotten hole while the darkness gathered and all creation conspired for my heart.

How long? I lay for an eternity. There was no time. Time had disintegrated in that black void. There was only emptiness, and that is Something; there was only being; there was only consciousness.

Like the light that comes up suddenly in a darkened theatre, daylight came quickly. Dawn came, and so myself came back to myself. I could see the pale outlines of my comrades to right and left, and I marveled to see how tame my tree could be, how unforbidding could be its branches.

I know now why men light fires.

Urgency and a certain air of inquiry and reproach characterized the manner of the Major as he drove his jeep through the coconuts, stopping at each squad mess along the line to commandeer the provender. Except for the urgency, he might have been a scoutmaster scolding his charges for having eaten their lunch by midmorning.

The Major's tour marked the death of the squad messes. Our brief escape from battalion authority was ended, and a battalion galley was being set up. But the Major found precious little food to cart off to a pyramidal tent which was set up about two hundred yards in from the beach. This was where we ate, and this was where we were introduced to our new diet of rice. The food had belonged to the enemy, and so had the wooden bowls from which we ate it. We preferred these to our own mess gear with its maddening capacity for making all food taste like metal. We ate a bowl of rice for breakfast and had the same for supper. Once a marine complained of worms in the rice to one of our two doctors.

"They're dead," he laughed. "They can't hurt you. Eat them, and be glad you have fresh meat."

He was joking, but he was serious. No one resented it. Everyone thought the doctor had a good sense of humor.

The day after our diet of rice began, the Major's unwonted urgency became clear to us. We were ordered up from the beach to new positions on the west bank of the Tenaru River. Our orders commanded us to urgency.

The enemy was expected.

2

The Tenaru River lay green and evil, like a serpent, across the palmy coastal plain. It was called a river, but it was not a river; like most of the streams of Oceania, it was a creek—not thirty yards wide.

Perhaps it was not even a creek, for it did not always flow and it seldom reached its destination, the sea. Where it might have emptied into Iron Bottom Bay, a spit of sand, some forty feet wide, penned it up. The width of the sandspit varied with the tides, and sometimes the tide or the wind might cause the Tenaru to rise, when, slipping over the spit, it would fall into the bosom of the sea, its mother.

Normally, the Tenaru stood stagnant, its surface crested with scum and fungus; evil, I said, and green. If there are river gods, the Tenaru was inhabited by a baleful spirit.

Our section—two squads, one with the Gentleman as gunner, the other with Chuckler as gunner and me as assistant—took up position approximately three hundred yards upstream from the sandspit. As we dug, we had it partially in view; that is, what would be called the enemy side of the sandspit. For the Tenaru marked our lines. On our side, the west bank, was the extremity of the marine position; on the other, a no-man's-land of coconuts through which an attack against us would have to pass.

The Japanese would have to force the river to our front; or come over the narrow sandspit to our left, which was well defended by riflemen and a number of machine gun posts and barbed wire; or else try our right flank, which extended only about a hundred yards south of us, before curving back north to the Tenaru's narrowest point, spanned by a wooden bridge.

The emplacement for the Gentleman's gun was excellently located to rake the coconut grove opposite. We dug it first, leaving Chuckler's and my gun standing some twenty yards downstream, above the ground, protected by a single strand of barbed wire strung midway down the steeply sloping river bank. We would emplace it next day.

We dug the Gentleman's gun pit wide and deep—some ten feet square and five feet down—for we wanted the gunner to be able to stand while firing, and we wanted the pit to serve as a bomb shelter as well, for the bombs were falling fiercer.

But furiously as we worked, naked to the waist, sweat streaming so steadily our belts were turned sodden, we were unable to finish the pit on the first day. When night fell, only the excavation was done, plus a dirt shelf where the gun was placed. We would have to wait for the next day to roof it over with coconut logs.

We felt exposed in our half-finished fortifications, unsure. The

dark made sinister humpbacks of the piles of soft red earth we had
excavated, and on which we sat.

But, because we did not know real battle—its squallish trick of
suddenness—we could not feel foreboding as we sat atop the soft
mounds, concealing the telltale coals of our bitter Japanese cigarettes in cupped hands, softly smoking, softly talking. We were uneasy only in that shiftiness that came each night and disappeared
each dawn.

No one went to bed. The stars were out, and this was enough to
keep everyone up, unwilling to waste a bright night.

Suddenly in the river, upstream to our right, there appeared a
widening, rippling V. It seemed to be moving steadily downstream.
At the point of the V were two greenish lights, small, round, close
together.

Jawgia whooped and fired his rifle at it.

To our right came a fusillade of shots. It was from G Company
riflemen, shooting also at the V. More bullets hit the water. The
V disappeared.

The stars vanished. The night darkened. Like our voices, the men
began to trail off to bed, wrapping themselves in their ponchos and
lying on the ground a few yards behind the pit. Only the Chuckler
and myself were left, to stand watch.

Lights—swinging, bumping lights, like lanterns or headlights—
glittered across the river in the grove. It was fantastic, a truck there,
as though we might awake next morning and find a railroad station
confronting us across that stagnant stream. The coconut grove was
no-man's-land. The enemy had a right to be there, but, by all the experience of jungle warfare, it was inviting death to mark himself
with lights, to let his truck wheels shout "Here we are!"

"Who goes there?" the Chuckler bellowed.

The lights bumped and swung serenely on.

"Who goes there? Answer, or I'll let you have it!"

The lights went out.

This was too much. Everyone was awake. The mysterious V in the river and now these ghostly lights—it was too much! We jabbered excitedly, and once again warmed our souls in the heat of our voices.

Shattering machine gun fire broke out far to the left. As far down as the sandspit, perhaps. There came another burst. Again. Another. The sharply individual report of the rifle punctuated the uproar. There followed the "plop" of heavy mortars being launched behind us, then the crunching roar of their detonation across the Tenaru. The conflagration was sweeping toward us up the river, like a train of powder.

It was upon us in an instant, and then we were firing. We were so disorganized we had not the sense to disperse, clustering around that open pit as though we were born of it. Falsetto screeching rose directly opposite us and we were blasting away at it, sure that human intruders had provoked the cry of the birds. I helped the Gentleman fire his gun, although I was not his assistant. He concentrated on the river bank, firing burst after burst there, convinced that the Japs were preparing to swim the river. The screeching stopped.

The Gentleman spoke softly. "Tell those clucks to quit firing. Tell them to wait until they hear the birds making a clatter, 'cause a smart man'd try to move under cover of it. That's when they'll be moving."

I was glad he gave me this little order to execute. I was having no fun standing in the pit, watching the Gentleman fire. I crawled out and told everyone what he had said. They ignored it and kept banging away. There came a lull, and in that silent space, I, who had had no chance to fire my own weapon, blasted away with my pistol. I leaned over the mound and shoved my pistol-clenching hand into the dark and emptied the clip. There came a roar of anger from the Hoosier.

"Dammit, Lucky, ain't you got no better sense'n to go firing past a fellow's ear? You like to blow my head off, you Jersey jerk!"

I laughed at him, and the Chuckler crawled back from the bank and whispered, "C'mon, let's get our gun."

We snaked up the bank on our bellies, for the night was alive with the angry hum of bullets. The Chuckler took the gunner's spot and I crouched alongside in the position to keep the gun fed. We had plenty of ammunition, the long two hundred and fifty–round belts coiled wickedly in the light green boxes, those same sturdy boxes which you now see slung on the shoulders of shoeshine boys.

The Chuckler fired and the gun slumped forward out of his hands, digging its snout into the dirt, knocking off the flash hider with a disturbing clatter, spraying our own area with bullets.

"That yellow-belly!" the Chuckler cursed.

He cursed a certain corporal who was not then distinguishing himself for bravery, and who had set up the gun and done it so sloppily that the tripod had collapsed at the first recoil.

I crawled down the slope and straightened it. I leaned hard on the clamps.

"She's tight," I told the Chuckler.

His answer was a searing burst that streaked past my nose.

A man says of the eruption of battle: "All hell broke loose." The first time he says it, it is true—wonderfully descriptive. The millionth time it is said, it has been worn into meaninglessness: it has gone the way of all good phrasing, it has become cliché.

But within five minutes of that first machine gun burst, of the appearance of that first enemy flare that suffused the battlefield in unearthly greenish light—and by its dying accentuated the reenveloping night—within five minutes of this, all hell broke loose. Everyone was firing, every weapon was sounding voice; but this was no orchestration, no terribly beautiful symphony of death, as decadent rear-echelon observers write. Here was cacophony; here was dissonance; here was wildness; here was the absence of rhythm, the loss of limit, for everyone fires what, when and where he chooses; here was booming, sounding, shrieking, wailing, hissing, crashing, shaking, gibbering noise. Here was hell.

Yet each weapon has its own sound, and it is odd with what clarity the trained ear distinguishes each one and catalogues it, plucks it out of the general din, even though it be intermingled or coincidental with the voice of a dozen others, even though one's own machine gun spits and coughs and dances and shakes in choleric fury. The plop of the outgoing mortar with the crunch of its fall, the clatter of the machine guns and the lighter, faster rasp of the Browning Automatic Rifles, the hammering of fifty-caliber machine guns, the crash of seventy-five-millimeter howitzer shells, the crackling of rifle fire, the *wham* of thirty-seven-millimeter anti-tank guns firing point-blank canister at the charging enemy—each of these conveys a definite message, and sometimes meaning, to the understanding ear, even though that ear be filled with the total wail of battle.

So it was that our ears prickled at strange new sounds: the lighter, shingle-snapping crack of the Japanese rifle, the gargle of their extremely fast machine guns, the hiccup of their light mortars.

To our left, a stream of red tracers arched over to the enemy bank. Distance and the cacophony being raised around us seemed to invest them with silence, as though they were bullets fired in a deaf man's world.

"It's the Indian's gun," I whispered.

"Yeah. But those tracers are bad stuff. I'm glad we took 'em out of our belts. He keeps up that tracer stuff, and they'll spot him, sure."

They did.

They set up heavy machine guns in an abandoned amtrack on their side of the river and they killed the Indian.

Their slugs slammed through the sandbags. They ate their way up the water-jacket of his gun and they ate their way into his heart. They killed him, killed the Indian kid, the flat-faced, anonymous prizefighter from Pittsburgh. He froze on the trigger with their lead in his heart; he was dead, but he killed more of them. He wasn't anonymous, then; he wasn't a prelim boy, then.

They wounded his assistant. They blinded him. But he fought on. The Marines gave him the Navy Cross and Hollywood made a picture about him and the Tenaru Battle. I guess America wanted a hero fast, a live one; and the Indian was dead.

The other guy was a hero, make no mistake about it; but some of us felt sad that the poor Indian got nothing.

It was the first organized Japanese attack on Guadalcanal, the American fighting man's first challenge to the Japanese "superman." The "supermen" put bullets into the breast of the Indian, but he fired two hundred more rounds at them.

How could the Marines forget the Indian?

Now we had tracer trouble of a different kind. We had begun to take turns firing, and I was on the gun. The tracers came toward me, alongside me. Out of the river dark they came. You do not see them coming. They are not there; then, there they are, dancing around you on tiptoe; sparkles gay with the mirth of hell.

They came toward me, and time stretched out. There were but a few bursts, I am sure, but time was frozen while I leaned away from them.

"Chuckler," I whispered. "We'd better move. It looks like they've got the range. Maybe we ought to keep moving. They won't be able to get the range that way. And maybe they'll think we've got more guns than we really have."

Chuckler nodded. He unclamped the gun and I slipped it free of its socket in the tripod. Chuckler lay back and pulled the tripod over him. I lay back and supported the gun on my chest. We moved backward, like backstroke swimmers, almost as we had moved when we stole the case of beer out of the North Carolina shanty, trying, meanwhile, to avoid making noise that might occur during one of those odd and suspenseful times of silence that befalls battles—noise which might attract fire from the opposite bank—if anyone was there.

For, you see, we never knew if there really was anyone there. We heard noises; we fired at them. We felt shells explode on our side and heard enemy bullets; but we could not be sure of their point of origin.

But, now, there was no enemy fire while we squirmed to our new position. We set up the gun once more and resumed firing, tripping our bursts at sounds of activity as before. We remained here fifteen minutes, then sought a new position. Thus we passed the remainder of the battle; moving and firing, moving and firing.

Dawn seemed to burst from a mortar tube. The two coincided; the rising bombardment of our mortars and the arrival of light. We could see, now, that the coconut grove directly opposite us had no life in it. There were bodies, but no living enemy.

But to the left, toward the ocean and across the Tenaru, the remnant of this defeated Japanese attacking force was being annihilated. We could see them, running. Our mortars had got behind them. We were walking our fire in; that is dropping shells to the enemy's rear, then lobbing the projectile steadily closer to our own lines, so that the unfortunate foe was forced to abandon cover after cover, being drawn inexorably toward our front, where he was at last flushed and destroyed.

We could see them flitting from tree to tree. The Gentleman's gun was in excellent position to enfilade. He did. He fired long bursts at them. Some of us fired our rifles. But we were out of the fight, now; way off on the extreme right flank. We could add nothing to a situation so obviously under control.

"Hold your fire," someone from G Company shouted at the Gentleman. "First Battalion coming through."

Infantry had crossed the Tenaru at the bridge to our right and were fanning out in the coconut grove. They would sweep toward the ocean.

Light tanks were crossing the sandspit far to the left, leading a counterattack.

The Japanese were being nailed into a coffin.

Everyone had forgotten the fight and was watching the carnage, when shouting swept up the line. A group of Japanese dashed along the opposite river edge, racing in our direction. Their appearance so surprised everyone that there were no shots.

We dived for our holes and gun positions. I jumped to the gun which the Chuckler and I had left standing on the bank. I unclamped the gun and fired, spraying my shots as though I were handling a hose.

All but one fell. The first fell as though his underpart had been cut from him by a scythe, and the others fell tumbling, screaming.

Once again our gun collapsed and I grabbed a rifle—I remember it had no sling—which had been left near the gun. The Jap who had survived was deep into the coconuts by the time I found him in the rifle sights. There was his back, bobbing large, and he seemed to be throwing his pack away. Then I had fired and he wasn't there anymore.

Perhaps it was not I who shot him, for everyone had found their senses and their weapons by then. But I boasted that I had. Perhaps, too, it was a merciful bullet that pounded him between the shoulder blades; for he was fleeing to a certain and horrible end: black nights, hunger and slow dissolution in the rain forest. But I had not thought of mercy then.

Modern war went forward in the jungle.

Men of the First Battalion were cleaning up. Sometimes they drove a Japanese toward us. He would cower on the river bank, hiding; unaware that opposite him were we, already the victors, numerous, heavily armed, lusting for more blood. We killed a few more this way. The Fever was on us.

Down on the sandspit the last nail was being driven into the coffin.

Some of the Japanese threw themselves into the channel and swam away from that grove of horror. They were like lemmings. They could not come back. Their heads bobbed like corks on the horizon. The marines killed them from the prone position; the marines lay on their bellies in the sand and shot them through the head.

The battle was over.

Beneath a bright moon that night, the V reappeared in the river. The green lights gleamed malevolently. Someone shot at it. Rifle fire crackled along the line. The V vanished. We waited, tense. No one came.

Lieutenant Ivy-League strode up to our pits in the morning. He sat on a coconut log and told us what had happened. He smoked desperately and stared into the river as he talked. The skin around his eyes was drawn tight with strain and with shock. His eyes had already taken on that aspect peculiar to Guadalcanal, that constant stare of pupils that seemed darker, larger, rounder, more absolute. It was particularly noticeable in the brown-eyed men. Their eyes seemed to get auburn, like the color of an Irish setter.

"They tried to come over the sandspit," the lieutenant said. "There must have been a thousand of them. We had only that one strand of wire and the guns. You should see them stacked up in front of Bitenail's gun. Must be three deep. They were crazy. They didn't even fire their rifles." He looked at us. "We heard firing up here. What happened?"

We told him. He nodded, but he was not listening; he was still intent on that yelling horde sweeping over the sandspit. When he spoke again it was to tell us who had been killed. There were more than a dozen from H Company, besides more than a score of wounded. Four or five of the dead were from our platoon. Two of them had been hacked to death. A Japanese scouting party had found them asleep in their hole on the river bank and sliced them into pieces.

It is not always or immediately saddening to hear "who got it." Except for one's close buddies, it is difficult to feel deep, racking grief for the dead, and now, hearing the lieutenant tolling off the names, I had to force my face into a mask of mourning, deliberately adorn my heart with black, as it were, for I was shocked to gaze inward and see no sorrow there. Rather than permit myself to know myself a monster (as I seemed, then) I deliberately deluded myself by feigning bereavement. So did we all.

Only when I heard the name of the doctor who had joked about the wormy rice did a real pang pierce my heart.

Lieutenant Ivy-League arose, still staring into the river, and said, "I've got to get going. I've got to write those letters." He turned and left.

We got the second gun emplaced that morning. Then, the Hoosier and I sneaked off to the beach.

Our regiment had killed something like nine hundred of them. Most of them lay in clusters or heaps before the gun pits commanding the sandspit, as though they had not died singly but in groups. Moving among them were the souvenir hunters, picking their way delicately as though fearful of booby traps, while stripping the bodies of their possessions.

Only the trappings of war change. Only these distinguish the Marine souvenir hunter, bending over the fallen Jap, from Hector denuding slain Patroclus of the borrowed armor of Achilles.

One of the marines went methodically among the dead armed with a pair of pliers. He had observed that the Japanese have a penchant for gold fillings in their teeth, often for solid gold teeth. He was looting their very mouths. He would kick their jaws agape, peer into the mouth with all the solicitude of a Park Avenue dentist—careful, always careful not to contaminate himself by touch—and yank out all that glittered. He kept the gold teeth in an empty Bull Durham tobacco sack, which he wore around his neck in the manner of an amulet. Souvenirs, we called him.

The thought of him and of the other trophy-takers suggested to me, as I returned from the pits, that across the river lay an unworked mine of souvenirs to which I might rightfully stake a claim.

When I had shot the Japanese fleeing down the river bank, something silver had flashed when the first one fell. I imagined it to be the sun's reflection off an officer's insignia. If he had been an officer, he must have been armed with a saber. This most precious prize of all the war I was determined to get.

I slipped through the barbed wire and clambered down the bank. I left my clothes at the water's edge, like a schoolboy on a summer's day, and slipped into the water. I had a bayonet between my teeth; still the schoolboy, fancying myself a bristling pirate.

I swam breaststroke. Not even the fire of the enemy would induce me to put my face into that putrid stream. The water was thick with scum. My flesh crept while I swam, neck stiff and head erect like a swan's, the cold feel of the bayonet between my teeth, and my saliva running fast around it so that it threatened to slip out at any moment.

I paddled carefully around the body of a big Japanese soldier, lying in the water with one foot caught in the underbrush. He swayed gently, like a beached rowboat. He seemed unusually bloated, until I perceived that his blouse was stuffed with cooked rice and that his pants were likewise loaded to the knees, where he had tied leather thongs to keep the rice from falling out. "Chow hound," I thought, and felt an odd affection for him. My feet touched the slime of the river bottom. I had to advance about three yards up the bank. My feet sank so deep in the soft mud I feared momentarily that I was in a bog. The mud came up to my calves and made greedy sucking sounds with every step, while surrendering little swarms of fiddler crabs that scuttled away in sideways flight.

Dead bodies were strewn about the grove. The tropics had got at them already, and they were beginning to spill open. I was horrified at the swarms of flies; black, circling funnels that seemed to emerge from every orifice: from the mouth, the eyes, the ears. The beating of their myriad tiny wings made a dreadful low hum.

The flies were in possession of the field; the tropics had won; her minions were everywhere, smacking their lips over this bounty of rotting flesh. All of my elation at the victory, all of my fanciful cockiness fled before the horror of what my eyes beheld. It could be my corrupting body the white maggots were moving over; perhaps one day it might be.

Holding myself stiffly, as though fending off panic with a straight arm, I returned to the river bank and slipped into the water. But not before I had stripped one of my victims of his bayonet and field glasses, both of which I slung across my chest, crisscross like a grenadier. I had found no saber. None of the dead men was an officer.

I swam back, eager to be away from that horrid grove. My comrades, who had covered my excursion with our guns, mistook my grimace of loathing for a grin of triumph, when, streaked with slime, I emerged from the Tenaru. They crowded around to examine my loot. Then, I went to chow.

Coming back, I noticed a knot of marines, many from G Company, gathered in excitement on the riverbank. Runner rushed up to them with my new field glasses.

He had them to his eyes, as I came up. I thought he was squinting overhard, then I saw that he was actually grimacing. I took the glasses from him and focused on the opposite shore, where I saw a crocodile eating the fat "chow-hound" Japanese. I watched in debased fascination, but when the crocodile began to tug at the intestines, I recalled my own presence in that very river hardly an hour ago, and my knees went weak and I relinquished the glasses.

That night the V reappeared in the river. Everyone whooped and hollered. No one fired. We knew what it was. It was the crocodile.

Three smaller V's trailed afterward.

They kept us awake, crunching. The smell kept us awake. Even though we lay with our heads swathed in a blanket—which was how we kept off the mosquitoes—the smell overpowered us. Smell, the sense which somehow seems a joke, is the one most susceptible to outrage. It will give you no rest. One can close one's eyes to ugliness or shield the ears from sound; but from a powerful smell there is no recourse but flight. And since we could not flee, we could not escape this smell; and we could not sleep.

We never fired at the crocodiles, though they returned to their repast day after day until the remains were removed to the mass burning and burial which served as funeral pyre for the enemy we had annihilated.

We never shot at the crocs because we considered them a sort of "river patrol." Their appetite for flesh aroused, they seemed to promenade the Tenaru daily. No enemy, we thought, would dare to swim the river with them in it; nor would he succeed if he dared. We relied upon our imperfect knowledge of the habits of the crocodiles ("If they chase you, run zigzag: they can't change direction.") and a thick network of barbed wire to forestall their tearing us to pieces. Sometimes on black nights, in a spasm of fear, it might be imagined that the big croc was after us, like the crocodile with the clock inside of him who pursues Captain Hook in *Peter Pan*.

So the crocodiles became our darlings, we never molested them. Nor did any of us ever swim the Tenaru again.

3

Our victory in the fight which we called "The Battle of Hell's Point" was not so great as we had imagined it to be. It was to be but one of many fights for Guadalcanal, and, in the end, not the foremost of them. But being the first in our experience, we took it for total triumph; like those who take the present for the best of all worlds, having no reference to the past nor regard for the future.

From the high plateau of triumph we were about to descend to the depths of trial and tedium. The Japanese attack was to be redoubled and prolonged and varied. It would come from the sky, the sea and the land. In between every trial there would stretch out the tedium that sucks a man dry, drawing off the juice from body and soul as a native removes the contents of a stick of sugar cane, leaving it spent, cracked, good for nothing but the flames.

And there is terror, coming from the interaction of trial and tedium: the first, shaking a man as the wind in the treetops; the second, eroding him as the flood at the roots. Each fresh trial leaves a man more shaken than the last, and each period of tedium—with its time for speculative dread—leaves his foundations worn lower, his roots less firm for the next trial. Sometimes there is a final shattering: a man crouching in a pit beneath the bombardment of a battleship might put a pistol to his head and deliver himself. Sometimes it is partial; another man might break at the sound of a diving enemy plane and scream and shudder and wring his hands—and rise to run. This is the terror I mean; this is the terror that strangles reason with the clawing hands of panic. I saw it twice, I felt it pluck at me twice. But it was rare. It claimed few victims.

Courage was a commonplace.

It formed a club or corporation, much as do those other common things upon which men, for diverse reasons, place so great a value; like money, like charity. For it is the common on which the exclusive rests. Our muddy machine gun pits were transformed into Courage Clubs when bombs fell or Japanese warships pounded us from the sea. There was protocol to be observed, too, and it was natural that the poor fellow who might break into momentary terror should cause pained silences and embarrassed coughs. Everyone looked the other way, like millionaires confronted by the horrifying sight of a club member borrowing five dollars from the waiter.

But there was a bit more charity in our clubs, I think. We were not quite so puffed up that we could not recognize the ugly thing on our friend's face as the elder brother of the thing fluttering within our own innards. You today, me tomorrow.

A month had passed, and it seemed to us the falling bombs were as numerous as the flies around us. Three times a day and every Sunday morning (the Jap fixity of idea, nourished on the great success of Sunday morning at Pearl Harbor) the coconut grove was sibilant with the whispering of the bombs. It sounded like the confession of a giant.

At night Washing Machine Charlie picked up the slack. Washing Machine Charlie—so named for the sound of his motors—was the nocturnal marauder who prowled our skies. There may have been more than one Charlie—that is, more than one Nipponese pilot making the midnight run over our positions—but there was never more than one plane at a time overhead at night. That was all that was needed for such badgering work.

Like the dog whose bark is worse than his bite, the throb of Charlie's motors was more fearsome than the thump of his bombs. Once the bombs were dropped, we would be relieved, knowing he would be off and away. But the drone of Charlie's circling progress kept everyone awake and uneasy for so long as Charlie cared—or dared. Dawn meant departure for Charlie, for then our planes could rise to chastise him, and he would become visible to our anti-aircraft batteries.

Charlie did not kill many people, but, like Macbeth, he murdered sleep.

To these trials was added the worst ordeal: shelling from the sea.

Enemy warships—usually cruisers, sometimes battleships—stand off your coast. It is night and you cannot see them, nor could you if it were day, for they are miles and miles away. Our airplanes cannot rise at night to meet them. Our seventy-five-millimeter pack howitzers are as effectual as popguns opposing rifles. The enemy has everything his way.

We could see the flashes of the guns far out to sea. We heard the soft *pah-boom, pah-boom* of the salvos. Then rushing through the night, straining like an airy boxcar, came the huge projectiles. The earth rocks and shakes upon the terrifying crash of the detonation, though it be hundreds of yards away. Your stomach is squeezed, as though a monster hand were kneading it into dough; you gasp for breath like the football player who falls heavily and has the wind knocked out of him.

Flash. Pah-boom. Hwoo, hwoo-hwoee.

They're lowering their sights...it's coming closer...oh, that one was close...the sandbags are falling...I can't hear it. I can't hear the shell...it's the one you don't hear, they say, the one you don't hear...where is it?...where is it?

Flash!...Pah-boom!... Thank God...it's lifted...it's going the other way.

Dawn blinks across the river. They go. The planes on the airstrip behind us rise in pursuit. We emerge from the pits. Someone says he is thankful the bombardment continued all night, for if it had ceased, an attack by land might have followed. Someone else calls him a fool. They argue. But nobody cares. It is daylight now and there are only the bombings to worry about—and the heat, and the mosquitoes, and the rice lying in the belly like stones.

The eyes are rounder. The tendency to stare is more pronounced.

We hated working parties. We were weak with hunger. We manned the lines at night. By day, they formed us into working parties and took us to the airfield. We buried boxes of ammunition there. Digging deep holes, lugging the hundred-pound crates, we only got weaker.

Once, returning from a working party, the bombers swept suddenly overhead. I fled before the crashing approach of the bombs they scattered throughout our grove. I leapt into a freshly dug slit trench with three others. I crouched there while roaring air squeezed my stomach. Behind me crouched another man, his face against my bare back. I felt his lips moving in prayer over my skin, the quivering kiss of fear and faith.

When I returned to the pits, they told me that the other working party, the one that I had missed, had been obliterated by the bombs. That was when Manners died, and the gay Texan.

Chuckler made corporal. He made it in a battlefield promotion. Lieutenant Ivy-League had recommended him for a Silver Star for our work on the riverbank in the Hell's Point fight, specifying that our action in moving the gun from place to place may have discouraged an enemy flanking attack. The regimental commander reduced the citation to a promotion of one grade. Ivy-League had not mentioned me in his recommendation. I have no idea why not. Though it was Chuckler who had first grabbed our gun, it was I who had proposed the moves—and Ivy-League knew it. I resented being ignored, although I tried to conceal it, and Chuckler, embarrassed, did his best to pass over it, trying to make a joke of it. But he deserved both promotion and citation, for he was a born leader. I never forgave Ivy-League, and I think this marked the beginning of my dislike for him.

————

They brought us mosquito nets. We still slept on the ground—a poncho under us if it was dry, over us if it was raining. But the mosquito nets were a boon. Now we could use our blankets to sleep on, rather than to guard our head against mosquitoes. The poncho could be rolled up for a pillow; if it rained, it went over us. But the nets really came too late. We were full of malaria.

They brought in supplies. Each squad got a toothbrush, a package of razor blades and a bar of candy. We raffled them off. The Runner won the candy bar. Despairing of dividing it among ten men, he fell into a torment of indecision, until everyone assured him he should eat it himself. He slunk off to the underbrush to do so.

Oakstump continued to reinforce his private fort. Every time I saw him it seemed he had an ax in his hand or a coconut log on his shoulder. Once he carried a log so huge that it gouged a hole in his shoulder; a wound which, in civilization, would have required stitching.

Everyone kept saying hopefully that the army was coming in next week to relieve us.

Everyone was in despair. We heard that the army relief force had been destroyed at sea.

Chuckler and I visited the cemetery. It lay to the south off the coastal road that ran from east to west through the coconuts. We knelt to pray before the graves of the men we had known. Only palm fronds marked the place where they were buried, although here and there were rude crosses, on which were nailed the men's identification tags. Some of the crosses bore mess gear tins, affixed to the wood like rude medallions, and on those the marines had lovingly carved their epitaphs.

"He died fighting."

"A real marine."

"A big guy with a bigger heart."

"Our Buddy."

"The harder the going, the more cheerful he was."

There was this verse, which I have seen countless times, before and since, the direct and unpolished cry of a marine's sardonic heart:

And when he gets to Heaven
To St. Peter he will tell:
One more Marine reporting, sir—
I've served my time in Hell.

Other inscriptions, and most often the dead man's name, were made by pressing bullets into the ground, so that the round brass end of the cartridges gleamed above the earth. Chuckler and I lifted our gaze from the cemetery to encompass the entire level plain sweeping back to the hills. Chuckler raised his eyebrows sardonically.

"Plenty of room," he said.

"That's for sure," I said.

We said a prayer before the grave of one of the dead from our own platoon.

"You know," Chuckler said, rising, "he had two hundred bucks in his kick before Hell's Point. He won it in a poker game."

"Yeah?"

"When they went to bury him he didn't have a dime."

We plotted the death of a rat that had become attached to our machine gun pit. We swore we would kill it and have fresh meat. Its habit was to scurry across the gun embrasure, almost flitting, it moved so fast in the half light. It seemed the rat grew bolder as we grew weaker from hunger, until in our extremity it actually sauntered across the embrasure! We never caught it. If we had, I doubt that we would have eaten it.

———

One night we were shelled by cruisers. A projectile landed in the river mud not far from us; the pit shook like jelly. No one spoke, until No-Behind said hopefully, "Must be a dud." I said, "Didn't you ever hear of a delayed fuse?" and everybody giggled, except No-Behind, who drew his breath sobbingly. I had to slap him.

Another night—a very black night—we huddled in the pits while the sounds of battle came to us from the hills on our right. We were alerted for an attack. We sat wonderingly the whole night, all of it, until morning brought the news that the first half of the battle of Bloody Ridge had been fought. The Japs had been repulsed.

When night fell again, the battle was resumed. We sat again in the black pit, waiting. This time there was almost no crackling of small arms fire, only the thump and crash of artillery—our artillery, we hoped. We took turns peering from the pit for signs of the enemy on our front, or crawled out on the river bank for a better look. We could only hope the Raiders and Paramarines would hold, up there in that black-and-scarlet hell, where the issue had become so close that our own artillery was falling upon our own positions, abandoned by the defending marines and overrun by the attackers. It was a most unbelievable barrage our one-hundred-and-five-millimeters threw out. I was nowhere near either end of it, yet it made my teeth ache.

Morning was a blessing. It chased away fear of the Japanese breaking our line up in the hills, pouring through the gap, spilling into the groves behind us. We knew the Japs had been beaten. Strange, how the anxiety of that vigil could be almost as wearing as the actual fight.

The Hoosier said it next day.

We were gathered in the shade of the only tree on the river bank. Hoosier sat leaning against the trunk, whittling on a stick.

He kept on plying the stick with his knife, slicing off long curly slivers of white wood, seeming not to care whether or not anyone heeded his words.

"They're gonna whittle us," he said, shaping his sentences proportionate to the slivers. "They come in last night against the Raiders, same as they come in against us. Sure, we beat them. So'd the Raiders. But ever' time we lose a few chips. Ever' time we lose a couple hundred men. What do they care what they lose? Life is cheap with them. They got plenty more, anyway." He waved the stick. "They got plenty of sticks, but we just got the one, we just got us. Fellow from the Fifth came by this morning and said the Japs was unloading two more troop transports down at Kokum. They keep on whittlin' us. Ever' day we lose ten, twenty fellows from the bombing. Ever' night Washing Machine Charlie gets a couple. When they hit us with them battleships, I dunno how many we lose.

"But they got it all their own way," he continued, grunting as the knife cut into a hard spot, " 'cause we ain't got no ships and we ain't got no airplanes 'cept a coupla Grummans that cain't get off the ground half the time because we ain't got no gasoline. They got the ships and they got the airplanes and it looks like they got the time, too. So Ah'm telling you"—the knife cut through and the stick broke—"they're gonna whittle us."

The Chuckler sought to make a joke of it.

"What's eating you? You never had it so good. Here's a guy getting lamb's tongue in his rice and he wants to get back to civilization and stand in them long lines for his war bonds. Whaddya want—egg in your beer?"

"Don't be a damn fool, Chuckler. Ah'm not kidding. They're gonna wear us down."

"No egg in my beer," said the Runner. "Just give it to me straight, just let me have mine in a nice tall glass like they have at the Staler. Carling's. Carling's Black Label."

Hoosier arose and looked down at us with a glance of wearied exasperation. He strode away, and we sat there in silence. We felt like theology students whose instructor takes his leave after presenting the most compelling arguments against the existence of God. Our faith in victory had been unquestioning. Its opposite, defeat, had no currency among us. Victory was possible, that was all; it would be easy or difficult, quick or prolonged, but it would be victory. So here came the disturbing Hoosier, displaying the other side of the coin: showing us defeat.

It shook us, and it was from this moment that we dated the feeling of what is called expendability.

All armies have expendable items. That is, a part or unit, the destruction of which will not be fatal to the whole. In some ordeals, a man might consider his finger expendable, but not his hand; or, in extremity, his arm but not his heart. There are expendable items which may be lost or destroyed in the field, either in peace or in war, without their owner being required to replace them. A rifle is so expendable or a cartridge belt. So are men.

Men are the most expendable of all.

Hunger, the jungle, the Japanese, not one nor all of these could be quite as corrosive as the feeling of expendability.

This was no feeling of dedication because it was absolutely involuntary. I do not doubt that if the Marines had asked for volunteers for an impossible campaign such as Guadalcanal, almost everyone now fighting would have stepped forward. But that is sacrifice; that is voluntary. Being expended robs you of the exultation, the self-abnegation, the absolute freedom of self-sacrifice. Being expended puts one in the role of victim rather than sacrificer, and there is always something begrudging in this. I doubt if Isaac would have accepted the knife of his father, Abraham. entirely without reproach; yet, for the same Master, he would have gone gladly to his death a thousand times. The world is full of the sacrifices of heroes and martyrs, but there was only one Victim.

If we were to be victims, we were as firmly secured to our role as Isaac bound to the faggots. No day passed without accentuating it.

"Lieutenant, when are we getting off this island?"

"Search me. I don't know."

"Couldn't you ask the Colonel?"

"What makes you think he knows?"

"This food is rotten, Lieutenant."

"Yeah, I know—but you'd better eat it."

"I can't take another mouthful of this wormy rice."

"Eat it."

"But how can they expect us to—"

"Eat it."

"But it gags me."

"Okay. Don't."

"I think I've got malaria. Here—feel my forehead."

"Cheez—I think you're right. It's hot as hell. You oughta turn in to the sick bay."

"Nah."

"Why not?"

"What's the point? They'll only give me some aspirin. If my fever gets real bad, they'll only put me in a tent with the rest of the bad ones. They won't let me go home. They won't take me off the island. Nobody leaves. So what's the point."

"Yeah, I guess you're right."

"Sure I'm right. So I'd rather suffer among friends. I'm telling yuh—nobody's leaving this island, not even in a pine box."

"You can say that again. Ain't we got our own cemetery?"

It was so lonely. It was the loneliness of the night watch, listening to the myriad moving things and straining to detect, beneath this irregular rhythm of nature, the regular sound of man. Loneliness. This was the pit that yawned beneath our yearning, our constant reproach of the world at large.

In another sense, in an almost mawkish sense, we had gotten hold of the notion that we were orphans. No one cared, we thought. All of America's millions doing the same things each day: going to movies, getting married, attending college commencements, sales meetings, café fires, newspaper drives against vivisection, political oratory, Broadway hits and Broadway flops, horrible revelations in high places and murders in tenements making tabloid headlines, vandalism in cemeteries and celebrities getting religion; all the same, all, all, all, the changeless, daily America—all of this was going on without a single thought for us. This was how we thought. It seems silly, now.

But it was real enough, then, and I think we might have become unwarrantably bitter alongside that evil river, had there not come at last a tearing, liberating change; we were ordered to new positions.

We left the river. We left without notice. We swung our packs onto our backs and our guns onto our shoulders, and walked over the wooden bridge where the Tenaru doubles back, past the crocodile lair, and up a hill and down into the fields.

4

It was a respite. The fields were like a mid-week holiday that saves a job from drudgery. It was a recess, a winter vacation. Fear seemed almost to vanish. It was as though we were members of an archaeological mission, or a hunting party. Only the absence of lights at night reminded us of the triune foe: the dark, the jungle and the Jap.

Even the terrible heat in these stifling fields of kunai grass could not distress us, for we had built our machine gun pit twice the size of its predecessors on the Tenaru and could take refuge in its cool confines. Our pit was indeed a fort, perhaps as big as a kitchen, six feet or more down. Overhead were double thicknesses of logs, a few inches of dirt and a heavy sodding of wild grass which took root almost as soon as we had planted it and which, from a hundred feet distant, gave the pit the aspect of a hillock.

With our great field of fire rolling away from us like the vast unharvested sea, and with our nasty network of barbed wire like a wicked shoal to ensnare the unwary, we felt that we need reckon with only a direct hit from a bomber or a battleship.

We retired behind our defenses to loaf and to nurse our "tropical ulcers." This is a name which we conferred upon any running or festering sore, and most especially upon those which ate into the outer covering of the bone. There were few of us whose legs and hands were not dappled with these red-and-white rosettes of pain; red with blood, white with pus and often ringed with the black of feeding flies.

Yet, there was luxury in the fields. We had beds. A supply of Japanese rope had been discovered in our area. We made beds with it, driving logs into the ground to shape an oblong, and plaiting a mattress of the rope.

What comfort! Dry, warm, and above the ground. No mere voluptuary in his bed of feathers and satin, with his canopy stretching silkily overhead, with his bell-pull next to his hand and his mistress curled at his feet, could have surpassed us for pure pleasure.

Chuckler and the Hoosier slept alongside each other, erecting their beds only inches apart, as did all other watch mates, such as Runner and myself. Their beds were about a dozen yards distant in the scrub between the pits and the jungle. It seemed that almost every night, while Runner and I lay whispering to each other, we would hear the thunderous progress of a land crab through the brush. We would hear, too, the snoring of the Hoosier, and we would cease to whisper and wait.

Then there would be silence, like the pause between notes of music. It would be broken, simultaneously, by an indignant shriek from Hoosier, a shout of laughter from the Chuckler and an unbelievable clatter-and-crash that was the land crab scuttling to safety.

"Dammit, Chuckler, it ain't funny."

"Whatsa matter, Chuckler? What happened?"

That would be Runner, his voice strangled with suppressed laughter.

"It's the crab again. Hoosier's crab. It came through again and cut the rope and pinched Hoosier's ass."

Hoosier's reply shocked the night.

But laughter rose up to assuage the injury, great shouts of it leaping skyward until even the aggrieved Hoosier could not remain aloof.

Now how can a man be frightened with things like this happening around him?

Our airplanes had begun to challenge Japanese supremacy in the air above us. Aerial dogfights raged daily over Henderson Field, and because we were in such proximity to the airstrip, many were above our pits. But we had now such a well-developed fear of airplanes that we would not come aboveground so long as the bombers lingered or the shrapnel of anti-aircraft bursts kept falling.

Only Scar-Chin persisted in what had once been a general delight in watching the show. He sat on the roof of the pit, ejaculating like a child at the circus, stirring not a foot even when the thump of the bombs was dangerously close, or when we in the pit below could hear the tinkle of falling shrapnel or the whizz of bomb fragments. He supplied us with a running description of the battle.

"Oh, boy—there goes one!" We would hear the shriek of a plunging plane. Then a shattering blast. "Oooh. That must have been a five-hundred-pounder. Hey, Chuckler, Lucky—c'mon up. You don't know what you're missing."

"The hell we don't," Chuckler growled, and then, raising his voice, "Whaddya mean—there goes one? Whose?"

"Ours."

We would exchange raised eyebrows. The Runner, or someone, would shake his head. "The bastard doesn't care who wins!"

"Look at them! Look at them! They've got them. They've got them on the run. The Japs are running—they're taking off."

Sometimes, in exasperation, or when the bombs came closer than usual, someone would shout up to him, "C'mon down here, Scar-Chin. C'mon, you crazy bastard, before you get your ass blown off."

Scar-Chin would chortle, "What's the difference? They can knock it off down there, too. Makes no difference where you are. If you're gonna get it, you're gonna get it, and there isn't anything you can do about it. When your number comes up, that's it, brother. So why worry?"

There was no arguing with him, nor with his fellow fatalists. Kismet was all the fashion on Guadalcanal. You could hear them saying, It Is Written, in a hundred different ways: "Why worry, you'll go when your time comes."—"Poor Bill, it must have been his time to go."—"Phew! I sure thought that one had my number on it."

There is almost no argument against fatalism. Argue until you are weary, but men like Scar-Chin still lounge among the falling bombs. Tell them they don't believe it, when they say, "You go when your time comes." Suggest that it is they, through their own foolhardiness, who choose the time. Impress upon them that they are their own executioner, that they pull their own name out of the hat. Remind them that even if it is fatalism that they want—as opposed to common sense—they still must choose it: they must even choose no choice.

It is a fine argument, an excellent way to pass the time while the bombs fall and Scar-Chin—that disturbing fatalist Scar-Chin—lounges above without a word of rebuttal, himself alone among the exploding steel.

On a hot day, I withdrew from the mud-floored pit to the thin shade of the scrub, where I threw myself face downward to nap. I awoke with the earth trembling beneath me. I awoke sweating with fear. The earth quivered and I knew it to be an earthquake. I was horrified that the earth might open beneath me and swallow me up; I was disappointed that it did not, that I saw no great fissures. Perdition must be like this; the earth opening, the final betrayal, the nothingness under the feet and the eternal wailing plunge.

My belly was rumbling so with hunger and gas that the Runner complained he could not sleep at night. He mistook it for the faraway thunder of enemy battleships. One night I awoke to hear him scrambling from his sack and racing for the pit.

"Everybody up!" he shouted. "Everybody up! It's the battleships again!"

"Hey, Runner," I hollered at him. "Get back here, before you blow your top. That's no battleship—that's my belly."

He came back, cursing me half-heartedly, a sort of sheepish, hopeless imprecation.

Of course, Runner had good cause to fear battleships whenever he heard a muffled rumbling. While we were in the fields, the shelling from the sea rose to a thunderous pitch. The earth would quiver beneath those blows, and they were nearer here than on the river.

The first salvo was as sudden and unexpected as an earthquake. No one ever heard its ghostly *pah-boom, pah-boom* far out to sea, nor heard the rushing of projectiles through the air until that triple, tearing crash of the detonating shells rent sleep as the screech of braking tires rends the serenity of the living room.

Hateful cursing in the dark, feet pelting to the pit, struggling and jostling at the entrance like New Yorkers in the subway. Another night lost, another sleep conceded to the enemy. They were still whittling us.

We had been nearly two and a half months on Guadalcanal the

night the worst shelling came, and I remember it chiefly because it was the night I nearly panicked.

The crash of the first shells tore so suddenly into a deep sleep that I could not control myself. It seemed they had exploded in my back pocket; the next ones surely would make bits of me.

I clawed frantically at my mosquito net. I tried to butt my way through it, tried to bull through gossamer. Then the next cluster landed, no nearer than the first; I drew breath and lay stock-still for a moment, as though to straighten out of the panting pretzel into which panic had twisted me.

Deliberately, I reached beneath me to clutch the mosquito net at the bottom of the fold and lift it free. Carefully, I climbed out. Determinedly, I stood erect. Then I kicked myself in the behind and walked to the pit.

It was the worst shelling, but I slept through it.

Having regained control of myself, having been spared the stigma of a public funk, I was completely confident and relaxed. I was unafraid, so I slept.

Chuckler found papayas on the banks of the Ilu.

We ate them in the morning before chow, while the cool of the night and the morning's moisture was in them.

Lieutenant Ivy-League heard of them, asked for some, and seeing we had finished them, organized a papaya party to go in search of these succulent melons.

But there were no more papayas on the banks of the Ilu. Instead we found something better. Our papaya parties became swimming parties. We would station sentries on the farther bank and take our pleasure in that wonderful river. It was the same one in which we had bathed and drunk the day of our landing; still swift, still cold, still a delight to hot and sweating flesh.

The tropics has its own anodynes, what the modern world calls "built-in." Such are the cool milk of the coconut or the swift-running little rivers that come dancing down from the hills. Streams like the Ilu and the Lunga kept us in health. I have no statistics to support me, but my own observations were that those of us who bathed frequently in them were those least afflicted by ulcers or malaria.

But our rediscovery of the Ilu came too late. We had had only a week of her charms, when we were notified to stand by to move out. We were going to new positions.

"The army's here."

"Like Hell!"

"I'm telling you, they're here. I saw them myself." It was the Chuckler, expostulating angrily with one hand, while the other clutched a white sack slung over his shoulder. "I was down the beach—at Lunga Point. I saw them land."

"What's in the sack?" asked the Runner.

The Chuckler grinned. He squatted on his haunches in the manner we had when there was nothing to sit on and the ground was muddy, and he began to laugh.

"I never saw anything like it. I was down on the beach right where the Lunga runs into the bay and I saw their ships. Some of them were still coming ashore in L.C.T.'s, and there was a whole bunch of them in the coconut grove there when suddenly somebody hollers 'Condition Red!' Poor bastards, I felt sorry for them. They'd had a rough time the night before. That big naval shelling was for them. I heard the Japs got here too late to sink their transports, so they threw the stuff into the airfield, anyway. It didn't hit the doggies, but it sure scared hell out of them.

"Anyway, they was in no condition for an air raid. They started digging and scrambling around. One of their officers gets a bright idea and the next thing you know they're all taking off for cover in the jungle."

Chuckler's face crinkled.

"You shoulda seen it. It was the damndest thing. No sooner are the doggies gone, when a whole raggedy horde of Gyrenes comes running out of the jungle. It was like it was staged. The doggies vanish into the jungle on one side, the planes come overhead and start bombing the airport and these raggedy-assed marines come slipping out of the jungle on the other side and start looting everything the doggies left behind. Then Condition Yellow comes and they melt right back into the jungle. The coconut grove looked like a cyclone hit it. When the doggies came back, half their stuff was gone."

It was a great joke on the dog-faces and the sort of comedy marines enjoy most.

"You mean you was just watching this all the time?" asked the Hoosier disbelievingly.

"Hell no! I just watched 'em pour out of the jungle. When I seen what they were doing, I joined in."

"What'd you get?"

The Chuckler opened his bag—also stolen—and disclosed his swag. It was the plunder of a judicious thief. No frippery, no useless ornament or artifices of that artificial world back home, like electric shavers or gold rings or wallets, nothing but solid swag of the sort that was without price on our island, things like socks or T-shirts or bars of soap or boxes of crackers. That was what the Chuckler stole, and we applauded him as the men of Robin Hood might have sung the praises of Little John upon his return from a light-fingered excursion into Nottingham Town.

It was but a few hours before we learned that this very army outfit was going to take our place in the lines. We were glad to hear it. Their arrival on Guadalcanal meant that we were no longer surrounded. Henceforth, contact with the outside world would be common. The fate of Wake Island no longer haunted us. Our navy was back. The worst that could happen to us now was Dunkirk.

So we were glad to see the soldiers when they came trudging up to our pits. They came after another air raid; a very close one. But the Thing had not infected them yet. War was still a lark. Their faces were still heavy with flesh, their ribs padded, their eyes innocent. They were older than we, an average twenty-five to our average twenty; yet we treated them like children. I remember when two of them, having heard of the Ilu, immediately set off for it, picking their way through the barbed wire, like botanists off on a field trip.

I shouted at them to come back. I cannot say exactly why I shouted; perhaps because they seemed not to show the proper respect for danger.

The barbed wire seemed to them an obstacle course, the enemy jungle a picnic ground. Their curiosity was childlike, their very backs bespoke trust, and they mocked my own dark memories of this island.

"Get the hell back here," I shouted, and they returned.

Their officer said, "What's wrong?" and I replied, with exaggerated concern, "Some bombs landed out there. They may be delayed action." He was gratified, and thanked me. "Thank God for somebody who knows these things." It made me feel like a prig.

So we said good-by. We left them in the fields. We let them take possession of our magnificent field of fire and our solid pits and our precious sleeping sacks of rope, our barbed wire and the Ilu, and we climbed onto waiting trucks.

We had lived on the sands of the beach, and mud of the river bank, the trampled kunai of the fields, and now we were going to the coral of the ridges.

Up, up and up we went, around and around, climbing roads that seemed to coil about our ridge like a spiraling serpent, until we came to the uppermost level and they told us to get down.

That was how we came to the Ridge.

5

The Ridge rose like the backbone of a whale from the dark and wind-tossed sea of the jungle around us. It rose to command a panoramic view, not only of the bay but of all northern Guadalcanal.

Lieutenant Ivy-League was urging us on, half trotting in front of us, as though he were the football coach coming onto the field before the lumbering, equipment-laden varsity. He led us down to the extreme southern point of the whale, where the snout curved down into the jungle. We had been given an extra machine gun to operate. He divided our squad into two.

"Chuckler, you take one. Lucky, you take the other."

Urgency seemed to pitch his voice higher, and we became concerned.

"See," he said, pointing out over the jungle, "that's Grassy Knoll."

Someone snickered. "Anyway, if we never get to it, we can always say we saw it."

The lieutenant bit his lip and said: "Intelligence says the Japs are massing out there. They're expected tonight." Now he had no difficulty with his audience.

"This is where the Raiders and the Paramarines held them. But they may try here again. That's why you've got the extra gun." He turned to glance down into the jungle. "That's the trail to Grassy Knoll down there."

No one spoke, and he motioned for me and my squad to follow. We jumped down the side of our Ridge spur, a sheer six-foot drop. The lieutenant pointed to a sort of low cave dug in the side of the hill.

"Put your gun in there," he said, and left, promising to send warm chow before nightfall.

It was a trap.

It was a trap, trap, trap.

It was a blind eye, an evil eye, a cyclopean socket glaring out of the side of the clay-red hill down into the choked ravine whence, even now, night drifted toward us.

We looked at each other.

"Okay," I said. "Let's get the gun in there."

We set the gun up wordlessly. But there was no room for more than two men—myself and my assistant. He was Cincinnati, a blond, square, smooth-talking Ohioan who was to distinguish himself in Australia by lending his comrades money at ten percent.

The others—Runner, Oakstump, Red the medical corpsman, and Amish the Pennsylvania Dutchman—scattered out on the hillside. I could hear them inching up it, getting farther and farther away from the trap. I said nothing. Who could blame them? I felt like a man with his arms pinioned. It was impossible to fight from our position. They would be upon us before we knew it. The file of little brown men padding up the trail would burst upon us from but a few yards away. Should we repel them, it would be the shock of but a moment; our cave was so poorly concealed, so poorly chosen, a hand grenade would finish us at the first try.

They would hardly need to take aim.

If they came tonight, we would die in our postage-stamp machine gun pit. We could not get away. Worse, we could not stop them; we could not even give them pause. It is one thing to die, another to die uselessly.

Night was upon us. We sat in the blackness, the sound-enhancing stillness, listening to our own breathing like a dying man feeling for his pulse, starting at the sound of the earth crumbling softly around us. Below, the jungle stirred uneasily.

We began to curse. Softly, ever softly, we cursed the stupidity of the officer who had laid out the lines, the thoughtlessness of Ivy-League; we cursed things singly or in pairs, generally or in the particular; and when we had done, when we had drawn off the venom of hopelessness, I turned to Cincinnati and said, "Start tearing the gun down. We're getting the hell out of here. We'll move up on top of the hill. I don't know about you, but I'm not planning to die without a fight."

He whispered, "You can say that again," and began to take the gun apart, while I crawled out of the cave to warn the men on the hillside.

I called softly to them, "Runner . . . Amish . . ."

"That you, Lucky?" It was Amish, surprise and just a tinge of suspicion in his voice.

"Yeah, it's me. Look. We're coming up, we're bringing the gun up on top of the hill. It's a trap down here. Keep us covered while we move and tell Runner to warn Chuckler and the others so they won't shoot at us."

He whispered, "Okay," and I crawled back inside the cave. I said to Cincinnati, "You take the gun and the water can and I'll take the tripod and the ammo box."

He said nothing, and then I whispered, "Let's go." We didn't bother to try to crawl out with our cumbersome gear. We kicked out the sandbags protecting the cave mouth and scrambled out and up and away from that claustrophobic pit.

We were sweating when we had done setting up the gun again, but it was with relief. There was elbow room. Now a man might fight.

But we had become unstrung. Not ten minutes later, I leaned forward and laid a hand on Cincinnati's arm, thinking I heard movement below and to the left.

When I thought I heard a sibilant command like "Over here!" I whispered, "Here they come!" and snicked the gun bolt.

We waited for the little brown men, for the silhouette of the mushroom helmet against the black bulk of the jungle.

But no one came.

No one came all night, though we heard gunfire and the smash of mortars. In the morning we learned that the attack had come against the army. against the very unit that had replaced us that day. They sat in our great big pits, behind our barbed wire and our field of fire, and they massacred the Japs.

We felt disappointed; not that they had not come against us on the Ridge, but that we had not been in the fields to mow them down. We were glad they had not hit us on the Ridge, exposed as we were. They would have swept over us, though we might have held them up.

We learned that morning, too, that we had been expendable for the evening.

"Didn't you know?" asked one of the other gunners who was stationed farther back on the Ridge. "We were under orders to shoot anything that came up the hill."

"Yeah? Supposing we came up? Supposing it got too hot and we pulled back?"

The man shrugged. "What d'ya think we would do—ask to see your liberty card? We'd'a shot your ass off, that's all."

Hoosier's eyes went big and he swore indignantly.

"Well I'll be go-to-hell!"

No one criticized me for moving the gun. Lieutenant Ivy-League agreed to it when I showed him that from the spur we could command the entire trail with plunging fire, as well as the ravines below it, and that we also might set up a cross fire with the Gentleman's gun, above and beyond up to the right. Also, should my gun be overrun, the Gentleman could deliver a plunging fire into it.

What a fortress we made of that Ridge snout!

We stripped the sides of the ravines of their cover. We leveled plateaus and covered them with barbed wire. We sowed the remaining jungle with booby traps fashioned with hand grenades. We filled gallon cans with gasoline and fastened these to trees at points where our guns had been sighted in, so that we could fire incendiary bullets into them and set them alight. We got one-hundred-and-five-millimeter shells from the artillery and buried them in the jungle, preparing them for detonation by electric wires running down from our pits. We dug rifle holes between the pits, and later, trenches running from hole-to-hole-to-pit, so that the ridges commanded by our guns and the riflemen of G Company were honeycombed with fortifications. Finally, we explored the jungle front for all the flat ground, where the enemy might be most inclined to set up mortars or machine gun fire, or where an attack might most likely be mounted, and these we registered with our guns, sighting in on them, each man carefully measuring his own hand span, so that he could fire at night and hit the target.

All the while, a terribly bright sun beat down on us. There was not a single tree on the Ridge. We had no shade, except to duck into the pits; and by mid-afternoon even these had become unbearable.

Sweat streamed from us and the ulcers yawned on our hands and legs. What bitter desperate anger at the sight of blood from a barbed-wire prick, and the hopeless foreknowledge of the flies that would be upon it. Only constant motion kept the greedy, filthy flies away. High as we were, we were not too high for them. We had outclimbed the mosquitoes, but the flies fed on us unceasingly.

Sometimes the pus built up painful pressures, whereupon Red, our corpsman, would draw a pitted, rusty scalpel from his kit and probe the wound. He would look at a particularly wicked sore and whistle, "Phewee! How long have you had this one?"

" 'Bout a week."

"That so?" he would inquire mildly, like a man discussing his neighbor's zinnias, and then drive his knife into the sore with all the verve of the man who likes his work.

Brick, from my squad, suffered terribly from the ulcers. His legs were thick with them. He suffered from the heat, too, as did Red. It was an ordeal for both of them, both having the fairest skin to match their flaming hair and light-blue eyes. But they reacted differently.

Brick succumbed. Each day when the sun reached its zenith he retired to the pit and lay with his face against the cool water cans, a wet piece of cloth on his brow. Sometimes he passed out, or became so exhausted he was unable to move. Only assignment to working parties at cooler points on the lines, or a blessed visitation from the rain, saved him from his daily agony.

Red became a mole. He kept his helmet forever jammed down over his eyes, and covered his body as though he were in the Arctic. He withdrew within himself.

He ceased to talk to us, except to dispense medical counsel with an aplomb rivaled only by an outrageous ignorance of his subject, or else to carry on a sort of frantic monologue concerning his chances of being assigned to duty near his home town of Utica, should he survive Guadalcanal.

But that helmet! He wore it always. He wore it for fear of the heat and for fear of the bombs. He slept with it on. He bathed with it on. It was not uncommon to see him, standing in the middle of the stream near E Company's lines to our rear, his body ridiculously white—his helmet on!

To mention it to him, to shout "Red, take that damned helmet off!" was to draw a look of animal hatred. Under the helmet, his face became small and sharp and hateful, like an animal with pointed teeth.

Soon the helmet became a fixation with us. We wanted it off. It was a sign that Red was going loco—and after him, who? We schemed to rid ourselves of it.

"The only thing we can do, is shoot it full of holes," said Chuckler. We were squatting on the hillside, where we always did, midway between the Chuckler's pit and mine. Red sat apart from us, mole-like, his helmet slumped over his inward-looking eyes. Hoosier reflected and grinned slyly. "Who's gonna do the shooting?"

"Me," said the Chuckler.

"Oh, no, you're not. We'll draw straws."

The Chuckler protested, but we outvoted him. It made no difference. He won the draw.

The plan was for Runner to engage Red in conversation while I came up behind him and knocked off his helmet. Chuckler was to spray it with machine gun bullets while it rolled down the hill.

Runner strolled over and sat down beside Red, wondering out loud if it would be possible—once we were delivered from Guadalcanal—to obtain a soft billet upstate. Red immediately shifted the venue to Utica, and the question to his heart. I stole up behind him and knocked off his helmet.

Chuckler's gun gave roaring, stuttering voice.

The twin shocks of the loss of his helmet and the sound of the gun sent Red to his feet as though from a spring released. He clutched his head, his unkempt flaming mop, as though the top of it had gone off with the helmet. There was terror on his face. Everyone was jumping, waving his arms and whooping.

"Let 'er go, Zeke!"

"Yip, yip, yip—yahoo!"

"Hey, Red—too bad your silly head ain't in that helmet!"

"Shoot 'er, Chuck—shoot the sides out of the blasted thing!"

"Yaaaa—hoo!"

Filled with holes, the helmet rolled out of sight beneath the hill. Runner yelled to the Chuckler to cease fire and dashed down to retrieve it, setting it atop a barbed-wire pole where it was shot into a sieve. Then it was brought up the hill and flung at Red's feet.

He gazed at it in horror. He turned to look at us and there was not even hatred in his eyes, only gathering tears and the dumb pleading look of the animal that has been beaten to the ground.

We had half hoped that he would laugh. But he wept and ran up the hill to the Battalion Aid Station.

There he stayed, until a new helmet was found for him and he could be persuaded to return to our pits. When he did, his manner was more distant than ever and his chin strap was never again un-done. Nor did anyone dare joke with him about the time we shot his helmet into bits.

It was November, three months and more since we had landed. The Japanese had been coming at our Division perimeter all of October, it seemed, always attacking over a narrow front, penetrating slightly during the night, and then, in the morning, being driven back with terrific loss. Yet they kept coming. Hardly a battalion of our three infantry regiments—First, Fifth and Seventh—had not fought its battle. So had the doggies of the 164th Regiment. But the Japanese kept coming. We could see them, sometimes, pouring off the beached transports down at Kokumbona.

Sometimes the old Airacobras would rise off the field and lumber down to the transports to bomb and strafe them. We cheered and danced as they passed overhead, en route to the carnage. We watched, fascinated, as the Airacobras dived to strafe or to release their bombs in that slow, yawning, dreadful parabola.

But they kept coming. They had heavy artillery, now; at the Matanikau River they had used heavy tanks. They kept coming at our lines, kept being thrown back; but every night we expected them. Time had become a terrible catchy rhythm, like the breathing of a child frightened by sounds in the dark. Each night we held our breath, the men of the First Marine Division and the soldiers who had joined us—on the ridges, in the ravines, looking seaward from the beach, guarding the rivers, crouching in airport shelters—all held their breath like a single, giant organism, harking for the sounds of the intruder in the dark. Each morning we released it—a long, slow, silent exhalation.

... They kept coming.

With them came more and more of their airplanes, winging in from Rabaul silvery and bright, like flying fish, high up in that most blue sky. Sometimes, before or after the bombers had dropped their loads, dogfights would growl over our Ridge so close that it seemed we had only to put out a hand to touch the combatants.

From such a melee one day, a Zero took to playing with us, strafing us. Chuckler became so angry he dragged his gun out of the pit and set it up to return the fire. He was aware of the difficulty of hitting a streaking Zero by firing a puny thirty-caliber machine gun over open sights, yet he could not bear huddling in the pit while the Jap made sport of us.

He swore at the Zero as it banked gracefully, and he struggled to get his gun in position, shouting at me, "C'mon, Luck—give me a hand."

I ran to assist him. But the Zero had turned and was coming back. Before I could reach him, it was upon us with a roar. Seeing the puffs of dust its bullets kicked up, hearing the musical tinkle of its empty shells falling on the Ridge, I turned and ran. Chuckler had sprawled flat. I ran. It was behind me, roaring, spitting, tinkling. I jumped off the hillside above the cave which I had abandoned the first night. I heard it roar over me before I hit the ground six feet below.

Atop the hill Chuckler was cursing wildly. I scrambled back up, helped him to get the gun erect and loaded, and squatted beside him to feed it. We waited for the Zero's return.

It banked and made for us.

"C'mon, you son of a bitch," Chuckler growled. "You won't find it so easy this time."

The tinkling had begun again; the dust puffs were dancing toward us; our gun was hammering—when, from behind the Ridge, appeared two Airacobras flying wingtip-to-wingtip, and the Zero disappeared. I say it disappeared. I suppose it blew up, disintegrated under the impact of the cannon which the Airacobras mounted in their nose. But I heard no explosion, perhaps because by then our Ridge had become a perfect cauldron of sound, what with the dogfighting, the bombing of the airport and the answering *wham* of the airport anti-aircraft guns.

It was the AAA guns that gave us as much pause as did the enemy. Most of their flak bursts were directly overhead, and often our ridge would sound like a xylophone registering the falling shrapnel.

We took cover, as much from fear of this brimstone rain as from enemy bombs or bullets. It was not pleasant to be walking the Ridge, far removed from cover, and to see the beautiful enemy host approaching and the black shell clusters popping into sight around them—and then to hear the rattling of the shrapnel.

On a clear day in mid-November I passed through the Battalion Command Post, just as Condition Red was shouted, just as the bombers, flying very high in a tight V, appeared in the sky. Our anti-aircraft threw up a black cloud of explosive, forcing them to veer off and to jettison their bombs, which crashed harmlessly in the jungle.

Soon I was alone. Everyone had gone below ground. I ran from hole to hole, seeking admittance. But all were full. At last I came to the officers' shelter dug in the hillside. With the fragments falling around me in a chilling fugue, I swept back the burlap over the entrance and gazed into the unblinking formidable glass eye of Captain High-Hips. What disdain! It was as though the holder of a coach ticket had sought to enter a parlor car! His hostility was as curt as a slap in the face. In that moment I hated High-Hips and all his class.

I muttered an apology and let the burlap fall back in place. I retired to the solitude of the Ridge and the rain of shrapnel, vowing: Let me rather die out here than be tolerated down there. But I was not scratched; only my sensitivity suffered.

Souvenirs reappeared while we were on the Ridge. I had not seen him since the Tenaru. He was now one of a half dozen sharpshooters serving as regimental scouts. At intervals of a week or so he could descend into the jungle on an expedition to Grassy Knoll. With him was an old-time Marine sergeant, a blocky taciturn ancient with wild bushy red hair and an enormous red beard that gave him the appearance of hell's Santa Claus. He never spoke while they moved down our hill with braked step. But Souvenirs loved the banter which his presence provoked.

"Hey, Souvenirs, got your pliers?"

Souvenirs grinned, tapping his rear pocket. "You know me, boys. I'd sooner forget my rifle."

"How about it, Souvenirs? I'll give you ten bucks for that Bull Durham sack around your neck."

"Yeah, I know what you mean. How about a pint of my blood, too, huh?"

"How many teeth you got in that sack?"

"That's my business."

"A hundred?"

"Guess again, boy. Guess up a storm."

Grinning crookedly beneath his handlebar mustache, Souvenirs disappeared into the jungle. But his famous Bull Durham sack full of Japanese gold teeth had left his admirers engaged in excited speculation.

"I wonder how many gold teeth the sucker really has in his sack?"

"I dunno—but a fellow from his old squad in F Company says he got fifty of 'em from Hell's Point alone. That was three months ago, and he's been going out on those patrols pretty steady since then. He's got at least seventy-five of them gold teeth in that sack."

"Must be a couple-thousand-dollars' worth. Hell's fire! I'd like to have that when we get back to the States. I'd get me a hotel room and a—"

"What the hell makes you think you're gonna see the States again?"

"Where d'ya think we're going when we get off of here?"

"Another island, that's where! Anybody thinks he's gonna see the States again is as crazy as hell! They'll have your ass on another landing so fast you won't know whether to sweat or draw small stores. Ain't nobody around here gonna see the States, not for a long time, anyway, unless he gets carried back."

"Aw, blow it!"

We were growing irritable. Our strength was being steadily sapped, and a sort of physical depression afflicted many of us. Often a man expended his whole strength going to chow, working his way down the slippery hill to the galley tent set in a ravine, and then climbing back up it. Sometimes, if the rain had been especially heavy, a man might skip chow; just forget about it, even though his belly might be growling. The hill would be too slippery.

The rain.

The rainy season was upon us. On our exposed Ridge it fell upon us in torrents. A man was drenched in seconds, his teeth chattering and his hands darting swiftly to his precious cigarettes, transferring them to the safety of his helmet liner, cursing bitterly if he had waited too long before becoming conscious of their peril.

After cigarettes, we were concerned about our ammunition. On the downward slope of the hill, the rain water ran into our pits and holes as though they were sewer receivers. We had to dash for the pits and lift the boxes of machine gun belts out of the water's way, piling them atop one another on the earthen gun platform. Any dry place in the pit was reserved for ammunition. He who sought refuge from the rain had to sit on the water cans.

There were whole days of downpour when I lay drenched and shivering, gazing blankly out of my hole, watching as the sheeted gray rain whipped and undulated over the Ridge. At such times, a man's brain seems to cease to function. It seems to retreat into a depth, much as the red corpuscles retreat from the surface of the body in times of excitement. One ceases to be rational; one becomes only sentient, like a barnacle clinging to a ship. One is aware only of life, of wetness, of the cold gray rain. But without this automatic retreat of reasons a man can go only one way: he can only go mad.

Barnacle-like, I had made a discovery during the downpour. I had found that even in wetness there is warmth.

I was the only one on the Ridge with a cot. I placed it in my hole. Over this, I had stretched a poncho on which I had sprinkled dirt. We were not permitted so much as a stick above the ground for fear the enemy might find a target. I ditched my hole, and there were times when my homemade drainage and my poncho combined to keep me dry; but when it rained heavily or persistently, I was done.

The hole filled with water which rose right through my cot and soaked me. At times, I might be lying in an inch or so of water with a foot of water beneath my cot. It was cold. It went right to the bone, because the intense heat had made our blood so thin.

At last in disgust I hauled my cot out on the hillside. The hell with it! Let the Jap shoot, if that near-sighted creature could see through the rain, if he was so stupid as to want to.

I placed one dripping blanket under me and pulled the other over me. It was warm! It was sodden, but it was snug; it was wet, but it was warm; it was miserable, but it made me laugh.

See me now, if you will, and you will see the war in the Pacific. Look at the Ridge rearing like a whale from the wild and dark green jungle sea, sweep that tan hillside with your eye and search for a sign of life. You will see none. You will see only the gray rain falling, the rain and a cot and a solitary man huddling beneath a blanket.

Ah, but he's happy! He, and only he in all the world, knows of the warmth within a wet blanket!

Runner came down with malaria. They kept him at the Battalion Aid Station for a few days, then sent him back to the lines. He was still feverish, but there was nothing they could do for him. He lay in his hole, unable to eat. When the chills came, we piled our blankets on top of him. When the fever broke and the sweat began pouring off him, he lay back and grinned. He could barely talk, but he whispered, "It feels so good. It feels so good. So nice and cool."

In mid-November we knew that the crisis had come. Our division had thrown back the Japs time after time, even gone on occasional offensive; we had hung on against stiff odds, until the battle seemed to be even. But crisis was unmistakable in mid-November.

It was in the air, a part of the atmosphere; just as a man might sense a hostile presence in the dark, we felt the thing coming against us: the great Japanese task force moving down from the north.

If it succeeded we would all go down.

But crisis never comes without being preceded by false optimism. So, too, was our crisis heralded by the appearance in the bay of a flotilla which sailed so gaily in, it seemed certainly to be the long-awaited reinforcements.

"Keeripes!" Scar-Chin shouted, even his aplomb shattered. "The navy's come! The navy's back! Look in the Channel. Look, look! A cruiser and three destroyers!"

We pelted up the hillside to the Ridge crest, whence unfolded the vast panorama of northern Guadalcanal, the sea and the surrounding islands. From this distance the Channel seemed but a blue lagoon.

But there were the warships. We hugged each other and danced— Chuckler, Runner, Hoosier, Oakstump—all of us. We strained our eyes for a glimpse of the transports. They were not in sight yet.

Then came the question.

"Who says they're ours?"

Silence.

The ships' guns gave answer. They were firing on our island!

Here in broad daylight, arrogant, armed with a contempt more formidable even than their guns, they hurled salvo after salvo into the airport, sank the few small craft we had in sight, executed a sweeping about-face in the Channel and departed the way they had come. Their stems dug into the boiling water as derisively as a woman flouncing her skirts.

Chagrin.

Not even our malodorous vocabulary could command a word base enough to express our vexation, our bitter exasperation, our cursing, foaming disappointment.

Back we went down the hill and spent the rest of the afternoon trying to make light of it, desperately trying to release the pressure being generated by this new dread which no one dared to name.

No one seemed to want to go to bed that night; even though it was dark, all stayed hunched around Chuckler's pit groping for the cheerfulness of the bright nights when we would stage impromptu vaudeville, trying to force a gaiety that was not there.

At last all crept to their holes. The naval battle awoke us. The voice of the imperturbable Scar-Chin came roaring out of the black, "Kee-ripes! It's a naval battle! You can see it! C'mon, ya jerks, c'mon up here."

I think of Judgment Day. I think of Götterdämmerung; I think of the stars exploding, of the planets going off like fireworks; I think of a volcano; I think of a roaring and an energy unbelievable; I think, of holocaust; and again I think of night reeling from a thousand scarlet slashes and I see the red eye of hell winking in her wounds—I think of all these, and I cannot tell you what I have seen, the terrible spectacle I witnessed from that hillside.

The star shells rose, terrible and red. Giant tracers flashed across the night in orange arches. Sometimes we would duck, thinking they were coming at us, though they were miles away.

The sea seemed a sheet of polished obsidian on which the warships seemed to have been dropped and been immobilized, centered amid concentric circles like shock waves that form around a stone dropped in mud.

Our island trembled to the sound of their mighty voices. A pinpoint of light appears in the middle of the blackness; it grows and grows until it illuminates the entire world and we are bathed in pale and yellow light, and there comes a terrible, terrible rocking roar and there is a momentary clutching fear to feel Guadalcanal shift beneath us, to feel our Ridge quiver as though the great whale had been harpooned, as though the iron had smacked into the wet flesh.

Some great ship had exploded.

We could not even guess what or whose. We had only to lie on our hillside, breathless, watching until the battle was done, and then to retire to the pits to await dawn with murmuring voices and beating hearts. Were the result not so vital, we would have seemed like baseball fans anxious for the World Series scores.

It was the beating of many motors on the airport that told us we had won.

From the moment of dawn the airplanes rose from the airport in pursuit of the enemy fleet. The sound of their motors was as triumphant as the March from *Aïda,* and we cheered and jigged and waved our arms at them passing overhead, urging them on, shouting encouragement, beseeching them for direct hits, to blast the Nipponese armada from the surface of the sea.

It was electrifying. The noise of the airplanes was never absent from the air above our heads. They came and went all day, even the most decrepit among them; and we never tired of saluting them. All Guadalcanal was alive with hope and vibrant with the scent of victory. We were as doomed men from whose ankles the iron bands have been struck. A great weight was lifted from our shoulders. The enemy was running! The siege was broken! And all through the day, like a mighty Te Deum rising to Heaven, came the beat of the airplane motors. Oh, how sweet the air I breathed that day! How fresh and clean and sprightly the life that leapt in my veins! To be delivered is to be born anew. It was as though we were putting aside our old selves, leaving those melancholy beings behind like a pile of soiled and crumpled clothing, exchanging them for newer persons, for the garb of gaiety and hope.

So the tide turned on Guadalcanal.

Chuckler found a scorpion in his clothes box, a canned-soup crate which he kept in his hole. "Hey, Luck!" he shouted, "I got a scorpion in my box! C'mere." I gazed at the crabbed creature with its fearsome tail. "Let's see if they really commit suicide." Chuckler found a stone. He struck the bottom of the box sharply with it, driving the scorpion into a corner. His last blow struck perhaps a quarter inch from the cowering scorpion's body. We waited. We watched in fascination as the tail quivered, came slowly aloft, arched over and plunged into the scorpion's back. It seemed to be convulsed, then to lie still: dead. "I'm a son of a bitch!" Chuckler ejaculated, releasing his pent-up breath. "How d'ya like that!" He was for overturning the box and emptying out the dead scorpion, but I suggested we wait a few minutes to be sure. We withdrew to squat on the hillside. In five minutes we returned. The scorpion was gone. "I'm a son of a bitch!" Chuckler said again, this time in exasperation. "You can't trust nobody. Even the scorpion's a phony!"

6

Chuckler and I began to forage for the platoon. Lieutenant Ivy-League set us free, like bird dogs, and each day we buckled our pistols over the sun-bleached trousers which we had cut off above the knee, slipped empty packs over our shoulders, secured our helmets and departed from the Ridge.

We had to make the descent on foot, but once we had gained the fields and the coastal coconut groves, we were able to hitchhike. Our destination was the food dump set up not far from our first defensive positions on the beach. Food had begun to enter Guadalcanal in abundance after the defeat of the Japanese naval force. But in the manner of distribution characteristic of every army since Agamemnon's, it had not even begun to reach the frontline troops. It was being funneled into the galleys and the bellies of the headquarters units and all the other rear echelons quartered safely behind the lines, those effetes who are at once the envy and the contempt of every frontline trooper who ever had recourse to sanitary stick and slit trench.

We considered all this food ours. We considered it ours whether it resided within the barbed-wire enclosure of the food dump or in the store tents of the rear echelons. We would get it by stealth, by guile, or by force: we would steal it, we would beg for it, we would lie for it.

At first, when Chuckler and I would drop off the tailgate of the truck on which we had hitched a ride, we would approach the heavily guarded food dump by crawling on our bellies. Once close to the fence—out of sight by the army guards who sat atop the piles of cases, rifles over their knees—we would scoop out the dirt under the fence and squirm under.

Stacks of crates and cartons gave us cover while we crept quietly along, searching for canned fruit, baked beans, spaghetti, Vienna sausage—even, prize of all prizes, Spam! Yes, Spam! Perhaps the processed pork that everyone called Spam was the bane of the Stateside mess halls, but on Guadalcanal, Spam was a distinct delicacy. Often we would risk a bullet in the back for Spam, softly looting a case of it at the foot of the very stack upon which the sentry sat, like mice filching cheese from between the paws of a sleeping cat.

Soon we had no need of stealth. The food dump had become the most popular place on the island. The roads became clogged with plunderers like ourselves, pistols swinging at their hips or rifles slung over shoulders, converging outside the fence like a holiday crowd outside of Yankee Stadium. There were now so many holes dug beneath the fence that one might gain entry at any point. Inside, bearded, gaunt, raggedy-assed marines roved boldly over the premises, attacking the cases with gusto, tearing them open to seize what they wanted, leaving the rejected articles exposed to wind and sun with the indifference of pack rats. When a man's bag was full, he sauntered off—contemptuous of challenge from the guards.

Inevitably, such a swarm of thieves depleted the dump and thus brought on more stringent security. We shifted to the ships. Friendly vessels riding at anchor had become a common sight in our channel since the naval battle.

We hoped to exchange that marine commodity—taletelling—for cups of delicious navy coffee, and perhaps even for candy bars!

We would wait until a boat had been emptied, before approaching its coxswain.

"Hey, sailor, how about a ride out to your ship?"

No insolence, here. We played the childlike warrior begging a simple pleasure, the poor little match girl outside the candy shop on Christmas Eve. We played on the sailors' sympathy, inducing them to overlook the very plain law forbidding marines to visit the ships. We cared for no law ourselves (what could the punishment be?) but the sailors had to be persuaded, as did the Officers of the Deck once the landing craft swung under the ship's beam and we called up our request to come aboard. Often he shouted down in anger.

"No! Coxswain, take those marines back to the beach. You know it's against regulations to bring troops aboard. Shove off, y'hear me?"

"But, sir, I just wanted to come aboard to see a friend of mine. From my home town. Wouldn't it be okay if my buddy and me came aboard to see my friend? We lived next door to each other. He's my best friend and I haven't seen him since the war started. He was with my grandmother when she died."

All depended now on the officer's acumen, or his willingness to be taken in. Should he ask for the friend's name, all was lost. Should he be stupid and believe us, or should he fall into the spirit of the thing and grin at our obvious fabrication, we would grasp the rope ladder and climb aboard.

Once gaining the run of the ship, we would trade our tales for coffee, our souvenirs for food and candy. A coterie forms quickly about us in the galley. We are the cynosure.

"Y'mean them Japs really was hopped up when they charged you?" a sailor asks, refilling outstretched coffee mugs.

"Sure," comes the answer. "We found dope on them. They all had needles and packages of dope. They'd hop themselves up before the charge and then they'd come at you banzai-ing." (No drugs were found on the Japanese.)

"Did the marines really cut off their ears?"

"Oh, hell, yes! I knew one fellow had a collection of them. Got most of them at the Battle of Hell's Point—the Tenaru, y'know. He hung them out on a line to dry out, the dope, and the rain rotted them all away. It rained like hell one night and ruined the whole bunch."

"You wouldn't believe it, but half of them Japs can speak English. We was hollering into the jungle one night things like 'Tojo eat garbage' and 'Hirohito's a son-of-a-bitch'—when all of a sudden this Jap voice comes floating up to us, an' whaddya think the bastard said?—'T'hell with Babe Ruth!' "

We bask in their laughter and extend our cups for more coffee.

A particularly receptive ship might even unlock the ship's store in our honor, and we would return to the Ridge, packs filled with candy bars, razor blades, bars of soap, toothbrushes and sundry trophies of the hunt. Let it be admitted that we were not unselfish in division of the candy bars; for these we considered rightful tribute of the forager. We kept them to ourselves.

One day, hearing that the Eighth Marine Regiment—the "Hollywood Marines"—had reached our shores, and that they had brought with them a PX, Chuckler and I girded for our greatest foray.

There were two tents and there were two sentries—each standing with rifle and fixed bayonet in front of a tent. Behind was thickest jungle. Oh, unguarded rear! Oh, defenseless rump! Did they think the jungle impenetrable! Did they count themselves safe, with this paper posterior of theirs?

Astonished, Chuckler and I withdrew to the nearby battery of Long Toms to take counsel. We looked at each other and exploded in delighted anticipation of the discomfiture of the Eighth Marines.

We made our plan: I was to enter the jungle to cut my way up to the rear of the bigger tent. I would have both of our packs. After fifteen minutes, Chuckler was to stroll back to the PX clearing to engage the guards in conversation. The moment I heard voices, I was to cut my way into the tent, fill the packs and carry them back into the jungle.

The cool murk of the jungle was to my liking, as I began to creep toward the tent. My stiletto was very sharp and I had no difficulty sawing through the lianas and creepers blocking my path. It was the necessity for extreme caution that made my progress slow. I had to be careful not to disturb the birds or the crawling things, for fear they might betray me. I was sweating when I reached the rear of the tent; the handle of my knife was slippery. I heard voices and realized that I had been longer than had been anticipated.

A thrill shot through me at the touch of the hot coarse canvas. My stiletto slid through the drum-tight façade with an almost sensual glide, and in a moment I had cut an opening. It was close within the tent and the odor of creosote filled my nostrils. I had to widen the opening to let in light and air.

Cartons were stacked one upon another. I peered at the letters on their sides; they were mostly cigarettes; it was a joke, there were plenty of cigarettes on Guadalcanal. But there were other boxes and soon my sweat-soaked eyes fell upon a carton of filled cookies. Without another glance at the remaining cases, spurred by the rising and falling voices of Chuckler and the sentry, I bent to the task of transferring the contents of one carton into the packs.

Even as I worked I had to quell the greed rising within me: "Go on," it said, "take more. Carry it out into the jungle by the boxful." I hesitated, but then I decided to fit my larceny to my needs and resumed my work.

When I had filled one pack, I rose to draw a cautious breath and to listen for the voices. Chuckler's deep laugh came floating through the canvas walls. I bent to the other pack, reassured. My eye fell upon a partially opened carton.

It contained boxes of cigars!

If cookies were worth their weight in gold on Guadalcanal, then cigars were worth theirs in platinum. In value, cigars could be surpassed only by whiskey, and there was no whiskey on Guadalcanal. Neither had there been cigars, until now. I had stumbled on what was probably the only store of them on the island!

I was for emptying my pack of the cookies, until I saw that there were but five boxes of cigars, which would just fit into the other pack. Quickly, I stuffed them in, and then, arranging one pack on my back and holding the other before me, I slipped from the heat and smell and tension of the tent into the cool and murk and relief of the jungle.

Covering the packs with branches, I rejoined Chuckler.

He grinned with delight when he saw me approaching.

"Hey, what the hell you doing down here," he shouted. "I'll bet you're up to no good." He nudged the sentry. "Better watch him. He's one of them dead-end kids from Jersey. He'll steal you blind."

He grinned at me again and I could see the rash devil dancing in his eyes. But the guard thought it not hilarious and a certain nervous tightening of both mouth and rifle hand gave warning. That Chuckler! It was not enough that we should put our heads in the lion's mouth, but we must tickle his throat as well!

My answering chuckle was a hollow thing, and after a few moments I had him by the arm and was leading him away.

"You crazy bastard," I whispered, when we had got a safe distance from the sentry. "You want to tip him off?"

I shrugged hopelessly and we departed, to return softly about two hours later to retrieve our loot.

We came back to bask in the adulation of the Ridge. We shared the cookies with our buddies and kept the cigars for ourselves. For days afterward, our pits were visited by a stream of officers—and once even a major from the Marine air units—all seeking cigars; all smiling, now, at the jolly enlisted men; all full of fake camaraderie and falser promises.

We gave them none.

We knew that we were winning. We knew it from the moment the P-38's—the Lightning fighters—appeared in our skies. They came in one day as we crouched in the ravine at chow. Pistol Pete had crashed his desultory shells not far from us, only a few minutes before. All of us braced for flight when we heard the roar of their motors and, looking up, saw the gladsome sight of their twin tails streaking over the jungle roof. We cheered wildly, and when Pistol Pete's shells came screaming in again, we cursed him good-humoredly out of hope renewed.

Going back to the Ridge—where the others waited to be relieved for their turn at chow—it was necessary to pass the stream which served as our washtub. Two men—Souvenirs and his scouting partner, the red-beard who looked like hell's Santa Claus—were washing there. They shouted at each other as they scrubbed their bodies. We stopped to listen, and Chuckler asked, "What the hell's going on?"

Red Beard replied, "This simple tool thinks we've had it tougher here than the marines on Wake Island." He glanced contemptuously at Souvenirs and then appealed to us—"How stupid can you get?"

"Whaddya mean stupid?" yelled Souvenirs. "Trouble with you old salts you figure nobody's any good who came into the Corps after Pearl Harbor. How do you know about Wake, anyway? You weren't there—and I still say it was a picnic compared to this place."

Red Beard was aghast. Even as he turned to let Souvenirs soap his back, he shrieked at him in fury. "Picnic! Don't talk like a man with a paper ass!"

"Aw, blow it . . . I'll bet the newspapers say this place was twice as bad as Wake. How many times they get bombed there?"

"Who cares? How many of them are left?"

"They didn't all get killed. Most of 'em was taken prisoner. Did we ever surrender? Huh? How about that?"

Red Beard turned again, automatically reclaiming his soap from Souvenirs, hardly pausing to launch his counterattack.

"Don't give me 'at bull about quitting. That's all I ever hear you boots whining about. At Wake they said, 'Send us more Japs.' But you guys say, 'When do we go home?'" His lip curled over his beard, and he raised his voice mockingly, "When does Mama's boy go home to show the girls his pwitty boo uniform?"

So the battle raged, so it ended, as it always does, unresolved. The Marine Corps is a fermenter; it is divided into two distinct camps— the Old Salts and the Boots—who are forever warring: the Old Salt defending his past and his traditions against the furious assault of the Boot who is striving to exalt the Present at the expense of the Past, seeking to deflate the aplomb of the Old Salt by collapsing this puffed-up Past upon which it reposes. But the Boot will forever feel inferior to the Old Salt; he must always attack, for he has not the confidence of defense. The moment he ceases to slash at Tradition with the bright saber of present deeds, the instant he restrains that impetuous sword hand, trusting instead to the calm eye of appraisal—upon that change he passes over to the ranks of the Old Salts and ceases to be a Boot forever. Youth rebels and age conserves; between them, they advance. The Marines will cease to win battles the moment either camp achieves clear-cut ascendancy.

Awareness of this began to dawn upon me as we trudged back up the hill. I was grateful to Red Beard for having reminded us of the men at Wake, and I was confident that he, upon reflection, would lose some of his contempt for us.

We were back at the pits when Hoosier broke the silence: "You think Souvenirs was right—what he said about the papers? About Guadalcanal being famous?"

"Hell no!" Chuckler laughed. "I'll bet we ain't even made the papers."

"Ah dunno, Chuckler," the Hoosier said thoughtfully. "Ah kinda think he was right, m'self." He turned to me. "Hey, Lucky—you think mebbe they'd give us a parade in New York?"

The answer came quickly from Chuckler, his eyes glittering at the thought of it. "Saay! Wouldn't that be something? That's not a bad idea, Hoosier. Think of all them babes lining the street." He paused, and the familiar expression of good-natured disdain returned. "Aw, forget it! You know they ain't gonna give us no parade. They don't even know we're alive. Who the hell ever heard of Guadalcanal, anyway!"

"Ah'll bet they have," Hoosier returned, his calm bordering on the smug. "Ah'll bet you we're famous back home."

"Well, I'll bet you ain't getting to parade in New York," Chuckler came back. "If we're that famous, if we're that good—they'll be using us for the next one. We'll get to parade all right—right up Main Street, Rabaul!"

"You can say that again!" came the Runner's gloomy second. He had been silent, biting a thumbnail to shreds. In an instant he had brightened at the thought of the parade and turned to me, speaking in a voice muffled by his munching, "Supposing they do give us a parade, where'd it be, Lucky—up Fifth Avenue?"

"No. You're thinking of St. Patrick's Day. That's where the Irish parade. Probably it'd be up Broadway—from the Battery."

"Battery!" the Hoosier exploded. "What they gonna do, charge us up?"

Chuckler nodded. "Everybody. Everybody's gonna get charged up on good old New York firewater. Right, Lucky?"

"Right. Thirty-day leave for all hands."

"And two babes for every man—one white and one dark."

Hoosier broke in sulkily, "Ah ain't gonna parade. The hell with 'em. Ah ain't paradin' for nobody. Soon as we get off the ship Ah'm gonna break ranks and lose m'self in the crowd."

"Wouldn't that be something?" said the Runner excitedly. "Supposing we came off the ship and everybody broke ranks and melted into the crowd. They couldn't find you in a New York crowd. We'd all be gobbled up. Everybody'd be drunk, and they couldn't do anything to you. Everybody'd be drunk, even the officers."

Everyone fell dreamily silent, a quiet that was finally broken by the wistful voice of Hoosier.

"Ah bet they do, Chuckler—Ah bet they give us a parade."

Two changes had been wrought: the skies of Guadalcanal had become American, and mail was coming through steadily. Both events improved our humor; so it was that a great ripple of mirth ran over the Ridge upon the arrival of a letter from my father.

I read the letter squatting on the hillside, my buttocks just above the wet ground. A torrential rain had fallen, filling the holes and pits in what seemed but a moment, subsiding suddenly and succeeded by an astonishing swarm of antlike insects so thick that one had to close one's eyes and shield one's mouth from them. Their tiny carcasses covered the ground when they fell (it seemed that they lived but a minute after that rain) and so it was that I was careful not to soil my freshly washed pants in either mud or the myriad of dead insects.

"Robert (my father wrote), your blue uniform is ready. Shall I send it to you?"

Ah...

There came to mind, swiftly and sharply, a set of marine dress blues. I saw that gorgeous raiment. I squatted, stuck up on our Ridge like Stylites on his pole, surrounded by wilderness and wetness and the minute corpses of millions of ephemeral ants. I squatted, clothed only in trousers cut off at the knee and a pair of moccasins stolen from an army duffle bag and I contemplated this vision of glory.

"Robert, your blue uniform is ready. Shall I send it to you?"

In an instant it had caught the fancy of the Ridge. Until we left the Ridge, I was "Lucky, the guy whose old man wants to send him a set of blues." I would walk to chow, and the men from the other pits would greet me with "Hi'ya, Lucky—where's yer blues?" or "Hey, Lucky, yer old man send you the blues yet?" My very approach was enough for smiles, as though each of them was envisioning the First Marine Division drawn up on our Ridge, resplendent in dress blues with flags flying and bands playing, marching off into the jungle to do battle.

There was no boisterousness, no guffaws; merely the smiles and the sallies and occasional rib-poking, as though the very quaintness of my father's proposal were a thing to be cherished, like a family joke, a bit of whimsy to save one's sanity on this mad island of ours.

Everyone thought my father a hell of a guy, and they often inquired after his health.

Sergeant Dandy gave us the bad news. He had visited us the day before to take our measurements for new clothing, and the inference had been so encouraging that we had spent the night in happy speculation. We were sure it meant we were leaving Guadalcanal; the question was, for where?

But Sergeant Dandy's nasal cracker whine shredded our happiness like a whip.

"Stand by to move out in the mawnin'. Weah movin' out from the Matanikau in a new offensive. Get all youah foul-weather gear ready and be sure youah guns is oiled and youah ammunition belt's dry. Eighth Marines'll be up to relieve us in the mawnin'."

He stopped and we examined each other in silence. There was no pleasure on his straight-featured boy-man's face, not even a hint of malicious satisfaction at being the bearer of bad tidings. The heart of Sergeant Dandy was as heavy as anyone's. "Doan ask me whut it's all about. Doan ask me no silly questions. Jus' do what I tol' you." He turned and left.

After nearly five months, this.

Runner had malaria, Brick barely stirred from the pit except at night, Hoosier and Oakstump were subject to long periods of depression, Red had long since left us, I had dysentery, Chuckler was irritable—all of us were emaciated and weakened beyond measure.

But we were to move out on the attack. We could not move to chow without gasping for breath, but we were to move on the enemy.

We despaired.

In the morning, we crouched by our guns and waited for the order to dismantle them and move out.

It did not come.

Nor did it come the next day or the next, and Hope came creeping back, blushing, ashamed of her disloyal flight but commending herself to us once more with the promise never again to desert the ramparts.

Then one morning the word came to move out.

Sergeant Dandy gave it to us.

"Leave the guns behind," he said. "Take only your rifles and foul-weather gear."

He grinned.

"We're being relieved!"

It was December 14, 1942. We had been on the lines without relief since August 7. My battalion—the Second Battalion, First Regiment—was the last of those in the First Marine Division to come out of the lines.

Guadalcanal was over.

We had won.

We came clanking down from the Ridge in a chill drizzle, while the men of the Eighth Marine Regiment came clambering up. They wore kelly helmets, the kind which our fathers wore in the First World War and which the British still wear. They looked miserable, plodding up the slippery Ridge in the drizzle. We pitied them, even though all the worst was past. But we could not resist needling them, these men from San Diego in sunny California.

"Here come the Hollywood Marines."

"Yeah, will you look who's here. If it ain't the Pogybait Marines! Where's your PX, boys?"

"Aw, blow it . . ."

"Tch tch—will you listen to them talk! That ain't the way they do it in the movies. Shame on you!"

"Hey—what's the latest from Hollywood? How's Lana?"

"Yeah—that's it—how's Lana? How's Lana Turner?"

They tried to appear disgusted but they could not conceal the awe with which the reliever must inevitably regard the relieved. We went down the Ridge, haggard but happy; they came up it, full-fleshed but with forebodings. I have said we were happy; we were; we were delirious.

———

The next week we spent beneath an improvised tent on a hillside where the ridges meander down to the kunai fields, Chuckler and I visiting and revisiting the food dumps until we had collected so much food that I could afford to devour a gallon can of preserved apricots, making myself wonderfully, wonderfully sick to my stomach. I lay on my belly and felt the stretching pain and marveled: "I'm sick. I ate too much. It's the most wonderful thing in the world—I ate too much!"

Only desultory visits from Washing Machine Charlie served to remind us that the Japanese were still contesting Guadalcanal.

The following week was spent in a Garden of Eden. We marched to the mouth of the Lunga River to a tent encampment in a grove of coconuts. They gave us a ration of beer. Somehow we managed to gather enough of it to get mildly drunk every night. During the day, we swam in the Lunga, that marvelous river whose cold swift waters kept the malarial fire out of my blood. Swimming was often hazardous, due to the wags who delighted in throwing hand grenades into the water. Once I heard a mighty shout out on the seashore, and running over, was astonished to see the giant sting ray which some men had trapped in a native fishing net. Of course it was dead, punctured in a thousand pieces by having offered a thousand trigger-happy men the opportunity to "get their gun off."

Then we were sleeping alongside a road, waiting to embark the next day. On that day, they brought us our Christmas packages from home. We could not take them aboard ship with us, for we were not allowed to carry more than our packs and weapons. Chuckler and I had already asked Lieutenant Ivy-League to carry our remaining boxes of cigars in his sea bag; officers would be permitted to carry sea bags. It puzzled us to see the reappearance of sea bags—strictly the issue of enlisted men—and it angered us to see them handed out to officers.

This was the first piece of discrimination which we encountered, the first flip of the Single-Sided Coin, whereby the officers would satisfy their covetousness by forbidding us things rightfully ours, and then take them up themselves, much as politicians use the courts to gain their ends. So we devoured what we could of these Christmas gifts from home, and threw the rest away.

"Stand by to move out. Forrr-ward, harch!"

We ambled down to the beach, our gait, our bearded, tattered aspect unable to match the precision of that command. We clambered into the waiting boats. We stood at the gunwales and watched the receding shoreline.

Our boat putt-putted to a wallowing halt beneath a huge ship that listed so markedly to port that it seemed drunk. It was one of the old Dollar Line ships; the *President Wilson,* I believe.

"Climb up them cargo nets!"

As we had come, so did we leave.

We were so weak that many of us could not make the climb. Some fell into the water—pack, rifle and all—and had to be fished out. Others clung desperately to the nets, panting, fearful to move lest the last ounce of strength depart them, too, and the sea receive them.

These also had to be rescued by nimble sailors swarming down the nets. I was able to reach the top of the net, but could go no farther. I could not muster the strength to swing over the gunwale, and I hung there, breathing heavily, the ship's hot side swaying away from me in the swells, very perdition lapping beneath me—until two sailors grabbed me under the armpits, and pulled me over. I fell with a clatter among the others who had been so brought aboard, and I lay with my cheek pressed against the warm, grimy deck, my heart beating rapidly, not from this exertion, but from happiness.

Once belowdecks, Chuckler and I set out for the galley and a cup of hot coffee and conversation. We walked in and sat down, just as the last soldier who had been aboard this transport was rising to leave. He looked down at us as we sipped the coffee from thick white mugs.

"How was it?" he said, jerking his head shoreward.

"Rough," we answered, mechanically. Then Chuckler spoke up, "You mean Guadalcanal?"

The soldier seemed surprised. "Of course I do."

Chuckler hastened to explain. "I wasn't being wise...I meant, had you ever heard of the place before you got here?"

His astonishment startled us. An idea was dawning, gladly. "Y'mean..."

"Hell, yes! Guadalcanal. The First Marines—Everybody's heard of it. You guys are famous. You guys are heroes back home..."

We did not see him leave, for we had both looked away quickly— each embarrassed by the quick tears.

They had not forgotten.

FOUR

LOTUS-EATER

1

The glory was gone out of it now. Gone was Guadalcanal. Gone was the valor, the doggedness, the willingness to let the jungle pick our whitened bones. We were spent, fit only for the Great Debauch stretching gaudily ahead in Melbourne.

Say a requiem for camaraderie, mourn the departed fellowship that had bound us—officers and men—from the Carolina coastal marsh to the last panting lunge over the side of the *President Wilson*. It was dead.

They took us first to Espíritu Santo in the New Hebrides, where we arrived on Christmas Eve, each to receive a lollipop from the chaplain, while Lieutenant Ivy-League gladdened the hearts of his superior officers with our cigars—and there, for three weeks, they gave us the manual of arms and practiced that portion of their code which admonishes the officers to remember that as he would not mistreat his dog, so he should not abuse his enlisted men.

Then they took us to Australia.

———————

A happily blaring band played us onto the docks at Melbourne. It was our first sight of the Land Down Under, for we had been belowdecks since leaving Espíritu, driven there by a filthy storm in the Tasman Sea. We grinned at the band, and suddenly every one of us knew it was going to be all right.

I passed a red-haired WAAF and exchanged smiles with her, detecting in her gladsome eye a second hint of the good times to come.

They bundled us onto a train and got us rolling. We crowded to the windows. Then everyone began to shout and whoop, for the most astonishing thing was happening. The route was lined with women—cheering, hugging themselves and each other, dancing up and down, blowing kisses, extending to the United States First Marine Division the fairest welcome.

The train halted at Richmond, a suburb of the city, and we were herded into a fenced compound reminiscent of a cattle pen. On the other side of the fence were more girls, squealing, giggling, waving handkerchiefs, thrusting hands through the fence to touch us. Suddenly we were beside ourselves. We had not seen a woman since New Zealand, seven months before.

Then they opened the gate.

"Commm-panee! Tenn-shun! Forrr-rd harch!"

We stepped out grinning, slouching, our rifles slung—right past the girls. In all that moving column of faded light green there was nothing to suggest the military. So were born the Lotus-Eaters.

We were mildly surprised to find ourselves marching into a stadium. It was the Melbourne Cricket Grounds. Here were our quarters, double-decked bunks stretching up the cement steps in tiers. They had removed the benches, replacing them with our bunks, so that the effect was one of a huge horseshoe, from which sprang row on row of thin spidery structures—and this enclosing a large circular green field. We were to live out of our packs. We slept in the open, unprotected save by a sort of quarter roof above us. Rain whipped by winds to our exposed front would not fail to wet us.

But who was to complain? Still less, who was to care about such trivial inconvenience on this first day of our return to civilization; who would upbraid the unadulterated good fortune which had quartered us in the Cricket Grounds—almost in the heart of the city— while the other regiments, the Fifth, Seventh and the Eleventh Artillery, sulked in the suburbs? The city was ours, to be tasted almost nightly. We had not earned it; we had rather won it: our Regimental Commander had flipped the lucky coin with the chiefs of the Fifth and Seventh. Of all the regiments, ours—the First—was in the most advantageous position for the Great Debauch.

Discipline, already dissolved in the delicious squeals of the girls, all but disappeared that night.

We had received part of our six-months' arrears of pay in Australian pounds, but we had been issued no clothing; we still wore our disheveled dungarees.

Yet, perhaps a third of the Regiment prowled the streets of Melbourne. I was out alone—Runner, Chuckler, Hoosier and the rest were either on guard or unwilling to risk it.

The exhilaration of that night! At first I thought that it was my strange uniform and deep sunburn that marked me out for curiosity. But soon I came to realize that there was something more: I was the deliverer in the land he has saved. The smiles and winks of the Melbourne crowds assured me of it; the street-hawkers, too, with their pennants—"Good on You, Yank. You Saved Australia"—told me it was so. It was adulation and it was like a strong drink. I took it for a triumph and soon regarded every smile as a salute and every Melbourne girl as the fair reward of the sunburned deliverer.

The first was Gwen.

We met in a milk bar. Strange place for a marine with every appetite athirst after seven months of abstinence, but the pubs of Melbourne closed at six o'clock, and I did not know then that the hotels continued to serve drinks for a few hours thereafter.

I had marked her the moment I entered the place, and had seen the interest in her eyes. But now, as I sat alongside of her and drank a milk shake, she feigned indifference. I did not know what to say. So I asked her the time. She glanced pointedly at the watch so plain on my wrist, at the clock above my head, and said, "You're a Yank, aren't you?" Her words could not have been more exciting if she had said, "Let's go up to my room," for it mattered only that she should speak to me.

"Yes," I said, "we've just come from Guadalcanal." Her eyes went round as she answered, "Have you, now? That must have been terrible." So it went, polite words, formal words, words without meaning, but words alive with the call of sex—words converging on the result, so that in the end, after stops at hotels here and there, it was as though her first remark actually had been, "Let's go up to my room," for that was where we went.

There was the flickering light of a gas heater and there was the bed. But no more.

Gwen instructed her brash visitor in the inscrutable ways of women: there would be no bell-bottom trousers in her young life, there would be no Yankee's bastard to insult her declining years, there would be nothing—without there first being a ring on her finger.

Pretending a gravity most difficult under the circumstances, I arose from that unrewarding couch and reinvested myself in my uniform and my dignity. And I left.

I closed the front door softly behind me and stepped into the silent night, ruefully reflecting on the American motion picture that has persuaded the world that all Yankee males are millionaires, cursing the conceit of womankind that is convinced there is no man living who cannot be bamboozled.

Back in the center of Melbourne, outside the Flinders Street Station, the streets were moving with marines. If a third of our Regiment had been illicitly ashore earlier, now it must have been half. Some were still bearded. It was a motley, reminiscent of that horde that had swarmed from the Guadalcanal jungle to fall upon the packs of the dog-faces.

This time, they brandished bottles, hot dogs of the thick sausage-like Australian kind, meat pies, dishes of "icy cream"—whatever could be obtained from the all-night kiosks. There was singing, too. It seemed that overnight everyone had learned at least two verses of "Waltzing Matilda."

> *Once a jolly swagman camped by a billabong*
> *Under the shade of a coolibah tree;*
> *And he sang, as he watched and waited till his billy boiled:*
> *"You'll come a-waltzing, Matilda, with me!"*

I had enough money left to hire a horse and carriage that stood by the railroad station, and half a dozen of us piled aboard. I slipped forward and rode the horse.

So we came home—munching the delicious kiosk provender, pulling at the bottles and roaring with song, while the huge tame beast beneath me clop-clopped amiably along the pavement.

Next day we drank to the death of discipline. We drank to it literally—for every pack had blossomed with a bottle—and with our feet on the corpse, for only one formation disturbed the orgy of the ensuing week. My memory of that reveille was that it was a delectable farce.

"Everybody up! Everybody out!" a drink-thick voice of authority bellowed that morning.

Silence.

Then, like the dead stepping from open graves, perhaps a dozen of our two hundred sleeping figures rose mechanically from their cots and enshrouded themselves in their blankets. One or two bent to tug bottles from their packs before stumbling downstairs and out the gate to gather in front of the stadium wall.

Old Gunny—the one who had embarrassed the Major when Secretary Knox visited us in New River—came staggering out to call the roll. But he could not speak. He gazed stupidly at this handful of huddling mummies.

Lieutenant Ivy-League rolled out to receive the report.

Gunny about-faced with grave deliberation. He saluted with fingers awry, as though sticky with glue. "All preshen' 'n accounted for," he said, and sank gently on his face. Ivy-League examined him with mournful solemnity, half bent, as though to place a tender pat on Gunny's face. Then he looked owlishly at us, and said, "Com'ny dishmished . . ."

We returned to our sepulchers.

After that, they let us run.

Perhaps they let us run because the officers—from top to bottom—were just as eager to gambol. They paid us, outfitted us with new uniforms—including those green battle jackets which we wore eighteen months before they gained the Eisenhower name—they instructed us as to where and when we could get our meals, and they reminded us that prophylaxis kits could be picked up at sick bay. Except for those detailed to guard duty, everyone was free from noon on.

Even the guards found playmates. These—who often descended upon the Officer of the Day, requesting "a marine to go walking with"—were derisively called "weed monkeys," after their habit of lying in the tall grass of Victoria Park surrounding the Cricket Grounds.

The guards at the side gates and those outside on roving patrol were most favored by the "weed monkeys"—and soon it got to be a standing joke that for the first time in Marine Corps history there were men volunteering for guard duty. But the weed monkeys made things easier for those of us who had stayed out too late. One had merely to circle the Cricket Grounds until one came upon a rifle leaning against the wall—mutely testifying to the guard's delinquent occupation elsewhere and one had only to open his gate and slip in.

Each day brought a new pleasure, a fresh discovery. We discovered Australian beer, which compares favorably with that delicious Japanese beer; we found the bars plentifully supplied with Scotch whiskey; we learned that a "sheila" is a girl, a "cobber" a friend, that what was "bonzer" was excellent, that "fair dinkum" was the equivalent of honest-to-goodness and that the term "Yank" could fall from the Australian lips like a kiss or a curse.

In the first week we came upon an upstairs restaurant on Swanston Street, and here we discovered sparkling hock. We had asked for champagne, but the waitress said there was none to be had.

"We've got sparkling hock, though," she said in that Australian accent that is cockney. "It's nearly the syme."

"Does it bubble?" asked Chuckler, motioning with his hands. "You know—like ginger ale?" Chuckler would explain spaghetti to an Italian mamma.

The waitress grinned indulgently. "You Yanks," she said, and departed, returning with an ice bucket and bottle. The cork popped like champagne, the fluid sparkled like it—it tasted like it! For as long as our money lasted, we had found our beverage!

Chuckler and I clinked glasses with the exaggerated gravity of Hollywood.

"T'hell with war," he said.

"Me for peace," said I.

We finished the bottle, and innumerable others thereafter, along with innumerable meals of Australian steak and eggs—for the place became our headquarters. Here we dined most of our girls—and here we met Hope and Molly. Hope was possessed of that large beauty that has won many a Hollywood fortune: large oval face with fine silken brown hair falling round it, wide-eyed and wide-mouthed, a straight nose—a fine-featured face but a face empty, in repose, grasping. She was buxom too. Hope was a classic—the classic barmaid, the sort whose broad behind has left a lasting imprint on the pages of history. She took to the dynamic Chuckler immediately, and was his girl until we left Australia. Hope never liked me. She thought me conceited and haughty—"Posh," she called me.

Molly was different. In the days afterward, she was fond of slipping away from Chuckler and Hope—and then we would walk in the park, singing and teasing one another. She knew from the beginning where our friendship would end. She had not, like Hope, any thought of a life of ease in the bountiful United States. Her interest in me and the other marines she dated was warm and human, for ourselves as persons, not for ourselves as futures. Poor Molly, she loved much—too much.

"Tell me of America," she would plead, while we walked the park paths, our feet crunching softly in the cinders, the night air a caress on the cheek, our arms interlocked—for that place, for that moment, in love.

I would tell her. Sitting on a bench, I would tell her, or perhaps lying beside a lake while the breathtaking southern sky curved vastly away in a velvety star-dusted night. The fragrance of the flowering gum trees suffused that delicate evening.

"Oh, Luck—I hope they never make you go back."

"Me, too."

"But they will, won't they?"

"Don't worry about it, Molly. There's nothing we can do about it. It's the war."

"Yes, but without it, we would never have met. You can thank the war for that, anyway."

Soon the mood would pass, and she would be jesting.

"Ah, you Yanks. You're full of the blarney. All of that sweet talk and the fine manners—and there's only one thing you're all after."

We would rise and swing, arm in arm, along the path, racing each other sometimes, at other times singing. Molly liked my voice, God bless her. The only woman—the only person—who ever has. She thought I could sing, or maybe she only said she did to get me to sing the American swing songs she loved. But Molly could sing—with a fine clear pitch she could. There was one that was my favorite, a lilting little thing she'd sing in a soft low voice as we walked home.

Patrick—Michael—Fran-cis O'Brien
Would never stop cryin'
For sweet Molly-o.

Each morn-ing
Up with the sparrow,
As swift as an arrow
Just leaving the bow,
Into her garden he'd wing.
Under her window he'd sing—

"Sweet Molly O'Donahue
It's yourself that I'm asking
To go for a bit of a walk..."

But Molly and I quarreled over another girl, and we drifted apart, even though Chuckler stayed close to his Hope.

Sheila had caused the breakup between Molly and me. I met her on a tram, as Chuckler and I rode to St. Kilda, an Australian beach resort outside of Melbourne similar to Coney Island—but not so blaring, not so much a honky-tonk.

At the end of the line the bus lurched and Sheila fell backward into my lap.

I imprisoned her with my knees, and said, "Get up please."

"I can't get up," she said, laughing.

"Aren't you ashamed of yourself?" I whispered into her ear. "Australian girls are so forward."

"Please," she said, giggling, turning her dark head to look at me, "please let me go."

I looked at Chuckler. "What's she talking about, Chuck? Let her go? She can get up, can't she?"

He nodded gravely. "She likes it there."

Sheila cast him an indignant look and said in a strained voice, "Let me go, please."

"All right," I said, "if you go into Luna Park with me."

She pursed her lips, then said, "Right-o."

"Good," I said, and relaxed my knees. Sheila got to her feet. She introduced herself and another girl, and the four of us went into Luna Park together.

We went home together, too, taking the long train ride to one of the far-lying suburbs—and Sheila put both Chuckler and me up for the night in her mother's home. Chuckler stayed in a room in the house, but I was given an outlying cottage to sleep in. Actually, it may have been a stable at one time, for Sheila called the backyard "the paddock." A walk connected it with the house about fifty feet away. The mattress was soft and lumpy, but the sheets were cool and clean-smelling—I dropped off to sleep.

A noise aroused me, and I looked up to see Sheila closing the door. She turned and came toward me, holding a candle. She wore a nightgown.

"Hello, Yank," she said with a soft gaiety. "How d'ya like it in the paddock?"

I propped myself up on an elbow and nodded my answer. She sank to her knees beside the bed and looked into my face with laughing eyes. "I'm fond of you, Yank. I hope you'll be coming up to see me often." I looked at her and she leaned closer and said, "Anything you want me to do for you?" I looked at her and she blew out the candle.

I saw Sheila every chance I had for about a month, sometimes dining at our headquarters, sometimes going to a dance, sometimes taking long walks about the lovely town she lived in, where the wattle grew bright on the hill—sometimes drinking endless cups of tea in her parlor to moisten a throat gone dry with the telling of tales of America to her lame and widowed mother. Not till the end of this time, till she told me that she was going to Tasmania, did Sheila tell me that she was married.

After Molly and Sheila, no more affection.

Only the chase.

How does it go? How should I know. I am not a Casanova, nor is this a textbook for the amorous.

It is cold, yes; it is calculating, of course; but a man should not risk involvement when satisfying lust. He must never be romantic. He must leave romantic love to the unrequited poets who invented it.

At times the chase would end in strange coverts. There was the drink waitress with the strongly developed moral sense.

"You Yanks," she panted, "have no morals."

"How so?"

"Ah," she said, scathingly, "just look at your Hollywood. Why, you read about those stars every day—going on with each other the way they do. Married four and five times. They'd be run right out of Australia. We've still got some morals left!" She drew the cover up to her chin. "Not you Yanks—all you want from a girl is to sleep with her!"

Only a fool, or one no longer interested in the chase, would have pointed to the difficulty of her position.

The same evening my homeward steps crossed those of another marine, younger than I, who grumbled as he sought to remove lipstick smears from the collar of his tunic.

"Trouble with these Australian girls," he complained, "is that they ain't got no morals. They're too easy. Catch an American girl giving herself away like they do. No siree, buddy—they've still got morals."

The descendants of the Pharisee are legion. 'O God. I give thee thanks that I am not as the rest of men ... adulterers, as also is this Australian, as also is this American, as also is ..."

It was the drink waitress who was the enigmatic one. As often as I was in her company, I could not comprehend her. She affected to despise Americans, yet, if she did not see me, she saw another marine. She liked to keep my money, yet, everytime I offended her, she pulled it from her purse with an imprecation and gave it back to me. Hot-tempered, she was cold. Drink waitress, she did not like to drink. Scoffer at American music, she would travel miles to a jazz dance.

When we went boating on the Yarra, she trailed her hand languidly in the water and seemed so bored that I secretly rejoiced, for we marines had been getting soft and the task of rowing upstream had become an ordeal. At last, when she began to yawn, I put the craft about and made for the boathouse.

The moment we set foot upon the shore, she wheeled in white anger and blazed at me: "Fancy! Fancy a man like you—to take a girl out on the water and bring her back without as much as a sweet look!"

Next day, my chest and arms throbbed with pain—and I was not rueful that I would not row or see her again.

Sheila came back. On a Saturday night when I had to remain in the Cricket Grounds and had gone to bed early, someone awoke me and said, "There's a girl outside the gate asking for you, Lucky."

She had been in Tasmania only a few months, yet she seemed older. We walked in the park and talked. Sheila wanted to go to town, but I told her I could not—even though she was going back to Tasmania in the morning, I could not.

"But we can't just sit here in the park," she wailed.

"Wait," I said. "I have an idea. The others are on forty-eight-hour passes. I'll get their sleeping pads and blankets and bring them out here. You go get a couple bottles of beer." I gave her the money. "We'll have a picnic. Okay?"

She laughed and said, "Yank, yer a bonzer boy."

The bunks were darkly silent. I denuded Chuckler's and Hoosier's sacks, as well as my own, rolled all up into a huge cylindrical wad, and stumbled out into the park with it. Sheila came along with the beer, as I was spreading out our couch beneath a big tree. We sat on the pads and reached for the beer.

I groaned in dismay. She had forgotten to get a bottle opener.

"Don't fret, Yank," she said. "Here's a go," and she placed the neck of a quart bottle of Melbourne bitter to her mouth and bit off the cap.

Ah, those Australian girls, I reflected, as the wonderful amber fluid came foaming free.

"Y'know, this is a serious offense," she said, making herself comfortable beside me. "It's offending in the King's Domain."

"What's that?"

"All public property belongs to the Crown. Something like this is called offending in the King's Domain—and they can put you in prison for it."

"Bloody good show, eh?" I teased. "Poaching, what?...here's a go, Sheila—to His Majesty the King..."

We spent the night in the park, and she left me in the morning, left me when gray dawn drew back the curtain of the night—left me forever.

I gathered the bedding together and stumbled back to the stadium. To my horror, the companies were already forming for reveille outside the wall. With my roll of bedding I was as inconspicuous as an elephant, a most patent offender in the King's Domain.

But I resolved to brazen it out. Sinking my face deeply into the bedding, I broke into a half trot.

I shall never forget the look of incredulity that creased the brow of Old Gunny when I passed between him and H Company. I had gone but ten steps or so when a titter broke out. Then catcalls. Then roars of ridicule. I increased my speed. But it had spread to the other three companies and soon I was running a gauntlet of derision. Running I was, now, and with all of my speed—for the shouting and the laughter and the hooting had risen to a gale of sound that blew me through the gate and up the steps to the bunks.

If I had offended the King that night, my comrades had exacted ample justice in his behalf.

2

But two things might restrain a man in the Great Debauch: malaria and guard duty.

Malaria meant hospital, sometimes it meant shipment home. So determined were we to enjoy ourselves, though, that a man experiencing the dull, wearing discomfort of an approaching seizure would still go to town; nor was it uncommon to see such a hardy sensualist huddling against a lamppost, face whitened, teeth chattering, tunic clasped tightly about his shivering body looking for a taxicab to take him back to camp and a cot in sick bay.

That was how I saw Scar-Chin last. His malarial attacks had become fiercer as they became more frequent. This last time he lay in agony on a cot in sick bay, which was a made-over office beneath the stadium. He had the "bone-cracking" malaria, the malignant kind that bakes your body in an oven and stretches your bones on a rack.

I had come to say good-by, for I had heard he was to be shipped home. I could not be sure if he had recognized me; nor could I torture him by asking, for such suffering cannot endure the intrusion of another human person. So I took my leave of Scar-Chin, whom I loved, Scar-Chin of the sardonic wit and the steady nerve. I held his burning hand and said good-by. There came, I think, a glint of recognition, a quivering round the mouth as though he were marshaling those muscles for a smile. But I could not bear to watch him struggle. I dropped his hand and left.

For those impervious to malaria, only guard duty could keep us out of the fleshpots. When our battalion had the guard, no matter what company might stand it, we all had to stand by and remain within the Cricket Grounds.

It was like the old days at New River, almost as though life moved again around the old triad of huts, beer and oil. We would troop in from the drill field and clean up. We would divest ourselves of the long underwear and plunge into the cold showers.

Someone would grab the buckets—for beer this time, not oil— while the squad gathered at the foot of the mezzanine overlooking the field. Everyone would be there: Chuckler, Runner, Hoosier, Oakstump, Amish, the Gentleman, plus newcomers like Broadgrin—a wide-shouldered, pleasant-faced lad from the Louisiana bayous who had come in as a replacement on Guadalcanal—and Big Ski, another replacement, tall, rangy, sallow, given to talking out of the side of his mouth about his Army hitch in Hawaii and his wife back home. Big Ski was the only married man among us.

So we spent the night, sitting in the gathering dark, facing outward to the black puddle of the infield, singing or telling stories, hearing in the lulls the muted voices of other squads, similarly spent, all around that huge horseshoe enclosing the playing field. The songs we sang were not our own; America had still not given us a song to sing. We borrowed "Waltzing Matilda" and "Bless 'em All" from the Aussies, and "I've Got Sixpence" from the British, whom we had never seen.

Soon, even this mild sport came to an end, and the day that they marched us out to the camp at Dandenong we knew that the soft times were over.

Full marching packs again. Helmets clanking against gun barrels. Sergeants bellowing again, unable to conceal a certain pleasure. Pack straps pulling, cutting into the shoulders—the soft new flesh shrinking, and the veteran shrugging and shifting his load, remembering, desponding. All this again; like a detested acquaintance dropping in for a drink, stirring up old animosities and confiding that he expects he's back in town for good. So make the most of it— and wait for the others to move out.

"Commmm-panee!"

There it was.

"...Harch!"

Silence, just a jot of it, just that tiny bit of nothingness, devoid of sound or movement, dividing one infinitesimal measure from another, infinity itself, perhaps—and then that unmistakable sound, the soft shrugging sigh of troops moving in unison, followed by the flat, ragged rap of multitudinous feet upon the pavement—and we were off.

"My mother told me there'd be days like this—but never so many of them."

"Hey! Get that machine gun outta my face. Whatcha trying to do, make me a casualty?"

"Keep off my behind then, you jerk—and you won't win no Purple Heart."

"Yeah, Purple Heart! Purple ass, you mean, that's what he'll win."

Dogs by the dozen were marching with us. They raced up and down the line of march, barking playfully. They were so silly and lovable and faithful, we had to laugh at them; a sort of sentimental laugh that moistens the corners of the eyes.

"Look at them crazy mutts," said Chuckler. "We walk a hundred yards, and they run a mile. They'll be pooped out before we get halfway there."

He was right, although he could have shortened the distance. We had not gone four miles, before I saw the first of them lying exhausted along the roadway. His head was sunk between his paws and his tongue lolled sideways in the dirt, the lower half covered with dust. He watched us sorrowfully as we passed. Poor fellow, he was bushed. For the next mile, the way was littered with canine casualties. But they would not desert us.

I stopped feeling sorry for the dogs when I felt the blisters building up on the soles of my feet. They had issued some of us New Zealand Army shoes before the hike, and I was among these unfavored sons of the quartermaster. They were of heavy and astonishingly stiff black leather, with unbending soles and clickety heels.

They were not for us, accustomed as we were to our Marine "boondockers" of buckskin and crepe rubber, a wonderful soft and comfortable shoe designed to make no noise. But this New Zealand instrument of torture! This shoe of steel! This boot of pain! It was working on the soles of my feet with the exquisite delicacy of a vise!

Pain became my companion for the next ten miles, until all of me appeared to be concentrated in this incredible tenderness being pressed at every step against the cruel steel of my shoes. But I made it to our new camp, and when I presented myself to the battalion doctor, and he had examined the great blisters that now hung like udders from the balls of both feet, he said to me, "You should have walked the last ten miles on your hands." I agreed, and sighed with sensual pleasure as he cut them and let the water run out, bandaged them, and sent me hobbling back to my buddies.

I was not the only one who wore those brutal boots. There had been others, similarly afflicted. The shoes were not issued again, for they had come close to ruining the feet of a quarter of the battalion.

Our new encampment accommodated the entire First Regiment. It was set on the slope of one of the hills, which a land pitifully poor in altitudinous earth has called the Yuyang Mountains. But they were no more than hills; gentle, rolling rises, with here and there a narrow brook. Poor Australia. Here, too, nature has withheld her favors. There are no rivers as we know them: only brooks, and one of them flowed at the foot of the hill on which our tent camp was located.

Of course it was raining, and of course there was mud. The food was a slop of mutton and soggy vegetables. For fuel, there was a ration of split logs for the wood-burning stove in the center of each tent. For recreation there was an occasional weekend liberty, and a slop chute a mile down the road where they served the greenest, foulest beer I have ever drunk—brewed, I am sure (if the word is not concocted), in the PX officer's own lister bag, and served to us in our canteen cups in a room fit to hold twenty people, but filled every night with at least two hundred.

The weeks went by in night marches and night problems and

daily drill in the fields, no different from the days as a New River recruit; more boring, perhaps even galling, because it was expected of us—the celebrated victors of Guadalcanal.

Sometimes we would be issued a handful of rice, or the equivalent of what a Japanese soldier lives on, and be ordered to maneuver at night and make forced night marches of thirty miles or so, and sleep by day. I remember sleeping in a field, and being awakened by a huge gentle-eyed cow which nuzzled me in meek reproof for having chosen the tenderest pasture for my couch. From night problems we learned one lasting lesson: when a map and a compass come into contact with a second lieutenant, prepare yourself for confusion.

Throughout, there had been an insensible drawing in of discipline, like a rider slowly pulling back on the reins. But there came a sudden rearing halt when they reshuffled the companies.

Sergeant McCaustic had taken charge of H Company as First Sergeant. He was a slender man hardly above the minimum height requirement, possessed of filthy tongue, twisted by an openly sadistic temperament but saved from being a monster by an excellent sense of humor and a quick brain.

In Sergeant McCaustic I had found my personal hair shirt. We had come to an understanding within a day or two; that is, we had agreed that we were incompatible. When the time for reshuffling came, Sergeant McCaustic disposed of me with gleeful dispatch.

I expected it as I walked to the company tent with the others at the fateful call. It was raining, but Sergeant McCaustic ignored the raindrops plastering his thin locks against his narrow skull. He spoke with unconcealed glee as he stood there, surrounded by grinning, smirking platoon sergeants and buck sergeants, while the men half encompassed them in a crescent.

"All right, here it is. This company has been goofing off long enough—and it's all because of a few eight balls and yardbirds. So today we're getting rid of them."

A few of the sergeants held their hands up to their mouths. They were enjoying it. It was obvious that the "eight-ball list" had not been drawn up by McCaustic alone.

"I pity the companies that get them, that's all I can say," McCaustic continued in his rapid way of talking. "But here we go. The following named men are to be shanghaied,"—there were snickers—"that is, transferred, to E Company. As soon as their name is called they will return to their squad area, gather up their gear and fall out in front of the company tent."

Each time he called a name, McCaustic grinned. A sergeant or two would laugh. The mirth would pass from them out to the crescent. But the laughter in the crescent was never so hearty or unfeigned as was that in the sergeants' circle. For each name meant the disgrace of some man, the departure of a buddy, the rending of the fabric of a friendship smelted in Parris Island and New River and tempered in the crucible of Guadalcanal. Each time a name was called, something was lost, something immeasurable, perhaps not even felt by most of the men in the crescent; but lost, nevertheless, like a clod of earth slipping silently off the river bank and into the current and on to the sea.

He called my name. There rose the laughter, and I walked to my tent in grief.

Good-by Chuckler, so long Hoosier and Runner, farewell to H Company. My spirit sank within me. I wept as I walked, and now the rain was merciful, for I could bow my head and pull my helmet low as though to keep it out of my face. I got to my tent and packed my things. But now grief was mingled with humiliation and indignation and I began to hate Sergeant McCaustic with an unforgiving, unforgetting, unrepentant hatred. My hands hungered for his neck. I yearned to be alone with him in his tent, I burned with the intensity of my hate, and if God Himself had bidden me then to love this man I cannot answer for my reply.

I packed and left the tent. It was still raining, as I returned to the company tent. The crowd had dispersed. The other "shanghais" stood in dejection in the rain, their heads, like mine, sunk lower than was needed to avoid the raindrops, their cringing bodies eloquent of disgrace. Within the company tent there was a buzz of voices and the cackle of McCaustic's laughter.

We stood there until an E Company sergeant appeared. He cast us a lackluster glance and ducked into the tent, reappearing within a few minutes with our record books in his hands. He stuck these beneath his poncho and examined us with candor. He shrugged.

"Detail, tenn-shun!" he barked. We snapped to clumsily, encumbered by gear. "Right face." We turned. "Forrr-ward, harch!"

We sloshed away.

The shanghais—or transfers—had gone back and forth between all companies in the battalion, perhaps because the commanders thought that reshuffling would end old family quarrels. In the confusion of it, I sought sanctuary. I decided to go over the hill, but, for once, I would try to get away with it.

My plan was thin and involved. It was based on three events of the morning: I had awakened with my upper arms covered with big red weals; the E Company gunnery sergeant had mistaken me for my friend Broadgrin, who had been shanghaied with me; and in a few hours E Company was to march to Rye for a week of firing weapons. Broadgrin was to remain behind on a wood-chopping detail, as I learned from the gunny. But no one had told him.

I got Broadgrin to agree to go out to Rye and to answer my name at reveille on two mornings. I told him that when Gunnery Sergeant Straight-Talk came around to put me on the wood detail, thinking me Broadgrin, I would tell him who I was and that Broadgrin had gone out to Rye. I would also tell him that I had been ordered to the hospital for treatment of hives. Broadgrin, after two days, was to tell the top sergeant at Rye who he was, pretending to be puzzled that his name had not been called at reveille. He was to say he didn't know me.

My hope was that the top sergeant at Rye, once he found that I was absent, would hesitate to enter me as A.W.O.L. until he could determine the exact date of my departure. He would not like to admit to either the sergeant major or his company commander that he had been entering an absent man as present. He would wait, I reasoned, until he got back to camp and had the opportunity to pump me. Then, I would bluff him.

It was a slim chance, but I was desperate to be away from the unknown and unloved faces of my new companions. Broadgrin thought poorly of the plan.

"Hell!" he said, gloomily, "if it was me, I'd just take off. But, okay."

When E Company marched off to the boondocks, I lay on my cot in the tent. I heard Gunnery Sergeant Straight-Talk bellowing in his whiskey bass for the men of the wood detail. I heard him call for Broadgrin twice, and flinched at the ensuing silence. Then Straight-Talk bawled out his instructions and commenced his hunt for Broadgrin. I peeped out and saw him clump along the duckwalk from tent to tent, sweeping back the flap, peering in, clumping on again. A few tents away, I drew back and lay on my cot.

A shaft of daylight preceded Straight-Talk into the tent. I closed my eyes.

"What the damn hell you doing in your sack?"

I opened my eyes, feigned surprise, and jumped to my feet. I looked at him blankly.

"Ain't you Broadgrin?"

I shook my head silently.

"What's yer name, then?"

"Lucky," I said. "I came over from H Company."

"I know, I know," he mumbled, pulling out a soiled notebook. Peering at it, he fixed me with a bleary look. "You know Broadgrin?"

"Yes."

"You seen him?"

"Yes—he went out in the field with the second platoon."

He cursed in exasperation. His breath was fragrant with Aqua Velva, Sergeant Straight-Talk, known the battalion over for his fondness for after-shave lotion, must have drained the bottle that morning. Then he looked fiercely at me.

"What the hell are you doing here? Ain't you supposed to be out in the field?"

"No," I said, rolling up my sleeve. "See. I've got hives. Top Sergeant told me to go to the hospital."

Straight-Talk looked at the red welts and recoiled. To an old salt, there is nothing more horrifying than skin disease, any form of bodily uncleanliness; for these are men who have spent a lifetime in communal living and have seen the spread of epidemics. To them, everything is contagious. He left me, without further questioning.

I put on my liberty clothes, stuffed a few clean khaki shirts and field scarfs into a little traveling bag, and lay down again. At noon, while the wood detail was at chow, I retreated down the slope and out the rear of the camp where there were no guards, caught a tram to the Dandenong Station, and from there a train to Melbourne. I spent four restful days in Melbourne, at the home of a friend, doing the crossword puzzle every morning at Dave's, drinking only a little, reading, even, and returned to camp on the fifth day, a Friday.

It was payday. A desk had been set up in the company street, behind which sat the company commander, who would pay us once we had signed the payroll books spread out before him.

"All right," bellowed Gunnery Sergeant Straight-Talk, lapsing into the pay call formula, "line up in alphabetical order, irregardless of rank—regulars first, reserves last. Sign the book first-name-middle-initial-and-junior-if-you-are-one."

I had a premonition.

Gunnery Sergeant Straight-Talk called my name and surveyed the line with the fierce stare of the huntsman.

I stepped forward and signed the payroll.

The company commander looked at me steadily, with calm, appraising eyes. He paid me.

I sighed with relief, and turned—but an angry hand caught my shoulder and spun me.

"You Lucky?"

It was Straight-Talk.

"Yes."

"Get the hell up to the company office."

His breath was as redolent of Aqua Velva as ever, and I reflected, going up to the company office with sinking heart, that today being payday, the battalion PX would undoubtedly be out of shaving lotion by nightfall. I reflected, too, that I had never dealt with the E Company top sergeant before.

His anger had no conviction in it as I stood there, looking down at him, sitting at his desk. He had not the look of a passionate man, not at all the manner of a hard-boiled top sergeant. His rugged face, with its large nose and larger ears, failed to conceal the fact that he was probably not quite thirty, a tender age for a top sergeant in the Marine Corps.

"You'd better stay here," he said. "You're going to see the man."

"Why?"

"You've got a hell of a nerve asking that! For going A.W.O.L., that's why, and you know it—absent without leave." He looked at me sternly. "Where were you?"

I remained silent, my heart pounding and my head hoping that

Broadgrin had been able to answer one reveille—just one, that's all—and throw them into confusion.

"Where were you?" he repeated, not so forcefully.

"Out in the field," I said.

He snorted contemptuously. "Don't give me that. We know you weren't there. We know what you told the gunny, too. You went over the hill, didn't you?"

Silence.

His exasperation melted into cajolery, and he showed himself more adept at wheedling than at wrath. "Look, I know what's eating you, I know you got a dirty deal from McCaustic. So you got to thinking about it and flipped your lid and went over the hill for a few days. Okay, I don't blame you—maybe. Why don't you be smart? Why don't you admit it, and let me talk to the captain? He'll go easy on you. C'mon—don't go doing something stupid, now, and louse yourself up."

This is the appeal most difficult to resist, this is the other fork of the tongue. But I resisted that siren's call, and kept silent.

Now the top sergeant became petulant, and at last I said, "I'm willing to face charges."

"Go back to your tent and stand by," he snapped.

I made my departure, half exultant. Broadgrin must have protected me! Obviously, the top sergeant had no wish to bring me before the Battalion Commander, and this could be only because he was reluctant to admit that he had carried me present on his morning report for some days, when I was in fact A.W.O.L. My scheme was working. I sat in the tent and waited. In an hour, a runner appeared: "Top wants to see you."

Alone, the top sergeant greeted me with a question: "Can you type?"

"Yes."

"Okay, how'd you like to be my company clerk?"

Who can blame me if I smiled? At last I had seen it! If you cain't lick 'em, bribe 'em!

I agreed, and three days later the top came down with malaria and I became the Acting First Sergeant of E Company.

But it was a boring job, hardly less tedious than the duties of company clerk, which I resumed when the top had returned from hospital. My ten days of managing E Company were almost without incident, except that once a toady offered me a bribe of two pounds to keep him off the weekend guard, which I refused, but which I coerced him into spending on Chuckler, Hoosier, Runner and the rest when we met one night at the slop chute. Otherwise my ludicrous metamorphosis from company culprit into company straw-boss provided only exterior comfort; interiorly, it was a stultifying chore, and that was why I leapt at the chance to transfer to Battalion Intelligence.

The Artist, who had been in my training platoon at Parris Island, was in Battalion Intelligence—B-2, as it is called. He had been transferred there as a scout from G Company, having distinguished himself at the Battle of the Tenaru, where a Jap rashly bayoneted him in the leg.

Not long after the top sergeant had returned, Artist accosted me on the battalion street. Lieutenant Big-Picture, the Battalion Intelligence Officer, was with him.

"Here he is," he said to the lieutenant, motioning me over. "Here's the man I was telling you about." He introduced me. "I hear you used to be a newspaperman," Big-Picture said. I nodded. "How would you like to put out a battalion newspaper?" I was delighted, and so ended my brief and eventful career as an E Company rifleman, during which I never once shouldered a rifle.

Of course, I never came close to publishing a battalion newspaper either; it was merely one of Big-Picture's big ideas. It was a notion that flattered his vanity. There was not even a regimental or divisional newspaper; still, Big-Picture might boast of having a potential publisher in his Intelligence Section, might even—this being his nature—consider the wish to be a fact.

Even so, Big-Picture rescued me from the drudgery of the company office, brought me back to the field, and assuaged the pride wounded by McCaustic's "shanghai." I owe it to Big-Picture, also, that he cared nothing for my reputation as a rebel, not even that by then I was already a veteran brig-rat.

FIVE

BRIG-RAT

1

I have heard it said that General Smedley Butler was fond of observing: "Give me a regiment of brig-rats, and I'll lick the world."

It may be that Old Gimlet Eye never said this. But it is exactly the sort of thing he might have said, or, if not he, then many another Marine commander. For it is most especially a Marine sentiment, and when analyzed, it turns out to be not shameless or shocking, but merely this: a man who lands in the brig is apt to be a man of bold spirit and independent mind, who must occasionally rebel against the harsh and unrelenting discipline of the camp.

I am not attempting to exalt what should be condemned. I am not suggesting that because of their boldness or independence the brig-rats be forgiven and escape punishment. Brigged they must be, and brigged they were. Nor am I speaking of the habitual brig-rat, the steady malingerer, the good-for-nothing who is more often in the brig than out of it and who seeks to avoid every consequence of his uniform, even fighting. I speak of the young, high-hearted soldier whose very nature is bound to bring him into conflict with military discipline and to land him—unless he is exceptionally lucky—in the brig.

I speak of Chuckler and Chicken and Oakstump and a dozen others—and, of course, of myself.

George Washington's birthday was the day on which Chuckler and I smudged the purity of our record books. The division was to parade in Melbourne that day. We were to march up Swanston Street, hardly a month after our arrival in Australia, to accept the plaudits of a city and nation still mindful of the Jap threat that had existed on Guadalcanal.

But Chuckler and I did not want to march. We wanted to see the parade, and this, you will understand, is quite impossible to the person who marches in it, rifle glued to the shoulder, eyes straight ahead and unswervingly focused on the nape of the forward fellow's neck.

By some subterfuge we evaded this odious duty, and so it was that we were firmly entrenched outside the City Club, drinks in hand, when the First Marine Division marched in Melbourne on the afternoon of February 22, 1943. Around us rose the cheerful and delighted calls of the Australians, as our comrades swung past.

"Good on you, Yank!" "Ah, a bonzer bunch, indeed!" "Good-o, lads!" "Hurrah for the Yankee lads!"

The men wore field uniforms, combat packs and full combat dress. Rifles were slung and bayonets fixed; each man wore or carried the weapon which was his in battle. So they were impressive; lean, hard, tanned—clean-limbed and capable-looking. I swallowed frequently, and my eyes were moist as they passed by. Even the Australians—who have inherited the British fondness for heel-clicking, arm-swinging, strutting troops—even they finally fell silent at the noiseless passage of the First Marine Division, walking in that effortless yet wary way that marks the American fighting man moving to the front.

Soon, Chuckler sighted the waving red-and-gold banner of our regiment. We ducked out of sight, moving from our front row position back to the third or fourth. The First Battalion swung by. Then came ours, and our hearts beat faster. E Company, F Company— now, at last, H Company. There they were! There were Hoosier and Runner, Lieutenant Ivy-League and the Gentleman and Amish—all of them! Oh, what a proud sight! It was exhilarating, it was heady, it was as good as reading your own obituary or hearing your own funeral oration—to see them move so confidently and so proudly along, and to mark the admiration in the eyes of the Australians around us. Great day, indeed! We hoped it would never end, but it did, and there was nothing left to do but to substitute for this rare and genuine exhilaration that other artificial sort which is kept, corked and capped, in inexhaustible supply within bottles. So we turned around and re-entered the City Club.

And of course we drank too much.

By nightfall, we had had it. But Chuckler was due to stand guard at the slop chute that night. He took his leave, wavering slightly. But by the time he arrived at the Cricket Grounds, I was sure the waver would be gone. Chuckler had that faculty.

After a time, I too returned to camp, arriving there only by luck or the intercession of my guardian angel. I ran for a tram speeding up Wellington Parade, leapt for the platform, missed it, grabbed the handrail and was dragged for two blocks until a pair of strong-armed Diggers were able to pull me aboard, like a drowning man.

Wavering, I came erect and thrust out my chest: "Tha's nothin'," I said. "Las' night—I got hit by one!" There was laughter until I reached my stop and got off.

I found Chuckler standing glumly outside the slop chute entrance. He had hoped for interior guard, where he might sneak a beer or two.

"I'll get you one," I promised.

I returned with a big glass seidel, out of which Chuckler might take a surreptitious sip. There were more seidels, until Chuckler said, "I've got to go to the head. Here—cover for me." He gave me his pistol belt and helmet, and made off.

For a sentry to be drunk, and then to desert his post and surrender his weapon, is to combine cardinal sin with unforgivable offense. I was anxiously hoping that he would hurry back. But then an unfortunate thing happened.

Lieutenant Ivy-League came striding down the corridor.

I say it was unfortunate because Ivy-League was the officer of the day. More than that, he was still the man who had filched my cigars—the enlisted men's cigars, if you will. My anger was nourished by the alcohol within me and I drew Chuckler's pistol and pointed it at him and said, "Stop where you are, you lousy cigar-stealing son of a bitch—or I'll blow your gentleman's ass off."

Or words to that effect.

Whatever the phraseology, the pistol made the point. Lieutenant Ivy-League retreated, returning reinforced by the corporal of the guard (Smoothface, who had rejoined the regiment) and the sergeant of the guard. While Ivy-League engaged me in conversation, Smoothface and the sergeant were infiltrating. Suddenly they sprang. I had been outwitted—now, I was overpowered.

"Get that pistol and pistol belt," ordered Ivy-League, white with rage. "Now, find that damn fool Chuckler!"

There was no need. He came hurrying up, too late, alas! Ivy-League ordered him imprisoned. Quivering with fury, his hands clenching and unclenching, his lantern jaw so tautly set one could almost hear the molars grinding, Ivy-League surveyed us. Then—

"Brig 'em!"

Smoothface led us away. Unaccountably, as we neared the forbidding steel-cage façade of the brig, we were given a reprieve. The sergeant said something and Smoothface halted.

"G'wan up to youah sacks," he said. "Ivy-League'll see yawl in the mawnin'." He shook his head sadly, especially sorrowful as his gaze fell upon me. "Ah dunno what the damn hell's got into yawl, Licky. Tryin' to shoot the O.D.! Ah know a guy got ten years, just fer sockin' 'n officer."

Someone awakened me roughly in the morning. It was the sergeant of the night before.

"C'mon, get your clothes on. Full green. You're going to see the man."

He stood bleakly by as I hastily covered my long underwear with battle jacket and trousers. The sergeant might be bleak exteriorly, but I was positively frozen interiorly. What I had done the preceding night was now upon me: twenty years at hard labor would not be too severe punishment for assaulting the officer of the day!

Frostier than either of us, the battalion sergeant major awaited us outside the colonel's door. Tall, sharp-featured, his sandy hair thinning and the hairs of his military mustache bristling like bayonets, he seemed more a sergeant of Scots Guards than American Marines.

"The prisoner," he said, looking through me, heedless of my horror upon hearing myself so described—"the prisoner will enter the colonel's office when I give the order. Upon the command to halt he will come to attention before the colonel and remain there until dismissed. Teen-shun! Forrr-rrd harch! Prisoner halt!"

My eyes fell upon the pink bald pate of Mr. Five-by-Five, our battalion commander.

Mr. Five-by-Five got his nickname from his build—a few inches over five feet in height and almost that much in breadth. It was an affectionate nickname, and we were really fond of him, or at least had been on Guadalcanal, when not a day passed that did not bring Mr. Five-by-Five toiling up and down those mountain ridges to look over his lines and his men.

Now, the sergeant major was reading the charges, the crispness of his military style occasionally defeated by a difficulty with words.

Then he had finished and the colonel looked up and through me, as though my stomach were transparent.

"Lieutenant, let's hear your version of what happened."

Ivy-League's voice came floating over my shoulder. I felt Mr. Five-by-Five's eyes upon me while Ivy-League, talking in a strained voice—as though either he, too, were abashed by the colonel, or else he were reluctant to do what he had to do—related the night's events. He told the truth, including that most important piece of evidence, the fact that I had been drinking; for drunkenness goes a long way toward mitigating an offense in the Marine Corps.

The colonel studied me sternly. I stared ahead, trying not to swallow, trying to put steel into my stature, trying to keep from blinking, trying to keep my tongue moist so that I might answer quickly and clearly when spoken to—trying in every way to raise a false strength upon the sinking sands of my craven stomach. The colonel's manner was stern. I could learn nothing from his face, while he studied my record book, leafing the pages slowly, seeming to weigh these against the words of the sergeant major and of Ivy-League. Would he be cruel or kind? I could not tell. But I knew this, as every soldier knows in war: my future, my life, even, was his to dispose of. It is a most unsettling thought.

"How d'ya plead?"

Against my will, I cleared my throat and swallowed.

"Guilty, sir."

He studied the book again.

He raised his gaze and held my eyes.

"I'm not going to ruin your life," he said, and my stomach that had been fleeing seemed to pause, and turn. "I could put you away for a long time for what you've done. Being drunk is no excuse—a marine is supposed to be able to handle his liquor. You've got a good war record, though"—he went on, leafing the pages of my record book again—"and you seem to have a good background. So I'm not going to ship you back to Portsmouth, where the books says I should ship you—but I'm not going to let you get away with it, either." His face hardened.

"Five days' bread-and-water. Reduced to private."

The sergeant major's commands snapped out. I obeyed mechanically, so happy I almost missed the look of chagrin on Ivy-League's face, the look of the hunter whose prey had eluded him. Ivy-League did not want to ruin me, either, but he would have appreciated a stiffer sentence. Five days' bread-and-water! I could have got five years! I was elated and could have hugged the prison chaser when he appeared outside the colonel's office, rifle at port arms, and escorted me away.

Going to the brig in the Marine Corps—especially to the bread-and-water cell—is like going abroad.

First you must go to sick bay for a physical examination to determine if you are strong enough to stand such a diet and confinement; then you must visit the company office, to have the black marks entered in your record, and more important, to be sure you are docked in pay for the time you spend imprisoned; next you must revisit your company area to surrender your weapon and your gear to your property sergeant—and then, clad only in baggy, faded dungarees, the livery of the brig, you are ready for the door to clang shut behind you.

Back in your company, you are a dead man for five days. Even your bunk is denuded of pad and blankets. You are a cipher—the scapegrace whose picture is turned to the wall.

Every foot of the way in these progressions made at an odd, dog-like pace, there follows your prison chaser, trotting grimly behind, his rifle at high port, like a canoeist with paddle poised—your shadow and your shame. The large black circles adorning front and back of your costume are almost endowed with weight, you feel them so poignantly; for you know that these are there for the prison chaser to aim at, should you break for freedom.

The brig receives you, and you are nothing; even the clothes you wear belong to the brig and bear its mark; your very belt and razor blades have been entrusted to the brig warden—you have nothing—you are nothing.

The steel cage door clangs behind you, O cipher, and there is the brig warden standing there, suggestively flexing a length of rubber hose, and you realize that he has been chosen for his cruelty. Suddenly, things have become serious. There is no one to appreciate the humor of the situation. A chill rises from the cement floor and the heart within you freezes, gazing upon the brig warden with the cruelty shining from his black eyes.

It is cold and you are alone, and there against you stands the brig warden in his neatly pressed uniform, and behind him the United States Marines, and behind them the United States of America—and behind the brig warden, again in all reality, a door is opening and a voice commands, "Forrr-ward, harch!" and you walk in on stilts to greet your companions in the bread-and-water cell.

I had entered a shadowy world. I had entered a place that seemed a cavern hollowed out of the submarine rock of a subterranean river. But then I heard the murmur of voices, and the shadows seemed to take on substance and I heard a laugh—and then even this foul place seemed to brighten with that great flaming thing, the human spirit, and I realized, of course, that I was not in hell at all, but only in the brig for five days.

My eyes having adjusted to the gloom, I found myself in a room about twenty feet by fifteen, into which a murky light sneaked through a rectangle of thick glass high in one wall. The floor was of bare cement, as were the walls, and it sloped inward toward a drain set in the center. In the middle of the right-hand wall was a water tap, on which hung two or three metal canteen cups. The bread-and-water cell was a converted shower room, I noticed, now, that my shadows were leaning against the walls, regarding me with curiosity and expectation. A voice questioned from the murk.

"What're you in for?"

I swallowed and answered. There was an awesome silence. Then—

"What're you—crazy, man? What d'ya want to try to shoot the O.D. for?"

"He stole my cigars on Guadalcanal."

Somebody growled, "Too bad you didn't kill the bastard," and another asked, "What'd they give you?"

"Five days' bread-and-water," I answered.

This time there was a general ejaculation of disbelief.

"How'd you get away with it? Hell! I got thirty days' P-and-P just for going over the hill a couple of days. And you only get five! For what you did—they should've shipped you back to Portsmouth and brigged your ass forever!"

"Hell, yes! Tryin' t'shoot the O.D. Who do you know, fellah? Yer old man a general or sump'n?"

Suddenly a rifle butt smacked sharply on the door.

"Quiet in there!"

There was a low grumbling, and gradually silence fell upon the bread-and-water cell. My eyes were now fully accustomed to the bad light and I studied my fellow brig-rats. There was no one from my company, although I saw other men, from the battalion, whom I knew by sight. Every face seemed disfigured by that look of peevish dejection common to victims of petty persecution or to city youth or to disenchanted dilettantes; but not one but was mitigated by the suggestion that, let the prison gates fly open, and every trace of rancor or resentment would vanish. Apart from that look, aside from vain grumbling against the officers or N.C.O.'s who had landed them there, or direful but empty threats of vengeance, there was nothing to distinguish the brig-rats from the men on the outside; they were merely marines who had got into trouble.

The shadows still stood, no one sat, and I asked a man close to me why. He pointed to the floor and said, "They wet the deck. You can't sit down, unless you want a wet behind."

The floor was wet, and just then, the door flew open and a private began sloshing buckets full of water on the floor. Behind him stood another private, with rifle at high port. I felt myself go hot with anger. "Take it easy," said the shadow beside me. "You'll get used to it. The brig ain't no country club, you know. They wet the deck whenever they catch somebody smoking in here."

"Smoking?"

He nodded and I followed his eyes.

Hardly had the door closed on the bucket-wielding private, before two shades huddled opposite us lighted a blackened cigarette butt. They concealed the match flare by taking off both of their dungaree coats, and placing them, like a tent, over the head of one of them. They smoked by inhaling little bursts, expelling them quickly downward, and then dissipating the telltale clouds by quick, fanlike movement of the hands. It was a caricature, but no one thought it funny.

There were fierce whispers of displeasure, but the smokers ignored them, continuing to jeopardize the entire room for a pleasure that could derive only from the knowledge that they were breaking a rule. Certainly the way they smoked could not be pleasant.

"They're long-termers," the shade beside me explained. "They've each got about twenty, twenty-five days more to do. They don't care if they get caught, now—a few more days don't mean anything to them. That's how they get the cigarettes," he went on, "long-termers get a full meal every fourth day. When they march them down to chow with the regular straight-time prisoners, somebody slips them a cigarette. They smuggle it in by sticking it in their hair or between their fingers—or even in their mouth. They wait until it dries out."

The door flew open again, and I cringed—expecting more water. But it was mealtime.

"Rookie, rookie, rookie—come and get your chow," one of the guards chanted in a mock falsetto. Then he slid a big wooden box into the middle of the room, and slammed the door.

They fell upon it like ravening wolves! They leapt upon that box and tore at the loaves of bread within it with the fury of a mob plucking at the flesh of a fallen tyrant. With a single soundless bound they pounced upon it and wrestled and shoved and pulled until, each with a handful of bread crammed against his lips, they fell back against the wall, there to crouch like caged animals, munching wordlessly on their fodder, their eyes angry and suspicious, their shoulders hunched and their very bodies suggestive of a snarl. Occasionally, a shade would rise to his feet and draw a cup of water from the tap, or take a pinch of salt from the grains spilled carelessly in the bottom of the box.

This was bread-and-water.

It was repeated morning, noon and night; and I, who had stood off in horror when that first shattering leap had come, I found only a crust or so to reward my revulsion. Thereafter, I learned to leap upon the first syllable of the guard's mocking chant.

Night falls in the brig with the swift silent plunge of dark dropping on the jungle. There is no dusk. A last feeble ray of light dies in the air about you, and suddenly it is pitch dark. Suddenly, too, you are tired. The evening bread box has been and gone; there is nothing to expect, but the passage of a day and the approach of freedom. Better to sleep, to forget it, to pass the night in soft and blissful oblivion and to awake one day nearer release.

The guards appear with the blankets, two to a man; one to place between body and the still-damp concrete, the other for a cover. Like Robin Hood's men, we throw ourselves upon this rude couch and go to sleep. We, the prisoners, are more fortunate than our jailors; for while we sleep, a guard must stand among us. We repose in the hollow of the hand of God, even we prisoners do this, and our guard must stand sleepless and erect, wary and fretful even, that some prisoner may outwit him and escape. But we sleep.

Morning brings the melancholy. We stand or crouch, faceless and formless; waiting for the bread box; longing for the night and dreading the dawn; counting the days and cursing the explosion of time, the eruption of minutes into hours and hours into days and four little days into an era; hating the officers and inventing impossible means of vengeance; sinking, sinking, sinking so deep into the abyss of self-pity that soon the very world is thrown out of balance, and blankets and bread box become magnified beyond proportion, occupying a man's whole mind, usurping the dwelling place of the world by a process of inverse mysticism that destroys time in reverse, that is the very black and evil heart of despair.

But there is a morning that brings freedom. The prison chaser trots behind again, there are the visits to the sick bay and the company office, and then, release. The steel cage door clangs behind; behind are the melancholy inmates of the bread-and-water cell, ciphers once again, their faces featureless and irretrievable.

The thing has left its mark. Five little days, even, and there is a scar. There is the memory of a debasing thing to be shared with all birds whose wings have been clipped, with all caged beasts and imprisoned vagrants, with the lowest and the highest in the history of time.

Yet, a man who is getting out of the brig in which he has been imprisoned for the first time—if such a man has spirit and the sense to profit by misfortune—a man like this will turn and gaze upon the place and smile. Then he will laugh. Because who can hurt him now? He's had bread-and-water!

Chuckler was awaiting summary court-martial when I got out, and his counsel called me as a defense witness. Runner, too, was to appear, as a character witness.

All three of us were filled with fear when the day of trial came—Chuckler because of the gravity of his offense and the possibility that he might be remanded to the far graver trial of a general court-martial, Runner because his loyalty to Chuckler might lead him to an inadvertent disclosure of his own sins; myself for the same reason, fortified by the fact that I had already tasted the brig.

We were fearful, too, because at first glance, the court seemed such a travesty of justice.

I say at first glance, for from its make-up and its conduct, such it would seem to have been; yet it was no such thing at all, for it ended in a finding that was as just as it was practical.

A lawyer might still insist that Chuckler's court was a travesty. A lawyer might be convulsed with mirth by Chucklers' counsel, a brand-new second lieutenant, younger, even, than we, fresh from an uncompleted pre-law course in a New York City college, most obviously destined to be a politician rather than a pleader. A lawyer would sneer at the prosecution and the judges, all chosen from the ranks of lieutenants and captains who had but two years ago been college boys with no more pressing judgments to make than to decide whether or not to spend the weekly allowance on beer or books. Such was Chuckler's court. But it ended by reducing him from corporal to private and giving him ten days in the straight-time brig. No one, least of all Chuckler, could dispute such a wise and merciful sentence.

It is unfortunate that my memory is so miserably unproductive here; I wish I could recall more of that trial.

Once, I remember, the prosecution halted Chuckler's counsel as he questioned me on my friendship for the defendant. "That's a leading question," the prosecutor snapped, whereupon the defense counsel—at first startled that this typical courtroom phrase should be turned against him, the only man in the room with legal training—gathered his facial muscles together in a crushing look of contempt and continued his interrogation.

The judges, all too aware of the defense counsel's legal talent, uncrossed and recrossed their legs, fluttered their hands—and let the objection die.

So Chuckler lost his chevrons and drew ten days in the comparative comfort of the straight-time brig, and his only complaint when he finally emerged was that, unlike me, he had been incarcerated under a brig officer who delighted in shaving the heads of his brig-rats as clean as a rat's tooth. Poor Chuckler was a skin-head when he came out, and he displayed a heretofore unsuspected vanity by wearing an overseas cap pulled down over his shining skull until the beautiful blond hair grew back.

2

Military police were more numerous. The hated black brassard with its block white lettering—MP—was becoming a roving wet blanket.

When we boarded the Australian ship, H.M.S. *Manoora,* preparatory to maneuvers in Melbourne Bay, the MP's came down to guard the gate. They became the hair shirts of our existence. Only a clever man indeed might slip past them.

We were all eager to go ashore, hating the *Manoora* as we did—finding the ship's very name coarsely expressive of our dislike—hating the tedium of just waiting there for maneuvers to begin, eating, meanwhile, such barbaric food as tripe and boiled potatoes for breakfast, sleeping in hammocks below decks and spending our waking hours polishing the *Manoora*'s endless expanses of lacquered wood.

But one night came the news that the MP's had been withdrawn from the gate. Only civilian guards remained. Within an hour, the ship was emptied of marines. They clambered over the wire fence between docks and road, or even sauntered boldly through the gate, rightly anticipating no restraining hands being laid upon them by the aged civilian guards.

Chuckler and Runner and I and another Louisville lad, a cousin of the Gentleman's, called the Chicken for his tender years—now, not quite nineteen—came with us. We slipped ashore the bold way, the grapevine having informed us that the civilians didn't care.

We stopped at the first restaurant we found, one lying on the coastal road. The *Manoora*'s tasteless cuisine had so impoverished our palates that we were ravening for our favorite Australian dish: steak and eggs, with wine or beer, or sometimes even with pitchers of thick, creamy milk and plates of Australian bread—milky white and of the texture of cake, sliced thin and overspread with butter as thick as cheese.

The restaurant was a great barn of a place, with what seemed a gallery or mezzanine running around the single spacious room. This was reached by a stairway to the right. At the end of the room were swinging doors leading into the kitchen. To the left of these was a smaller private dining room, in which I noticed a round table with some stiff-backed chairs.

We ate our dinner, and began to drink. Chuckler had telephoned his girl, who was coming out by train to meet him; but this would be in another hour. So we drank, as did a half dozen other parties of dungaree-clad marines. Among them was a dark, handsome, slender fellow from E Company—their company barber in fact, the man who would cut hair for a few bob. He was quite noticeably drunk.

Some of the marines had girls and were dancing with them to the music of a juke box. Through the open front door one could see the pavement of the street glistening darkly in the light thrown from our room. It had been drizzling all day.

A jeep pulled up outside the door—appearing there so suddenly as to seem placed there—and a quartet of MP's burst into the room on the run. We scattered like frightened sheep, the effect of panic heightened by the sound of scraping chairs and overturning tables—but there was no sound of a human voice, not even a scream from the girls.

I darted up the gallery stairs, the MP's pelting madly after me.

Light gleamed through an open door, as I ran swiftly down the corridor. I slanted in and slipped the door shut behind me, bolting it. I ran through a room as a hammering started at the door, and came into a bathroom. There stood an Australian, half clad in trousers and underwear shirt, his face white with lather and a razor in his hand. His whole body asked the question: "What's up, Yank?" Breathing hard, my eyes casting about for exit, I said: "The MP's are after me."

"Oh, the bloody provos, eh? Well, 'ere's a go, Yank—over here, now, out the window with you. Out on the roof, see? They'll never follow you out there. There's a good lad, now. I'll take care of the bloody provos!"

I slipped out on the roof as the hammering continued. I crawled to the ledge and let myself down, hanging there by my hands. In a moment, I could hear the MP's talking to the Australian, but I could not distinguish their words. There was the sound of the window going up and flashlight beams slicing eerily into the oozing darkness overhead, then only the darkness, silence and the window going down again. The ledge was cutting into my fingers and the flesh strained so beneath my arms I feared it would part and leave only my arms hanging there. But I had to hang on. To haul myself back up on the roof again would have been a superhuman achievement. I could not let myself fall, for the sound would bring the MP's down on me, and I was afraid to move my head to look for them. I had to hang on, intolerable as the pain might seem, until I heard the jeep cough into voice and roll away.

Then I let go. It was not much of a drop, and I landed on pavement—for the Australian's room had fronted on the street. In fact, I might have been visible to the MP's, had they cared to glance my way. I held the darkness until I was sure they were out of sight, and then, swinging my arms to set the blood running freely again, I made for the shaft of light that came through the open doorway and slipped back into the restaurant.

I began to drink again, waiting for Chuckler and Runner and the

Chicken to reappear. But they did not. Other marines came drifting back, laughing, boisterously rehearsing their escape from the MP's, but no comrade of mine was among them.

"Hey, E Company," I asked of the group which included the handsome now-drunk Barber, "you seen anything of my buddies from H Company? The MP's get 'em?"

"Nope." Then they laughed. "MP's didn't get nobody. They all went up them stairs after you, you simple tool! How the hell'd you get away from them?"

"I told them I was from E Company, so they took pity on me," I replied.

"They'd know that was a crock o' crap," someone replied. "You don't see nobody from E Company hauling ass. They'd know it was H Company right away from the view."

We exchanged insults, and there might have been a fight, had not the Barber slipped in stupor from his chair. They bent to aid him and, as they did, the MP's came charging into the room again. They pounced so quickly there was no escape. I had moved toward the private dining room, but an MP intercepted me.

"Where you think you're going?"

"After my hat."

"Hat, hell! C'mon with me, buddy."

The other MP's had the Barber propped between them. His head rolled foolishly. His buddies apparently had escaped, sacrificing the Barber and myself to their retreat. One of our captors jammed the Barber's hat on his head and began to propel him out the door. I turned to the MP who held me.

"How about my hat?"

"Whaddya mean—hat?"

"It's in that room there. I've got to get it. You're not going to make me leave it behind, are you?"

"Okay. But I'm going with you."

I approached the other door with the MP crowding behind me. I opened it. Then I kicked sharply behind me, slammed it shut, crossed the room, yanked open the other door, darted through, pounded past the swinging doors, and ran into the kitchen, shouting: "Quick, which way out?" I followed the eyes of a waitress to the rear and lunged through another door. Here a courtyard confronted me, and beyond this a high stone wall topped with barbed wire. But the sound of the pursuing MP's impelled me across that courtyard like a cannon shot. Up against the wall I flung myself, grasping the ledge with clutching fingers, legs up, up, up, strain and over—and there I was, arching through the dark and moist night.

A shot!

The son of a bitch shot at me!

The force of my fall sank me to my knees. I felt my hands bleeding from flesh torn by the barbed wire. My coat was likewise torn. But I could think only of the shots and I felt a hot rush of anger.

But now I must defend myself against a pack of dogs that had gathered silently about me after I landed in their alley. Now they were snapping and yapping—making my progress through this dark lane impossible of stealth. Lights were coming on in the tumbledown houses which stood back to back in the alley.

I crept along, feeling my way, fending off the dogs, stumbling against fences.

A light came on in a house to my left. A door swung open and light flowed into the black. I crouched to avoid it. A woman's voice called out: "Who's out there?" I would have been foolish to pretend there was no one there. The dogs were growing more ferocious, growling deep in their throats, ringing me round now that they could see as well as smell me.

"It's an American," I said. "I'm a marine. The MP's are chasing me."

"The bloody provos," she growled, advancing to a back gate, her flashlight in her hand.

"Here, come over here. Go, you pack of mongrels, get away from here! G'wan! Scat!" She menaced the dogs with the flashlight, as I slipped through the gate. Her light fell on my hands.

"You're hurt," she said quickly. "Come, I'll fix you up. I used to be a sister. A nurse, you'd call it."

I followed her into the house. She cleaned the cuts, put mercurochrome on them, and bandaged them. I watched her. She was a plain, strong-faced woman in her early fifties. She was alone in the house, but it did not occur to her that she should be afraid.

"What are you running from the provos for?" she asked, bandaging me with precision.

"They're after me. They've been after me all night. We're aboard the *Manoora* and a lot of us went ashore tonight. But we're not supposed to be on liberty—and we're never supposed to be in work clothes like this."

"I thought so," she said. "I wondered to see you sloppy like that. Your lads are always so neat—all shined and creased like you'd just stepped out of the clothespress."

I followed her through a narrow and dark hall. She made it seem casual, as though she might be doing this night after night. I shrank behind a curtain separating her hall from her kitchen.

She opened the door.

Two shots rang out!

She slammed the door.

"Oops," she said, "they've just shot one of your mates!"

It might have been that it had stopped raining, so calm was her voice. "Oops," she said, reporting a fact somewhat more than commonplace—that the MP's had shot poor Barber through the thigh, and with a .45 bullet at that, as I learned later.

"He was running down the street, and just as I opened the door I heard the shots and saw him fall. Sshh, now—I hear them coming."

I shrank back further into the dark and saw to my amazement, that she was cautiously reopening her door.

"Ahhh," she sighed, closing the door softly, "they're going now." She raised a hand. I listened. There was the noise of a jeep in movement away from us. "Your cobber's all right, I guess," she continued. "He's alive, anyway. They're taking him away in their auto." I came forward, and she said, "Do they always do that?"

"No," I growled. "I never heard of it before. Did they really shoot him?"

"Oh, yes. I saw him fall."

"They'll be sorry," I said.

"What do you mean?"

"I wouldn't like to be that MP—not when that fellow's buddies find out who shot him."

"Well, I hope they give him a beating he'll never forget. Bloody provos!"

I thanked her and slipped out into the street.

To my left I could see the shore road and light breaking through the clouds above the water. I walked toward the bay, determined to find Chuckler or Runner and to slip back aboard the *Manoora*. I had had enough of playing hide-and-seek with MP's who turned the game into a pig-sticking excursion. I peered cautiously around a building, once I had gained the shore road, and saw the restaurant marked by the beam of light slanting out the front door. There were no MP's in sight. I crossed the road and descended wooden steps onto the beach.

Chuckler would be here somewhere with his girl. He had no other place to go, not clad as he was. The sand swallowed the sound of my footsteps so I whistled loudly lest I come upon them without warning and cause embarrassment. Thus whistling, I sat alongside a boat drawn up on the beach. Within ten minutes, Chuckler was by my side, appearing suddenly and silently out of the mist.

"Where's Hope?" I asked.

"Gone home. She took a cab to the railroad station. C'mon. We'd better get moving."

En route to the dock, our path crossed that of the Chicken. He grinned when he saw us.

"Damn, Lucky! I would've swore the MP's had your ass. I nearly split a gut when I saw you tear-ass up them stairs. I was runnin' myself—but I couldn't keep from laughing. They got Runner, you know."

"Runner!"

"Sure. He was the first one they grabbed. I seen it just as I took off."

Chuckler shouted with laughter. "Well, whaddya know? They finally caught up with old cautious. Runner in the brig at last!"

"Sure enough, Chuck," said the Chicken. "Ol' Runner's a member of the club now."

We fell silent approaching the gatehouse. An ancient Australian, attired in the uniform of the civilian guards, was coming off duty. He motioned us to him, and whispered: "Don't try it. The officer of the day is watching the gatehouse. He's arresting your lads as they come in."

We thanked him profusely and fell back to take counsel. We decided to climb the fence. We were over it in moments. But then, we found that the wharf was some feet offshore, and could be reached only by entering one of the small boats moored there, casting off and paddling with our hands.

In the lee of the wharf, I held fast to one of the pilings while first Chicken and then Chuckler shinned up. They did it so well and so silently one could hear the lapping of the water against the pilings above the sound of their going. I called up to them, softly, but got no answer. Fearing to raise the sentry, I did not call again, but secured the boat and shimmied up the piling.

A strange tableau was presented to my eyes the moment my head came above the level of the wharf. Chuckler and Chicken stood side by side, bodies poised for flight—but their hands held high above their heads while a helmeted sentry menaced them with his rifle. I sought to duck but the sentry had seen me. He motioned with his rifle, and I ranged my person and my hands in the desired attitude. From the sentry's very bearing we could tell that he was a recruit just in from the States. Almost no veteran would have detained any of his comrades so, nor would a veteran have been less than horrified at the thought of confronting one of his comrades with a rifle. Chuckler spoke softly to him.

"That rifle loaded?"

"Yeah," said the sentry, carefully watching his interrogator.

"Cartridge in the chamber?"

"Uh-uh. Nope."

We breathed more easily, and I, who had inched toward him during the conversation, suddenly broke for the dark hulk of the ship. I counted upon the sentry either not firing or else swinging to cover me, and thus giving Chuckler and Chicken the chance to bowl him over, knock him off the wharf into the water, or to scatter themselves in such a way as to make it difficult for him to aim.

But the sentry was both quicker and smarter than the three of us.

He sprang back to forestall Chuckler and Chicken and brought his rifle to his shoulder to cover me. He slammed the bolt home. When I heard that deadly snick of cartridge into breech, I froze. We all froze. We contemplated the sentry in incredulity and consternation.

"You stupid, chicken boot!" Chuckler hissed. "What the hell do you think we are—Japs? Put that damned rifle down!"

The sentry surveyed us open-mouthed, as though Chuckler's angry words had fallen upon some heretofore unsuspected ground of loyalty. His eyes seemed to see us again as different persons, not the abstract transgressors of a moment ago, whom his general orders commanded him to detain—but now flesh-and-blood marines from his own battalion, and he seemed to realize that he was menacing us with a loaded rifle that could kill. He began to lower it.

But it was too late.

Across the wharf and out of the great shadow cast by the ship came loping the officer of the day.

Involuntarily, I hardened the muscles of my stomach, as though bracing them for a bullet, when I saw it was Lieutenant Racehorse. For Racehorse was the most feared, the most capable, the most respected and the most bloodthirsty leader in the battalion. As I stood there with my hands raised, watching his approach, seeing him draw his pistol as he ran, bawling for the corporal of the guard, I saw him dimly in the past—walking along the Guadalcanal hills and practicing drawing his pistol from behind his back, practicing quick drawing and shooting, practicing, perhaps, with that very pistol he now drew and pressed into my belly as he came up.

He looked out at me from beneath his helmet, but I could read no emotion in that lean confident face with the flaring nostrils and the small wide-set eyes.

"Search them," he said, pressing the pistol deeper into my belly.

"What do you want to search me for?" I asked him. "You know me, Lieutenant. I'm no fifth columnist."

"Search them," Lieutenant Racehorse repeated, and the sentry obliged. He was blushing now.

"Give us a break," Chuckler said, and I was surprised to hear it. But then I remembered that Racehorse had come up through the ranks, and presumed that perhaps Chuckler was appealing to this.

"No breaks tonight," said Racehorse. His voice was high. "You should have thought of that before you jumped ship and went ashore without leave. And out of uniform, too." He looked us over coolly. "Sentry, get behind those men and cover them."

"C'mon, Lieutenant," Chuckler pleaded. "Give us a break. We didn't do any worse than any of the other fellows. Hell! The whole Second Battalion was ashore tonight. We're just the unlucky ones who got caught."

"No, you're not. I caught dozens of them coming through the

gate. And I let them all off. But not you. I watched that whole business from across the wharf. You guys are too smart—and if I had been that sentry you'd all be dead."

He marched us to the *Manoora* and up the gangplank and up to the forward part of the ship and down a ladder and into a white-washed hole lighted by a single glaring electric bulb. This was the *Manoora*'s brig. It was not a room at all, rather a seagoing Little-Ease, a vacancy occurring as port and starboard of the *Manoora* joined to point the prow. The ribs of the ship's sides were visible. One man could barely turn around, three not at all. We had been stuffed into the place, literally—and when the hatch clanged shut, we discovered a plate fastened to the bulkhead which bore this inscription: "This brig certified fit to contain one able-bodied seaman." We looked at each other, counted each other—and guffawed.

Then we fell asleep—Chuckler, being the heaviest, lying on the deck, I on top of him, and Chicken on top of me.

We awoke to the realization that we had put to sea. The prow rose and fell steadily, and we, stuck away in our hole up high, rose and fell in the exaggeration of our height. Our brig, like a rabbit hutch quivering beneath the hunter's footfall, shuddered and shivered with the *Manoora*'s motions and the throbbing of her motors. We rose and fell, sometimes dizzily, sometimes rushingly, sometimes with that long gliding rise, that fateful pause and dead bottomless drop that is the worst of all. But we were not sick, or even unhappy. The motion of the ship meant that the maneuver had begun, and this, we concluded, would mean that our commanders would be too busy to try us for our misdeeds.

But they weren't.

The bread-and-water cell blazed with good cheer. I entered with Chicken. There had been a deck court-martial before the Battalion Executive Officer. He had removed the Pfc. stripe I had only recently regained, fined me, and withal sentenced me to ten days' bread-and-water. Chicken fared as badly, though Chuckler had escaped the brig by forfeiting his second pair of corporal's chevrons.

When we entered, there were delighted cries of welcome—"Look who's back!" and "Welcome aboard, mate!" It was like a class reunion. Almost everyone had been in before, and everyone knew everyone else. Even the guards were alumni.

Our appearance interrupted an election. This was a regular occurrence, the election of a mayor of the brig—and it was the most fairly conducted contest in my memory. Only two things qualified a candidate: frequent incarceration and length of service. Elections had to be held as often as the present mayor's time expired and he happily vacated his office.

One of the candidates was concluding a windy oration, dark with dire promises of vengeance upon the officers, bright with pledges of innumerable blossoms for the incarcerated lotus-eaters. Our own Oakstump was his rival. His speech was solid.

"He's a bloody short-termer," Oakstump said of his opponent. "It's only his second time in." He thumped his massive chest. "I've got another fifteen days to do—and it's my fourth visit."

Oakstump was elected by acclamation.

"Congratulations, Mr. Mayor," I said to him, but his beaming reply was cut short by the arrival of the bread box. Everybody leapt—I lunging with them—so easily did men accustom themselves to privation.

Oakstump drew a canteen of water from the faucet. He tore a huge length of bread in two, surveying the halves thoroughly. "Guess I'll make a sandwich," he said.

I snorted, "What the hell with—air?"

"Salt," he said. "I always make a salt sandwich."

He stooped, grabbed a handful of salt from the box, and deposited it on one half of bread, smoothing it carefully. He patted it and placed the second half upon it.

"Just right," he said dreamily. "Just enough salt for this sandwich."

He began to munch, pausing to slip the water, so satisfied it seemed sinful. Had I not recalled Oakstump on Guadalcanal, mixing his wormy rice with the contents of a stray can of peanut butter and smacking his lips over the mess, I might have pronounced him mad. But this was Oakstump of the oxen back and matching brain and unconquerable palate—and I ask you, how can such men be defeated?

That night, our own H Company took over the guard. Runner was the bread-and-water sentry. Though he had been caught by the MP's during the *Manoora* episode, his luck had held—they had let him go.

When darkness fell and we had thrown ourselves down on our blankets, Runner slung his rifle, dug out a cigarette and lighted it for me. Soon, other cigarettes glowed in the dark.

"How about some food?" I whispered.

"Where? The galley's closed."

"Out at the kiosk by the main gate. You can get hot dogs."

"Okay—as soon as I get off guard. Keep it to yourselves, though, or the whole damn brig'll want hot dogs."

I fell asleep, happily anticipating a reawakening by Runner.

It was close to midnight when Runner awoke me. He had a brown bag filled with kiosk food. I awoke Chicken. Runner slipped out of the cell.

We devoured the food. What a banquet! Here was the lowly hot dog, but it was spiced with risk, flavored with prohibition and washed down with the nectar of a watering mouth.

He feasted us again the following night, and would have done it the next night, too, had H Company not relinquished the guard.

But the fourth night there came a stranger awakening.

A flashlight played impudently on my face.

"That's him," a voice said, and I was commanded to arise. So was Chicken.

We were taken outside, fearing, of course, the worst. But we were being freed. We were placed in the custody of a tall, gaunt newcomer to the battalion known as Eloquent, both for his passion for the polysyllable and for his expressive hands.

He marched us down the corridor toward the battalion sergeant major's, and we were startled to see men still going out on liberty. It was only nine o'clock, but we had been asleep two hours already.

"What's the catch?" I asked Eloquent.

"You were improperly confined," he replied.

"How come?"

"The Exec was a bit too enthusiastic. He wanted to throw the book at you, but he threw too big a book. On a deck court-martial you may reduce a man in rank or fine him or confine him. But you can't do all three, as he did to you."

"You mean I get my rank and money back?"

Eloquent gave me a pitying look.

"Don't be a dreamer. The sergeant major has a nice new court-martial all written up for you two."

"What's the punishment?"

"Loss of rank and fifty-dollar fine, same as before."

"But what about the four days of bread-and-water we just did?"

"You never did them."

Chicken and I stopped dead, rooted by impotent anger.

"The new court-martial merely says that you have been punished by loss of rank and the fine, and when it's entered in your record book that's how it will be. There won't be any mention of the brig."

"Yes, there will," I said, fighting a losing battle against my temper. "Because I'm not signing. Take me back to the brig and I'll finish the ten days." I turned to Chicken. "What about it—are you going back with me?" Chicken looked at me sheepishly. "I dunno, Lucky. I dunno as we can git back. Whut're we gonna do if the sergeant major says we got to sign? Yuh cain't fight City Hall, Lucky."

"There speaks a sensible man," Eloquent said grandly.

"You call that sensible?" I blazed at him. "That rotten major makes a mistake and we're supposed to pay for it! We serve four days we weren't supposed to serve, and we're supposed to forget it. Forget it in writing—make the lie official! That's sensible! Well, I say the hell with you and the sergeant major. You can tell the sergeant major to take his court-martial and your sensibility between thumb and forefinger and at the count of three he can stuff it smartly up his official—"

"Whoa, now, take it easy," Eloquent interrupted. "You can't take on the whole United States Marines. You're absolutely right, the major's absolutely wrong. But unfortunately you're a right private and he's a wrong major."

There was nothing to do but glower at him. He had put it well: a right private has no chance against a wrong major.

"Don't think I don't admire your spirit," Eloquent was saying. "It probably would have been appreciated more in the Middle Ages. But I would advise you to conform and sign the court-martial."

"C'mon, Lucky," said Chicken, "sign the silly thing, so's we can go out and get somethin' to eat. Yuh cain't fight City Hall."

I signed the court-martial, while the sergeant major sat wordlessly behind his desk. I signed it stiffly, detesting the very letters that formed my name.

I was relieved to get out of the office and to find that Eloquent could spare a pound until payday. We took it and slipped off to Richmond to devour steak and eggs, to drink beer and curse the major.

As far as the U. S. Marines are concerned, Chicken and I never served those four days. Nor were we ever reimbursed for the four days' pay we were docked while imprisoned.

"Let's face it, Lucky," said Chicken, chewing his steak with audible relish. "They got us on a one-way street."

Our days in Melbourne were drawing to a close. "When are you leaving?" the girls asked. "They say you lads will be leaving soon," said the people who invited us into their homes. They knew. They always seemed to know before we did.

Now we could not get enough pleasure; there were not enough girls; we could not drink enough. It was going to end soon. Drought would soon dessicate this torrent of delights, and we would be back on a desert. It was as though we were trying to store it up.

Then, one day in late September 1943, they marched us from the Cricket Grounds to the docks and onto the ships and back to the war.

Crowds of women had gathered dockside. There may have been men among all that vast and waving throng, but our eyes could see only the girls, squealing their good-bys as they had squealed and hugged themselves in greeting nine months before.

"Look at them, Lucky," said Hoosier. "Don't kid yerself they're out just to say good-by. They ain't only wavin', they're waitin'—they're waitin' fer the first boatload of doggies coming into the harbor."

"So?" shrugged Chuckler. "You'd do the same if you was them. You're just jealous."

"Hell, yes, Chuckler," Hoosier said, replying with eagerness. "Ah'm just beefin' because Ah'm on the wrong boat."

Just then, as though to fit the Hoosier's estimate of the farewell scenes, as though to summarize the Great Debauch now lying behind us, that period receding ever faster with the ever widening water between the docks and our stern, the men aboard the ship took to a farewell gesture of their own.

They dug from their pockets and wallets those rubber balloon-like contraptions for which they had no longer any use, and they inflated them. These they set adrift on the currents of wind whipping about the fantail. Soon the space between the docks and our departing transport was filled with these white and sausage-shaped balloons—dozens, then hundreds, then thousands of them—dancing in the breeze, bouncing up and down, seeming to flutter even on the wind of noise raised between the ever-separating camps, the hoarse and vulgar hooting of the marines and the shrill and pseudo-shocked shrieking of the girls—answering one another like rutting beasts in the forests, counterpointing one another like the coarsest concerto grosso.

In the diminishing distance we could still see the balloons.

Hail and farewell, women of the West. We who are about to die insult you.

SIX

VETERAN

1

Like all Liberty Ships, our vessel was anonymous. Oh, it had a name, but not one you would remember for longer than it took to pronounce it. Squat, dark, uncomfortable, plodding ship, it served only to take us from place to place, like a ferry, without character, without interest, without adventure—anonymous.

It was the first Liberty Ship within our experience, although it would not be the last, and of this unlovely brood, the Runner expressed our contempt. "You know," he said, gazing in disgust upon the crowded decks, talking above the ship's shuddering rattle, "they make these things on a weekend. They get a lot of people who have nothing to do and get them all together in one place. Then they get them drunk. On Sunday night they have another one of these." He waved his hand to embrace not only our bovine beauty but that entire cowlike line of transports plowing north along the Australian coast.

We ate on deck, and we also attended to our necessities on deck.

A galley shed had been constructed above decks and there were also topside heads. In a strong wind, we fought to keep our food down on those unmanageable instruments of exasperation we called our mess kits—or to keep it down in the stomach, once the wind blew from the heads.

We had resumed taking atabrine pills. When one arrived at the end of the line, canteen cup of coffee in one hand, meal and mess kit balanced precariously in the other, an officer waiting there commanded one's mouth to open. Whereupon a medical corpsman flicked a yellow atabrine pill into the cavity.

"Open your mouth, there."

"Ah, that does it."

"You missed, you fool!"

"Hey, there—watch your food. Ugh! You clumsy . . . watch it, watch it! . . ."

"I can't help it, Lieutenant—the damned ship rolled . . ."

"Damn it, men, be careful of those canteen clasps. You're spilling your coffee. Come on now, move on. You there, what are you blinking at? Move on, you're holding up the line. Careful, now, corpsman. You're missing too many of them. Careful, I tell you. CAREFUL!"

"Oops, I'm sorry, sir."

"It isn't a bad burn, sir—not even a second degree, I don't think."

"Damn it, corpsman! I told you—"

"Watch it, sir. She's rolling again. Ugh, smell that head. Watch it, sir! He's turning green. Watch it, sir."

So we plied our way up the Australian coast, sailing inside the Great Barrier Reef. We had the reef to starboard and shore to port. It was a natural protective barrier, and as we sailed at night, we were permitted to smoke on deck. No enemy undersea raider would risk snubbing its nose in such a submarine labyrinth.

We had no notion where we might be going, except to be sure that we were headed north and therefore back to war. By this time, the Japanese had been cleared from the Solomons, and most of New Guinea, and we had launched our northward, island-hopping progress across the watery wastes of Oceania. The frightful losses of Tarawa were uppermost in our minds.

But, as veterans, we would talk more and joke more about the place we were going than the condition of life we would enter; of the latter, we had no doubts. Conjecture kept our tongues wagging and our minds occupied during those days of ennui, when we would sit gossiping on the greasy canvas covering the hatches. Sometimes it would become a word game, or a slogan-inventing contest.

"Keep cool, fool, it's Rabaul," someone might say of the impregnable Japanese fortress on New Britain. Or: "The Golden Gate in Forty-eight," meaning that we still had five years of war confronting us before we would see San Francisco again. "Will you be on the roster when we get back from Gloucester?" was a macabre reference to Cape Gloucester on the further end of New Britain, while the prospect of invading Korea presented the incipient Freudians in our ranks (and there were many) with an unrivaled opportunity to rhyme Korea with that word which stands for one of the consequences of Freudianism in action.

Idle, immobile, bored—a man is easily irritated. Even the prospect of food exasperates, because to eat, it is necessary to assemble mess gear and to arise and get in line; and after the meal, it is necessary to clean the mess gear and to stow it away and perhaps face the infuriating prospect of another person encamped upon your place on the sunny side of the hatch.

There is candy to be bought from the ship's canteen; but this is even more infuriating. To get it, one must stand in line, perhaps for three hours, while the storekeeper attends to the wishes of the sailors in the ship's company, and then, when the time has arrived for the troops to make their purchases, risk the exasperation of an exhausted stock. The supply of candy seemed to give out each day, just as the marines prepared to buy, and then, miraculously, as though associated with the mysteries of some awesome sun god, to be replenished for the ship's company with a new sunrise. (But at night, we could perceive the votaries of the canteen deity sneaking from bunk to bunk down in the hold, offering to sell the marines five-cent bars of candy at a dollar a bar. They also sold us sandwiches at somewhat unfriendly prices.) Mostly, we gazed over the rail on the fantail of the ship, looking deeply into the wake boiling and churning in a pale green froth. Sometimes the screws would whirl frantically when the prow of the ship dug too deeply into a wave, lifting the stern free. It was as though the propellers felt naked in the sunlight and were hastening to reclothe themselves with the sea. Here on the fantail, mesmerized by the wake, lulled by the turning of the screws, you sank into a pleasant torpor. You need not think, you need not feel, you need almost not be, except to become integrated with the wave or to flow with the motion of the ship—and it was only when the prow plunged and the stern rose and the water fell out of sight that the movement of the blue sky swinging across your vision and the whir of the freed propellers served as reminders of reality and the moment.

We were permitted on deck at night, although we were forbidden to smoke once we had left the protection of the Great Barrier Reef. There were dark nights that suggested security similar to that of the Reef, but then there were starry nights that cast a pale and enchanting glow over all the world, seeming even to profit from the danger inherent in their illumination.

We sailed through narrow seas fringed by green jungles crowding down to steep banks in riotous luxury. We were coasting New Guinea. Suddenly, we were in a harbor, and our motion had ceased and we were unloading. One of the other transports seemed to have run aground about half a mile to our starboard.

"They can send that skipper home," said Chuckler.

"Yeah," Runner said. "He's probably one of those twenty-one-year-old captains they get from the Merchant Marine Academy."

But there was no more time for talk. We were going ashore. The crews were swinging the landing craft free of their davits and lowering them into the water, prodded by the bumptious urgings of the bosun's mates, come into their own now that there was an unloading to be done. We were drawn up on deck, and then, at the command, were clambering over the side, down the cargo nets, into the boats, and so ashore.

We saw quickly that this was no uninhabited island. There were no buildings, of course, but there was a harbormaster on the beach bellowing through his megaphone to direct the unloading, and there were lines of olive-green trucks waiting to carry both us and our stores away inland. But first we turned to unloading our ship, and in one of the intervals granted us, we took to swimming.

From the beach I saw a half-sunken fishing schooner about fifty yards away, and decided to investigate. I swam out, pulled myself aboard and made my way up to the point of the prow, which was out of the water. I was some fifteen feet from the surface when, on impulse, I dived off.

Falling, I saw to my horror a coral reef only about three feet submerged. I strained my body so as to make my dive as shallow as possible—but even so, I scraped the reef the length of my torso, and when I had swum hastily ashore and emerged on the beach, blood was streaming from a number of abrasions in such quantities as to startle a native who squatted there smoking a stick of tobacco.

But the cuts were superficial and were quickly dressed—with iodine, of course, probably only because it burns better. As I stood there, hands clenched and teeth on edge, a voice said: "That was a close call, Lucky. You're well named. Does it hurt much?"

I turned to confront Father Straight. I knew before I turned that it was he, for his was the only gentle or cultivated voice I had encountered in the Marines. Father Straight was our chaplain—the first, in fact, that the Second Battalion ever had. He had joined us in Australia just as we shoved off. I saw him our second day out when I noticed a crowd of marines encircling an elderly-looking man. They had such a respectful air, such a hungrily respectful air, and the man was so obviously not one of us, that it was easy to conclude his calling.

"It stings like hell, Father," I said, unconscious of any profanity in the word. Only the unprintables were thought unspeakable in a chaplain's presence, and then not always so. "But I was lucky it didn't cut my . . . it didn't cut me wide open."

"Yes, you can thank God for that."

Father Straight was a man in his forties, but he was still that radiant type that the Irish call a "black Celt." Looking at him, I saw that the sea voyage had spread a coat of tan over his visage, once white with the flour of civilization, and that the sedentary flesh about hips and waist had begun to vanish.

"How do you like the island, Father?" I asked.

"It's very exciting," he said, brightening. "This is my first time in the jungle." He eyed me like a stranger about to ask directions. I asked: "Anything I can do for you, Father?"

"Perhaps there is. In the excitement, they seem to have forgotten me."

"Stick with us," I said. "We'll take care of you."

He hesitated. "Will it be all right?"

"Sure. It's always fouled-up when we move."

"Swell," said Father Straight, and he accompanied us when we had loaded one of the trucks with the Intelligence Section's gear and climbed aboard. The truck climbed a series of small hills and finally deposited us in the middle of a field of kunai grass—our new home.

This is how the Marines train their men. Keep them mean and nasty, like starving beasts, says the Corps, and they will fight better. When men are being moved from one place to another, spare no effort to make it painful; and before they have arrived at their destination, dispatch a man ahead to survey the ground with an eye toward discomfort. For sustenance give them cold food, and for tools a

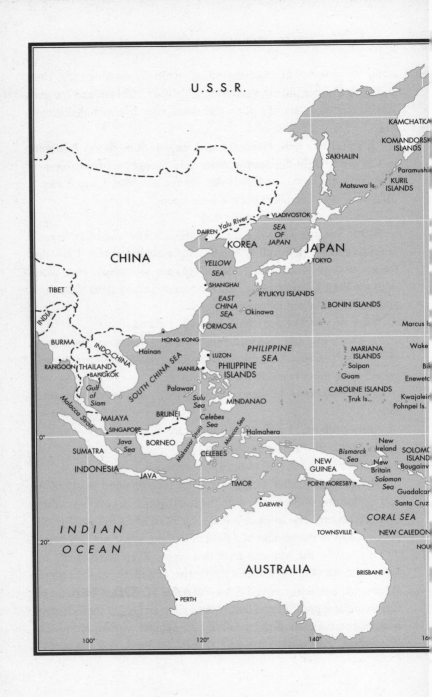

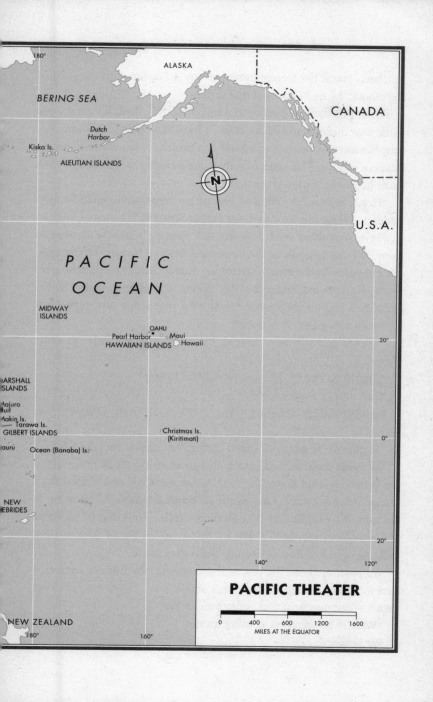

180°

ALASKA

BERING SEA

CANADA

Dutch
Harbor

Kiska Is.

ALEUTIAN ISLANDS

U.S.A.

PACIFIC

OCEAN

MIDWAY
ISLANDS

OAHU
Pearl Harbor   Maui
HAWAIIAN ISLANDS   Hawaii

20°

MARSHALL
ISLANDS

Majuro
Jaluit
Makin Is.
Tarawa Is.
GILBERT ISLANDS

Christmas Is.
(Kiritimati)

0°

Nauru
Ocean (Banaba) Is.

NEW
HEBRIDES

20°

140°

120°

PACIFIC THEATER

0   400   600   1200   1600
MILES AT THE EQUATOR

NEW ZEALAND

180°

160°

machete, and if the Commander has any influence with the gods of the clouds, he must see to it that it rains.

All of this had been accomplished. Rain fell, dusk fell, and word came that there would be no chow. I looked at Father Straight, forlorn beneath his helmet, wrapped in a poncho—regulation in every detail of clothing. He seemed naïve, like a child given a football uniform before he's played the game.

"Hey, Playboy," I yelled to one of my new Intelligence Section buddies. "Help me fix a sack for Father Straight."

Playboy ambled over and lent his lunging machete strokes to mine. We cut a swath in the kunai and made a bed of the cuttings. We cut poles in the brush, stretching Father Straight's poncho over them. He crawled under and lay down. Something rustled in his grass bed and he shot erect. He smiled sheepishly and sank back again. In a moment, it was dark.

"Take it easy, Father," I said. "We're going to rustle up some chow."

"That'll be swell," he said, boyishly. "Where?"

"Tell you in confession."

Father Straight laughed, "You can't steal from yourself, you know."

"Right. We're going to speed up the distribution process a little."

We made the road and swung aboard an empty truck returning to the beach. A mile down the road, we vaulted off and waited for a loaded inbound truck. One came, its hooded headlights glowing in the rain. We caught it as it slowed on a hill, riding it until we came abreast of our bivouac. There we threw off a case of tomato juice and one of baked beans, leaping clear after them.

We portioned out the major share among our friends, then hurried to Father Straight's lean-to. I shook him. "Here's some food, Father—but maybe you'd better bless it first."

"What?" he snapped, coming awake.

We laughed.

"Oh," he said, and even in the dark we could recognize it for an amused "Oh."

Playboy and I laughed again and crawled back into the rain. A pair of poor Catholics who had blithely spent the months in Melbourne jumping on the Ten Commandments, we went to sleep confident that we had found expiation in pilfered offerings of tomato juice and baked beans.

Not till morning did I think to inquire where we were.

"Goodenough Island," someone explained.

Playboy laughed wryly, "It's Goodenough, all right—good enough for marines."

We set to work erecting our section tents, goaded rather than guided by Lieutenant Big-Picture's disorganizing commands. We had three tents—two to live in, one to work in.

In this third tent reposed our skimpy map-making gear: a table, made of a length of plywood resting on wooden horses, some compasses, pencils, tracing paper and a square or two. A Marine battalion intelligence section carries little cartographer's gear. Actually, we were a section of scouts; the eyes and ears of the battalion commander; that is all, no matter how strenuously Big-Picture sought to magnify it.

But much as I delighted in the prospect of becoming a scout, Lieutenant Big-Picture would not hear of it.

"You're here to get out my newspaper," he said grandly.

"But, Lieutenant, we're going to be back in action soon. And I don't even know how to shoot an azimuth. I'd get lost in a telephone booth. All I want to do is to find out how to handle a compass and how to read maps."

"You don't need to."

"But, Lieutenant—we won't have time for a newspaper when we get into action again. What'll I do then?"

Lieutenant Big-Picture, at least two months my senior, waved a deprecating hand in the style he had cultivated since that magical day on Guadalcanal, when, alone of an entire intelligence section, Sergeant Big-Picture could tell the Battalion Commander what an aerial mosaic was, earning for this feat an on-the-spot commission as Lieutenant Big-Picture.

He waved an airily patronizing hand, and said, "When we get in action, you'll keep the battalion diary."

"What's that?"

"You'll find out when we go out in the field. Now, what about my newspaper? Let's hear your thinking on it. First things first—what will we need to start with?"

"A mimeograph machine."

"Check. Talk to the sergeant major about that. What next?"

"Paper."

"Sergeant major. Come again."

"Stapling machine."

"Same. Come on, let's have a real problem."

"Reporters."

"Well, yes, sure, reporters, of course—I mean, how many will we need?" He paused. "What the hell d'ya mean, reporters?"

"If we're going to have a battalion newspaper, sir, we're going to have to have news. That means we've got to cover the companies. So we'll need a man from each company designated as the company's reporter."

"What'll he report?"

"Everything that goes on in the company. I'll make a sort of newsletter from each, then we'll have a section for Headquarters news, maybe a Poet's Corner open to submissions, a message from the Commander and an editorial."

"Message from the Colonel! Editorial!"

"Yes, sir. It'll dress up the page a bit, maybe give the Commander a chance to boost morale."

"Now, wait a minute, my man. Wait a minute." Lieutenant Big-Picture held up a restraining hand. He strode up and down gravely. He sat down, assuming an attitude like Rodin's Thinker.

"You've got to be careful about this sort of thing, Lucky. You can't go blazing ahead. We've got to consider the company commanders. They might not like the idea of a man reporting news in their units. They might want to look his stuff over a little before he submitted it."

"Censor it, sir?"

"Watch yourself there! It's just that it's a ticklish thing and the company commander might want to be sure the reporter had things straight, the way they really happened. We have to move carefully on a thing like this."

"Yes, sir."

"So, I'll tell you what we'd better do. You check with the sergeant major and see what he can do for you in the way of paper and things. In the meanwhile, I'll have to talk this over with the company commanders. I've got a briefing scheduled for tomorrow. The significance of Stalingrad. And one more thing. That message from the Colonel idea, and the editorial. Forget it. D'ya hear? They're out!"

"Yes, sir."

I obeyed orders and consulted the sergeant major, who told me to get the hell out of his tent.

Lieutenant Big-Picture, having had a full night to reflect, stuck strictly to Stalingrad next day. The battalion newspaper had been scissored from the big picture as neatly as an inexplicable terrain feature from an aerial mosaic.

The screws of discipline were firmly turning. One Sunday morning we played volleyball in the kunai grass, not far from the mess tent shared by the Commander and Major Major-Share, our new and unpopular Executive Officer. It was past mealtime, except, of course, for such worthies as Major Major-Share, who might dine whenever he pleased.

As we played, the mess corporal on duty ran up to join us. Out of the corner of my eye, I saw the Major walking with that sideways cant of his from his sleeping tent in the direction of the mess tent. Then the mess corporal noticed him, but pretended unconcern. Someone cautioned him against keeping the Major waiting. Major Major-Share's temper was well known. But the mess corporal was of that peculiar breed of unhandsome men who, perhaps angered by the airs of their more favored fellows, suddenly startle them by the strength of some inexplicable and unshakable attitude. He kept on playing volleyball.

We kept getting nervous.

The Major kept waiting.

Tension was snapped by the rising bellow of the Major's voice.

"Sergeant major!" he roared, whirling to point an imperious charge in the direction of the now transfixed mess corporal.

"Sarr-jent! Maaa-jor!"

Out of his tent burst the sergeant major, on the d-d-d-double came the sergeant major, while Major Major-Share, drawing himself up like a monster frog, finally exploded in a collapsing roar.

"LOCK THAT MAN UP!"

And they led the poor corporal away.

We were going to leave the island. The scuttlebutt said it was because of the numerous cases of scrub typhus among us—but actually, as it turned out, it was to gather with the other regiments in a staging area, whence we would assault the Japanese once more. The war came closer. We were eager, now, for news of triumphs in the Pacific, even of Allied victories in North Africa, for these, too, would drive the now turning tide closer to the enemy shore, would reduce the ranks of a long-mobilized foe while the late-mobilizing Allied cause gained in size and skill.

And a week before we left, our own small cause and numbers were augmented by a single ally, but one so singular as to be almost an army in himself.

"There's an Australian out on the road," Lieutenant Big-Picture said. "Go out and give him a hand."

I walked through the grass to the road and met the Digger.

I met him as he sat amid the grandeur and confusion of a jeep piled so high with men and material that one thought immediately of the dwelling place of an acquisitive recluse, or of the frantically loaded vehicles I have seen rushing away from floods or earthquakes.

There were at least three billy-cans, those battered tins in which the tea-drinking Aussie boils his beverage; a flute; a corroded British helmet and a shiny new American mate; a kerosene lantern; a gasoline lantern; a case of Sterno; cans of tea and sugar; sacks of rice; three or four bulging haversacks crammed with a mixture of American and Australian uniform issue; a grass skirt; a trumpet, purchased, the Digger told me later, from "a Yank" for "fordeen bob"; a driver; the Digger and four bewildered Melanesian blacks from whose powerful shoulders hung packs, in themselves minor masterpieces.

I gazed enraptured, and so did a lounging crowd of marines gathered in the hope of humor. But there was to be no poking fun.

" 'Ere!" the Digger burst out irritably. "D'ya always sit round on yer bum when y'can see a bloke needs an 'and?"

I bent to help him unload, as did some of the others and when the contents of the jeep were deposited on the ground in a miniature mountain, the driver left with such speed that he raised a cloud of choking dust.

Irritability was most plain on the Digger's face, for he had pushed back his battered slouch hat with it; stained white puggree band—and one could take a good look at his small, leathery visage with its flippant line of black mustache. His natives were aware of his mood. They stood, hesitant and apprehensive, watching him. Perhaps he enjoyed their confusion, for he suddenly adopted a half-smiling, half-pensive pose, gazing over their heads at the thread of white against the distant mountain, the waterfall washing Mount Ni-tulolo's face. Or perhaps the Digger was concealing his own confu-sion, hoping too, by his ruminative look to impress us with his presence. At last he turned to me and said:

"Give us a go, Yank. 'Ere's yer Second bleddy Battalion, now, ain't it?—so 'ow about showing me to me billet?"

I led him back to his tent, which had been hastily erected behind ours. While I helped him to tighten the ropes—for this tent sagged so limply it might have been put up by an officer—I was startled by a sort of gibberish in the brush beyond, accompanied by the sound of wood-cutting. It was the Digger's natives. They had followed us through the grass, but so silently I had forgotten them. The gibber-ish was their Melanesian tribal dialect, for they all came from a sec-tion of New Guinea around Lae, where the Digger had been a coconut planter before the Japanese invasion. The wood-cutting was for the lean-tos they were constructing for themselves—they would most certainly not sleep in the Digger's tent, any more than he would permit them to eat any of our food. The sacks of rice were for their own mess.

I helped Digger draw a cot and other necessary gear from the quartermaster, and I promised to return after evening chow, when I would show him the river in which we washed.

When I returned, I was brought to a halt ten yards from his tent by the sound of a trumpet blaring into the island quiet. So incongru-ously blatant was it—it might as well have been a train whistle. There was a melody: it sounded like "There'll Be a Hot Time in the Old Town Tonight."

I poked my head inside Digger's tent. In the light of a kerosene lamp set on the ground, I saw him sitting on his cot with his shoulders hunched down and his face screwed up as he blew with all his might into a trumpet. When he saw me, he put down the trumpet, wiped his mouth, and said: " 'Ello, there, Yank—'ave a seat." He began to blow again, lifting his foot high and bringing it down slowly when he hit the difficult notes. It was "There'll Be a Hot Time in the Old Town Tonight"—recognizable, but not always faithful.

"Where'd you learn that?" I asked when he had finished.

"Yank sowljer I bought the horn from taught it to me," he said, bending down to light a Sterno stove, on which he was boiling water for tea. It was now too dark to visit the river.

"But that's an American song, you know."

"Bleddy well right. There's some things you Yanks can do. Now, there's a tune I like. On my oath, I'd say it's real American, too. That's the kind of thing I like about America. You can have your New York, Yank. Say," he paused hopefully, "you're not from Texas, are you?"

"No," I said. "New Jersey."

"Oh," he sighed, and busied himself fixing tea.

"Are you going to be with us long?" I asked.

Digger shrugged. "Indefinitely."

"What're you gonna do?"

He winked. "Secret, Yank—top secret."

"How d'ya mean?"

"I mean secret, me lad. I can't tell you, that's all. Somebody back in Australia tells me to pop off and join up with the bleddy Marines and here I am. Tea, Yank?"

I accepted and said, "But what about your native boys?"

"They're with me, that's all. I'm just attached to you blokes from here on, for better or for worse—and I'm hoping it's for better. I don't mind telling you, Yank, I'd feel a lot easier if I was with me own. You can't top the A.I.F.!"

"Like hell you can't! We'll top the Aussies any day. Ask the Japs how they rate the enemy. They rate us the toughest in the world, and after us the American soldier—and then the Australians!"

"Where'd you hear that?" he growled.

"I didn't hear it. I read it! I read it in one of your bloody own papers."

"Go on! You're daft! You're a bunch of schoolboys alongside the A.I.F." He glared at me and prepared to refill the white mugs he used for teacups. "Don't misunderstand me," he said, carefully sloshing the hot beverage from the billy-can. "I don't say you can't fight. I just say you've got a long way to go to come up with the A.I.F." He returned to his cot and raised his cup. "Here's to the American forces." We sipped, and then he added, "And thank God for the A.I.F."

We shoved off a week later. The Digger's "somebody back in Australia" had given him little time to join us. We were notified to stand by the day after the Digger's arrival.

We slung our weapons, slipped into our packs and strode down that dusty road to the harbor. It was choked with L.S.T.'s, and many of them were drawn up on the beach, their ramps down and their jaws yawning while troops, vehicles and guns walked, rode and bumped into their dark and spacious bellies.

We entered our ship. The ramp came up behind us, the jaws creaked shut, and we sailed away.

2

Rain.

The rain had come. Finschhafen on the southeast coast of northeast New Guinea received us in a wet and dripping embrace.

Once again we unsheathed our machetes to hack out living space in the sodden jungle.

Once again we squatted in miserable indolence, awaiting the order to attack.

Once again we heard the bombs, whispering as though lost in that blind black rain overhead, crashing wildly into the jungle.

Only the Digger's natives were pleased by the delay.

"Dis Noo Kinni groun," Buri said, his strong teeth flashing in a delighted grin. He removed his ever-present pipe while stooping to pat the mud fondly. "Noo Kinni groun," he said, almost crooning.

All of them—Buri, Kimbut, and the two others whose names I cannot recall—were from New Guinea. They were proud of it, inclined to look down their splay noses at the other Melanesians who live in the Bismarck Archipelago, the island group in the western Pacific north of eastern New Guinea. They were most especially disposed to scorn the "bush kanaka"—the non-sophisticates who dwelt in the interior beyond reach of the civilizing commerce of the coast. They all spoke pidgin English—the mark of the traveler in their tribes—and they taught it to me during our two dreary weeks in Finschhafen.

They told me of their life before the war—the unbelievably simple life of the food-gatherer, apart from the annual few months in the employ (I was about to say exploitation) of planters like the Digger—and I tried to tell them of our own complicated existence. But this was next to impossible. Only when I spoke of the buildings could they comprehend, and these I usually described with the aid of magazine pictures.

"You catchem one fella house," I said, pointing to the bottom story of the Empire State Building. "All right. You catchem 'nother fella house. He stop along top. All right. You catchem 'nother fella. You catchem plenty fella, all the same number grass belong donkey. Plenty fella stop along top."

They nodded, eyes big with wonder, sometimes perhaps a shade bigger than need be—for they were consummate actors, and impeccably polite.

The Finschhafen stopover was brief—perhaps ten days—saved from boredom only by the bombings and a pointless two-day patrol into the outback, where Buri amused us one wet afternoon, trying to provide hot tea by coaxing fire from two sticks of wood. It was a trick learned from the American comic books he was fond of studying—but it was an angry failure.

When we returned, we found the camp struck, and everything in readiness for departure.

A nocturnal patrol, mainly composed of men from our section, had reconnoitered under the enemy's nose in New Britain. They had been taken across the Dampier Strait in a torpedo boat and had paddled ashore in a rubber raft. The information they brought back with them—and they almost didn't get back, for their PT boat had been shot up in a running fight with a heavily armed Japanese barge—was exciting enough to send us to arms. Apparently the place where we would land was lightly defended.

The Commander called us together that night and delivered an eve-of-battle speech.

The men formed on the road running perpendicular to the beach, clustered in a thick irregular crescent around the Commander, who stood with his back to the brush. He spoke in deliberate but angry tones; he spoke like a man who hated the Japanese, as though he had suffered a personal affront at their hands and was bent on personal vengeance—as though this were a personal, not mechanical, war. His harangue seemed unreal; it was unreal, because it could never produce the desired effect.

"Kill Japs," the Commander was saying, "I want you to kill Japs. And I want you to remember that you're marines. We've got a tough job where we're going. And where we're going we won't have much room for ammunition. So you'd better be sure you see something before you shoot. Don't squeeze that trigger until you've got meat in your sights. And when you do—spill blood—spill yaller blood."

That was all.

We walked back to the tents.

It was Christmas Eve.

At the tents, Father Straight was preparing to say Midnight Mass. He had an altar erected beneath a pyramidal tent, and we gathered before this, kneeling in the mud and hunched against the fine rain falling, to witness the immolation of the Prince of Peace. Girded in the ugly, awkward habiliments of modern war we worshipped the Divine Son of the God of Battles.

Holy, Holy, Holy, Lord God of Hosts . . .

Father Straight spoke gently. He reminded us that not all of us would live to see another Christmas, that perhaps some of us might die this very day. He told us to be sorry for our sins, to ask the forgiveness of God, to forgive those who had wronged us—to prepare our souls for death.

We sang hymns. Nineteen hundred and forty-odd years ago the Babe had been born in Bethlehem, and we celebrated Him this night in a dark and misty forest that His Father had wrought. We sang hymns to Him: "Silent Night" and "Adeste Fideles" and "Hark the Herald Angels Sing."

Mild he lays his glory by
Born that man no more may die.

And tomorrow our hands would be stained with the blood of our brothers.

But we sang on, half-heartedly, half-hopingly; sometimes mechanically, sometimes with a desperate, driving poignancy; one hand on the heart, the other on the hilt of a bayonet; now convinced by the truth and urgency of what Father Straight had said, now despairing of words and ideas as fine and as gossamer as the mist around us. But we did not leave off singing, and when we had finished, we went to bed.

In the morning we marched down to the ships.

But they gave us a wonderful Christmas dinner. We were dispersed on the beach, along that expanse of smooth black volcanic mud where a single row of great oaklike trees leans seaward, like a bristling line of gigantic spears. There was turkey and mashed potatoes, bread and even ice cream, and we marveled to think that we could eat so regally on the eve of battle.

Then they brought us our Christmas mail. It was as though we kings, having finished banqueting, had clapped our hands and called for minstrels—and got them. We spent the remainder of the day picnicking on that smooth black beach.

When it grew dark, we boarded our assault ships, bound for the morning's battle on the shores of New Britain northeastward across the Dampier Strait.

Into the night we sailed—silent and songless—back to war.

3

On the sunless shores of New Britain, where the rain forest crowded steeply down to the sea, we of the First Marine Division came back to the assault, and it was here that we cut the Japanese to pieces, literally, when that devouring jungle did not dissolve them; and it was here that we pitied them.

Now, to pity the enemy either is madness or it is a sign of strength. I think that with the First Marine Division on New Britain it was a sign of strength.

We pitied him in the end, this fleeing foe, disorganized, demoralized, crawling on hands and knees, even, in that dissolving downpour, for in the end it was we—the soft, effete Americans—who had learned to get along in the jungle and who bore up best beneath the ordeal of the monsoon, and in these things lay our strength.

It was the jungle and the rain, too, that made New Britain so different from Guadalcanal. I knew that it was going to be different the moment that I ran down the ramp of our L.C.I. and across a narrow black beach, scrambling up a small steep bank to burst from sunlight into the gloom of the jungle. For, in that moment, the rains began to fall; and in that moment we began to hunt the foe.

The sound of cannonading and diving airplanes had already been stilled when the Commander—our new battalion leader—set up his command post about fifty yards in from the water. Our assault companies had moved forward to take up positions that formed a defense perimeter, a half-moon with its straight edge running along the beach. Across its widest point, it could not have been quite four hundred yards wide.

As a unit, we would advance no further. Here we would sit, alone, astride the coastal track while the remainder of the division conquered Cape Gloucester to the northwest. We had inserted ourselves as a defensive wedge between our division and the enemy believed to be below us to the south. To reinforce his comrades, the Japanese would have to come through us. So here we sat, alone, out of contact with our main force because we were in what the Commander called "radio defilade."

From here, the Commander sent our daily patrols. With that restless precision characteristic of him, he had been dispatching patrols into the unknown terrain from the moment of our landing. They came and went constantly; out and in, out and in, north, south and east, further and further, rolling out like feelers, like the tactile senses of our battalion—that military organism that lay there blindly in the jungle—hunting for an exasperatingly absent enemy.

To the north, one patrol discovered the body of an E Company scout who had been reported missing. The area bore marks of a struggle, as though he had fought hand to hand. His body bore dozens of bayonet wounds. They had used him for bayonet practice. In his mouth they had stuffed flesh they had cut from his arm. His buddies said he had had a tattoo there—the Marine emblem, the fouled anchor and the globe. The Japs cut it off and stuffed it in his mouth.

The Commander was angry.

Again—to the north—two Japanese officers had been caught snooping around our positions and had been killed. An E Company outpost, scouting the terrain at their front, had discovered a Japanese force, in platoon strength, sleeping on the ground. Sleeping! They fired into them, into these sleeping supermen of the jungle, withdrawing upon the approach of another enemy platoon.

So the enemy was there. But in what strength? If the Japanese platoons had been but patrols, then the foe was in sizable force. The enemy's actions, too, were mystifying. Sleeping indeed! Could it be they were not aware of us?

These must have been among the Commander's considerations when he called for a fresh patrol to the south, for from the south had come silence—and it would not do to have it suddenly erupt, to have ourselves pinched between two fires.

He chose Lieutenant Commando to lead the patrol, and I went along as scout. Commando, who had joined us in Australia, was a big powerful Frenchman with a slight accent that might have been the English of a French Canadian as well as the accent of a Frenchman. He gained his name through having been at the disastrous Dieppe raid. The fighting techniques he observed among the British commandos he sought to graft onto us. But he overlooked our own pride as marines and ignored the obvious difference between the terrains of Europe and Oceania—and so was often disappointed and offended when his well-meaning criticism was resented and rejected.

The track we were to follow began as a narrow path along the beach and slanted inward from the ocean to follow rising ground that soon lost itself in the luxuriance of the jungle. It twisted and turned as though blazed by a native, drunk on betel nut.

There were ten of us—a man in the Point, normally the position of the Intelligence scout, but now occupied by a G Company man, and the rest of us strung out behind him. Our alignment was not neat, of course, but deliberately staggered—and between each man was an interval of about twenty feet. At a sign from the Point—usually a raised hand—we melted into the jungle. No one smoked, of course, nor did anyone speak. Canteens, knives or ammunition clips were secured so as to make no noise. Weapons were carried cradled over the breast, ready to be swung down for instant firing or for the butt to be dug into the earth to break a fall. I kept my Tommy gun loaded and cocked, but with the safety catch on. A single motion of my right index finger would unlatch the safety and trip the trigger. Even those armed with rifles expected to shoot from the hip—because all jungle encounters are sudden, and because the density of the rain forest affords a visibility of about five yards. Who needs to aim at such range, even if there were time?

A patrol moves slowly in the jungle. Fear of ambush produces the most extreme caution, which reduces speed to a crawl. It is this literally. Each foot is firmly planted before the other is raised, utmost care is taken to avoid twigs, and a sort of crablike rhythm is produced as the eyes and torso travel in the alternating directions of the feet. Left foot, lean, look, listen, pause; right foot, lean, look, listen, pause.

At such speed, it would take a day to move a mile and return. Should the trail be hilly, or especially twisting, it might take longer. On this patrol, it had taken twenty minutes to go around one bend, precisely because that curve lay at the foot of a rise and because such a terrain feature is admirably suited for ambush. It holds the twin advantages of ground and surprise: the enemy can deliver a plunging fire into your ranks at the very moment when your own visibility is at zero. He might even allow you to gain the hill, permit you to pass him—and then fire from behind you—a most demoralizing trick.

We had safely negotiated the turn and had worked up a series of small hills—slick with mud—to reach high ground. We were on what might be called a cliff, or at least a steep bluff, from which the ground to our right fell away to the sea. The sound of the ocean breaking on the shore was just audible if one listened for it.

The birds and all the moving things were silent, and we were uneasy. Their quiet either was heralding our own approach, or it gave sign of an enemy. A rain was falling.

The Point was in view as we approached a curve. He crouched low to negotiate it, then softly on his belly to slither around it. Then his hand came up.

We vanished into the foliage.

The hand rose again, displaying four fingers. Four of the enemy.

I lay in some high grass that fringed this portion of the track, wondering if the thumping of my heart would betray me. Then it occurred to me that I could not see over the grass. Should the Jap pass by, I could see only his legs to shoot at. Then I remembered that the man in front of me occupied the left side of the track and that I must be careful not to hit him when I fired. When I recalled that the man behind me was to the left, I hoped that he would be as considerate.

Then I thought: perhaps we shouldn't shoot at all. There were enough of us to overpower them. Should I suggest to the lieutenant that we capture them, once they had walked into our trap?

But Commando had different ideas. As I looked behind me, he signaled to a man and whispered to him when he came over. The man went sneaking up to the curve where the Point lay. In a minute, the Point came sneaking back and conferred with Commando. In another minute, a rifleman whom I did not know crawled alongside me, unslung his rifle, adjusted a grenade launcher on the muzzle and prepared to fire grenades.

Commando came up.

"About a hundred yards, left," he whispered.

The rifleman nodded.

The Point returned to his vantage.

He raised a hand.

The rifleman fired. Again and again he fired. He must have sent five grenades arching up and down, and I could hear their explosions as they hit.

Back scurried the Point.

Commando eyed him eagerly—greedily, even.

The Point shrugged. His shoulders were more eloquent than his whispered observation: "I dunno. Mebbe. They were coming down a hill, four of 'em. You might've got the first guy. They hit the deck."

The lines of lust, drawn so bright and sharp on Commando's face, were fading now. His face grew softer, then sharp again with irritation. I looked up at him. He ignored me. He had ignored my presence from the outset, and I made a mental note to correct the lie he would undoubtedly tell when we returned to headquarters.

"I dunno, Lieutenant," the Point said again, and waited.

Commando's oval Latin face brightened. "Four of them, eh?" he said, his accent chopping at the last word. "Good." He leaned down and patted the rifleman on the shoulder. "Good work," he said. He looked sharply at me, and I realized that he had been aware of me and of my identity all along. I would be expected to confirm the falsehood.

Suddenly, I was cold and aching. The rain had pierced my clothes and my neck was stiff from craning. At that moment, the man who had replaced the Point raised his hand.

The Point hastened back to his position, and in a minute rejoined Lieutenant Commando, who had resumed his old post at this new alarm. They conferred, and then, the Point went back up the track.

My teeth were jarred when the Point opened fire, and the rifleman belched away again with his grenades.

When the Point came tearing past me, his face tense, running wide-legged like a horseman, and when the man behind him also blazed away and retreated, I knew what was going on.

Lieutenant Commando was playing commando.

This was street-fighting technique. One man fires and retreats, covered by the second man now firing, and then he, too, fires and retreats, and so on down the line, a tactic that can go on to infinity, or at least until one has retreated as far as one wishes—as far back as the generals, even—or until all the ammunition is consumed. No doubt this is an excellent technique for the cities of civilization, but it was as impractical in the jungle as ski troops in the Sahara, or, more to the point, the employment of our style of patrol in that same desert. Such a tactic fits a situation in which there is little or no concealment. Who could ask for more concealment than the rain forest of New Britain?

My contempt for Lieutenant Commando's misplaced tactics was confirmed the next moment, when the last man before me had fired and come running past me.

"Oh what a paper ass!" he said, cursing between clenched teeth. "Oh what a paper-assed shavetail son of a bitch." He looked at me and growled, "Commando sits on his brains," and when I saw that it was none other than the doughty Souvenirs, I felt as though my own judgment of the lieutenant had been fortified by an opinion from the Supreme Court.

It took but a moment, and then Souvenirs was behind me and it was I who had to fire now. I knelt and fired from the hip, pulling hard on the sling with my left hand to keep the muzzle from riding skyward, as submachine guns will do. I emptied my clip—a big one of thirty rounds—in the direction of the curve in the track, and then turned to run, but not before I had felt a fleeting repugnance for that insane clatter, shattering the jungle silence as it did, and a spasm of trepidation at the extreme exposure of my position.

We carried on the farce through each of the ten men and until we had disappeared behind another bend. Then, we set our faces for the perimeter and returned home, moving this time, at a much faster pace, for we had little fear of an ambush being set up in terrain we had already traversed.

The rain had stopped but the rain forest dripped on. Just before the perimeter, we turned a bend, and there, over the head of the man before me, I saw a monster spider, crouching in its web—one of those red and black horrors, with horrid furry legs stretching out crookedly from a body as large as your fist. At that moment it fell from its web upon the helmet of the forward men—encompassing it—and he, with a gesture of extreme loathing, swept his helmet from his head to send it clanking into the bush. I waited for him to retrieve it, turning to cover the trail behind us, and then we caught up with the rest.

Lieutenant Commando and I continued on to the command post after we had gained the perimeter. What looked like another patrol—a combat patrol, judging from the automatic weapons they carried—was drawn up outside the C.P. tent. The Commander was inside, talking earnestly to a young F Company officer, when we entered. His face relaxed when he saw us, and he grinned at the four fingers Commando brandished aloft. Even in the poor light of the tent, the Commander's blue eyes seemed to glint.

"Never mind," he told the young officer. Then he turned to us. "Glad to see you back, Lieutenant. We heard the gunfire. What was it all about?"

"We ran into an enemy point down near Tauali, sir," Commando answered. He took a map from the pocket of his dungaree coat, unfolded it, marked it at the point where we had shot up the countryside and handed it to him. "There were four of them, sir. We destroyed them with small arms fire and rifle grenades."

The Commander glanced up hopefully.

"Find anything on their bodies?"

"No sir," said Commando without hesitation. "We had no time to search them. It looked like they were the point for a main body of considerably larger size."

I looked at Commando from the corner of the tent to which I had retreated. I looked at him closely. If ever a man spoke with confidence or certainty, it was Lieutenant Commando.

The Commander shrugged.

"Too bad. We could use a little information right now. But then," he said, laughing, "business is picking up. We're killing the little bastards, and that's the general idea. Unless I miss my guess," he went on, obviously relishing the phrase and the notion, "unless I miss, my guess, they're getting ready to come calling any day now." He smiled again, showing his even white teeth. "That'll be all, Lieutenant. Good work."

Commando thanked the Commander and left. I watched him go, thinking: He is not a liar, he believes that he actually saw all that. Nor is he a coward, for I have seen him react to danger. Souvenirs is right: Commando sits on his brains.

Fortunately, Commando's report had no effect on the precautions of the Commander. We remained on a twenty-four-hour alert in the expectation that the Japanese might "come calling."

But they did not come that night.

In the morning, I was assigned to a fresh patrol ordered to explore the Tauali track. This one was led by Lieutenant Spearmint and it was one in which I was given my due and restored to the Point—but this may have been merely because I was the only one who had been over the ground before. Lieutenant Spearmint was sensible enough to take advantage of that.

Spearmint was a very capable, a very calm and a very sensible officer. He had been promoted from the ranks as had many of our leaders, but he had not been dazzled by the heights of his new eminence. As the surest sign of this aplomb in the face of such good fortune—for no sunnier smile of the gods seemed possible to us—Spearmint still chewed gum.

The clean-linen league, as we called the officer corps, had not conned him into a change of manners, and even now his jaws were working in slow, ruminative movement as he told us off into our positions and gave the command to move out.

"And remember, Lucky, let me know when we reach the spot where you hit them yesterday."

It was raining and the track was more slippery than ever—and so, our progress was even slower than it had been the day before. To the right, now faintly heard through the rustling of the rain, now inaudible, lay the ocean. These were the only sounds.

Word was whispered up to me that the lieutenant wanted to parley. I crept back to where he crouched by the side of the track. He had a map balanced on his knees and was holding his poncho over his head to shield the map from the rain. He motioned to me and I knelt in the mud beside him.

"Where are we?" he asked in a low voice.

A normal question, but it shook me. I had been concentrating so hard on the negotiation of those curves that I had forgotten to take bearings. My worries had been for the foe, not for direction.

I held my breath and listened for the ocean.

If I could hear it, and if it was on my right, it meant we were still traveling in the right direction. If I did not hear it or if I heard it on my left—it meant that we were lost.

I heard it—on our right—and I looked at the lieutenant's map to see the scale of miles, and then calculating the distance we had come, the bends we had passed, the distance to the ocean, I pointed to what seemed a corresponding point on his map, and said, "There."

Spearmint nodded. I peered up into his face. It was a controlled face, and looking into it now, I saw the lines of concern disappear from about his eyes and saw the gum-chewing begin again, and I obeyed without a word when he nodded and told me to move out once more.

It had stopped raining. The green of the jungle gleamed wetly while we worked up to the plateau where the fiasco under Lieutenant Commando had taken place. We came to an open place, a short expanse of low grass beneath a hole in the jungle roof, leading to a short sloping hill that disappeared around a curve before reappearing as Commando's bluff.

Halfway up this hill, imprinted as clearly as though cast in plaster of Paris, was the mark of a foot. It was a bare foot, a broad foot, a foot with a prehensile toe. It was a native's foot. It pointed at us, downtrail. It thrilled and mystified us. I had beckoned to Spearmint and was prepared to discuss it with him, but he looked nervously about him, and said, "C'mon, let's get up that hill. This is bad ground."

We trod carefully up the rise, for it was still slippery.

In the excitement of the footprint, I almost forgot to remind Spearmint of where we were, but then, I remembered, and said, "Lieutenant, this is where we hit them yesterday."

Spearmint looked concerned.

"What about the footprint?" I asked.

He looked at me thoughtfully and pushed his helmet back. He chewed his gum methodically, with his lips drawn back and the big teeth showing. It was as though he drew strength and spirit from that rubbery wad.

"What about it?" he repeated softly, more to himself than to me. "It's there, that's all. Nothing we can do about it. Worst thing is—it's just one print." He shrugged and returned to contemplating me. "We'd better stop here awhile. You take rear guard, back by that hill."

"But, Lieutenant," I expostulated, trying to conceal my chagrin, "I'm supposed to be in the Point."

"Go ahead," he replied, unruffled. "Do as I say. Rear guard."

I obeyed, feeling as though I had been degraded.

Just a trifle below the crest of the hill, and to the left, I concealed myself in the underbrush. I broke off a few twigs which obscured my line of vision, gaining, thereby, a clear view across this open expanse. I crouched there on my haunches, stewing, angry that I had been demoted to the rear. Though the rain had stopped, there was still not a single sound, not even the ocean.

A twig snapped.

I glanced up to see four men approaching me.

They were close together.

For a moment, I thought they were our own, and I wondered why another patrol had been sent out, and why that big fellow in the lead, Major Major-Share himself, had chosen to lead it.

They kept coming and I saw their mushroom helmets and knew that they were Japs.

I reached down and unlatched my safety and said to myself: "Wait, and then shoot up and through them and maybe you will get them all with one burst."

They were coming up the hill now. The big fellow had his head bent into it and his arms pumping, and he looked even more like Major Major-Share, as I swung my right foot wide to block the trail, and there, looking up at them, pressed the trigger and fired.

They fell screaming.

The big man threw his arms over his head and screamed and spun and fell with the clatter of his rifle, and those behind fell in other ways, screaming, too, with one rolling over and over, down the hill, to disappear from sight forever.

I had emptied my thirty-round clip and had but my twenty-round clip left. I had no idea if there were more of them, so I abandoned my position across the trail, falling back around the curve to the next man, who received me with parted mouth and starting eyes.

"Stay here," I said, and hastened back to Lieutenant Spearmint. He was not unnerved, but the sound of firing to his rear had not left him undisturbed. His face asked the question.

"A Jap patrol," I panted. "Four of 'em. I think I got them all. But there may be more."

I had no need to wait, for Spearmint was on his feet motioning for another man to join us and for everyone else to stay where they were, on the alert. "C'mon," he said. The three of us returned to the brink of the hill. "Any more of them?" I asked the man I had left behind, and he shook his head in the negative. I could hear groaning. I turned to the lieutenant. "Want me to give a look?" He nodded.

I lay on my belly and began to inch out on the slope. The big man lay where he had fallen. He was dead. There were two others lying further down the hill and just at that moment, just as I appeared, the furthest of them began to crawl away.

Explosions roared behind my ear. Lieutenant Spearmint's man had cut loose with a Tommy gun and had done so almost inside my ear. It jarred me. Thinking perhaps more enemy were coming, I scrambled back to the high ground.

"He almost got you," said the man who had fired.

"Who almost got me?"

"That Jap—the one I just let have it. He was sighting in on you."

The man was excited. He had a handlebar mustache and it seemed to quiver as he spoke. I looked at the lieutenant. His face reflected concern, but it was an anxiety for the safety of a patrol seemingly cut off by the enemy. I thought: this guy's crazy, the only live Jap out there is the wounded one. But I thanked him anyway.

Groaning rose from the hillside again, and the sound of movement.

The other man and I leaned out and finished off the wounded Jap. I fired short bursts, afraid of using up my last clip.

"Listen," said Lieutenant Spearmint, when the deed had been done. "You two stay here. I'm going to strike off to the right, toward the ocean. No sense going back the way we came—there may be Japs behind us. As soon as you see the tail man, pull out."

An intense silence had fallen, broken by what seemed to us the sound of movement down at the foot of the hill, where it ended in thick growth.

But our patrol made sound enough as it broke through the underbrush toward the sea, racketing like mastodons, so eager were they to be away from this mystifying plateau. When we saw the last man, we followed suit, but not before my comrade had swept the hillside with a long burst from his submachine gun.

Once we had passed the underbrush, we understood the reason for the noise. A field of smooth, wet, slippery rocks lay underfoot, covering a steep descent to the sea.

We slipped and slithered and bumped and rolled and clattered all that distance of a few hundred yards to the water, expecting that any moment would bring the enemy fire down upon us. It was a most awkward flanking movement, but it got us out of the box we imagined ourselves to be in.

We returned along the pebbly beach, sometimes walking through the ocean, sometimes cautiously climbing over steep rocks that thrust darkly into that flat gray sea. When Spearmint thought we had gone far enough, and when the ground to the right no longer rose so high above us, we left the beach and regained the trail.

After staking out a point and a rear guard, Lieutenant Spearmint called a rest. He approached me, taking off his helmet to mop the sweat from his brow.

"You'd better go back to the perimeter and let 'em know what the firing was about."

I turned. Spearmint suddenly grabbed my arm and said, "Oh, I forgot to tell you." He jerked his head in a backward motion and grinned and said, "Good work."

I felt better about that rear guard.

It was not far, now, to the lines—and I ran through the jungle at a dogtrot, eager to report my news and to bask in the admiration of my comrades. Suddenly the sentinel of one of our cossack posts confronted me over his rifle, and I grinned at him, flourishing four fingers aloft.

"Nice going," he said, "who got 'em, Lucky?"

"Me, I did," I flung back at him, still running—and relished the surprised "Hey!" that broke from his lips.

Ardor had given way to truth by the time I reached the remaining men of the outpost, and I held up only three fingers this time, exchanging grins with them, and continuing on to the C.P.

The Commander immediately sent out a fresh patrol, with instructions to pass through Lieutenant Spearmint's men and to investigate the track as far to the south as seemed wise.

But they found nothing. There were only the bodies of three Japanese soldiers, the signs of the escape of a wounded fourth, possibly a fifth—and that was all. Even the native's footprint had been obliterated. Nor did there ever come to us any explanation of how that enemy patrol came to be behind us. The swirling mists of the rain forest had enshrouded the incident in mystery.

In the dark of that night the Japanese "came calling."

Out of the jungle dark they rushed, out of the blackness of a night made wilder still by the wailing of a wind that might have been a hurricane.

I was not in it; in fact, no more than twenty or thirty marines were in it. It came against G Company, which occupied the center and highest ground of our perimeter. This eminence rose from around our C.P., except at the western or sea anchor, of course, so that the headquarters lay in the center of a horseshoe rising around us.

The attack came at two in the morning, just as the wind rose to a pitch of fury—when the night was full of its shrieking, and the tearing, crashing sounds of the jungle reeling beneath the lash of its eternal tormentor—when the surf, too, roared in pain behind us.

And all the while it rained.

On such a night it was impossible to know more than what the sounds might tell us. Because the noise was predominantly our own because not even a spent bullet fell in our declivity, we knew that we were not losing. But we knew no more.

I sat in our C.P. tent, fully armed, awaiting instructions from either the Commander or Major Major-Share. I had with me a thermal grenade, with which I was to destroy all of our papers, should the Japanese break through. Some others from the section had been impressed as ammunition carriers, but I remained in the tent, crouching wonderingly in the dark, spared the ordeal of carrying mortar shells to the "stovepipe" crews.

I could hear the carriers cursing as they plodded past the C.P. tent, the shamrock-shaped triple shell casings on their shoulders, and sometimes I could see them in the momentary, flickering light cast by exploding shells or lightning flashes—I cannot now remember which. Some sobbed with bitter, molar-grinding exasperation when they would have slid down the muddy slope for the second or third time, to be struck cruel blows by their heavy burdens or else forced to grope blindly for them in the dark and mud before resuming the ascent.

But the stovepipes needed ammunition. From their sounds it was plain that they were widening and making denser their rain of shells. They had raised a fearful racket and had almost obliterated the wild wail of the storm. Our machine gun fire had ceased, except for a sporadic burst. Once in a while there was the pop of a single rifle or the spreading crackle of many rifles firing simultaneously. There were no enemy sounds. The battle was dying. The mortars were its death rattle. We had won.

By the first light of day we learned what had happened.

Four Japanese soldiers and one officer had been taken alive, and had been brought down to the C.P., their arms bound behind them, knives at their throats, and from them we learned that the Third

Company, 53rd Regiment of the Japanese 17th Division had been dispatched from the main body at Cape Gloucester to Tauali, to defend against our landing.

Their passage had been through near impenetrable jungle and they had not arrived on the scene until two days after our own coming. Nevertheless, they attacked us. They attacked us, some one hundred of them against our force of some twelve hundred, and, but for the prisoners, we had annihilated them.

Were they brave or fanatical? What had they hoped to gain? Had their commander really believed that a company of Japanese soldiers could conquer a battalion of American marines, experienced, confident, better armed, emplaced on higher ground? Why had he not turned around and marched his men home again? Was it because no Japanese soldier can report failure, cannot "lose face"?

I cannot answer. I can only wonder about this fierce mysterious enemy—so cruel and yet so courageous—a foe who could make me, in his utmost futility, fanaticism, if you will, call upon the best of myself to defend against him.

Our dead were six men, among them the stubby, intrepid Obie, whom I had last seen in Melbourne so drunk he could barely stand, whose gun pit had been overrun when the Japs overwhelmed a section of the lines in their first silent rush up the hillside—Obie, who had helped to drive them out in the counterattack, and who had been alternately firing and hurling imprecations at them until one of their bullets took him squarely in the forehead. May he rest in peace.

The Japanese dead lay in heaps on the hillside, and they filled the trench where Obie's gun had been located. The souvenir-hunters were prowling among them, carefully ripping insignia off tunics, slipping rings off fingers or pistols off belts. There was Souvenirs himself, stepping gingerly from corpse to corpse, armed with his pliers and a dentist's flashlight that he had had the forethought to purchase in Melbourne.

I stood among the heaps of dead. They lay crumpled, useless, defunct. The vital force was fled. A bullet or a mortar fragment had torn a hole in these frail vessels and the substance had leaked out. The mystery of the universe had once inhabited these lolling lumps, had given each an identity, a way of walking, perhaps a special habit of address or a way with words or a knack of putting color on canvas. They had been so different, then. Now they were nothing, heaps of nothing. Can a bullet or a mortar fragment do this? Does this force, this mystery, I mean this soul—does this spill out on the ground along with the blood? No. It is somewhere, I know it. For this red-and-yellow lump I look down upon this instant was once a man, and the thing that energized him, the Word that gave "to airy nothing a local habitation and a name," the Word from a higher Word—this cannot have been obliterated by a quarter-inch of heated metal. The mystery of the universe has departed him, and it is no good to say that the riddle is solved, the mystery is over—because it has changed residences. The thing that shaped the flare of that nostril, that broadened that arm now bleeding, that wrought so fine that limply lying hand—that thing exists still, and has still the power to flare that nostril, to bend that arm, to clench that fist exactly as it did before.

Because it is gone you cannot say it will not return; even though you may say it has never yet returned—you cannot say that it will not. It is blasphemy to say a bit of metal has destroyed life, just as it is presumptuous to say that because life has disappeared it has been destroyed. I stood among the heaps of the dead and I knew—no, I felt that death is only a sound we make to signify the Thing we do not know.

I went back down the hill.

En route, I stopped off to see the Digger. He and his natives had a spot to themselves on high ground just behind E Company. He was glad to see me and he was quite plainly shaken. He made tea.

"Where in 'ell did yer Yanks learn to shoot like that?" he said. I held my tongue. "Blimey—that was a racket you made last night. I don't mind saying I was a bit nervy." He finished his tea in quick gulps, and eyed me half-sheepishly, half-grudgingly. "Yer marines are bleddy good. Bleddy near as good as the A.I.F."

It was the accolade.

The storm had subsided by morning. It had swamped two of our amphibian tanks and an L.C.V. But no one ventured down to the little black beach, for a new peril had arisen. At daybreak, a mysterious enemy gun had tried to range in on us from the hills. It could not be located. But all of its shells fell in the water.

I led a patrol every day now. Still unable to shoot an azimuth, able to read a map only with difficulty—yet I continued to lead patrols, listening for that good old reliable ocean.

Most of my patrolling was to the north, toward what was called Dorf Point—where the beaches were lined with the wreckage of those ungainly barges which the enemy had relied on for moving supplies, until that nocturnal traffic had been shot to pieces by our torpedo boats operating out of New Guinea. On one of these patrols, commanded by the tall, good-natured Lieutenant Easy from E Company, we came to a cluster of native huts. The interior had that musky odor of fish, which we had learned to associate with the Japanese. I thrust my hand into a tangle of bedding. It was still warm. The touch thrilled me.

"It's still warm," I said to Lieutenant Easy, looking up at him. "They must have just pulled out."

He nodded and gave the command to press on in pursuit.

But it was getting late, and we could not go much further from our lines, lest we risk night falling between ourselves and a safe arrival home. So we turned our faces to the south.

I fell back with the lieutenant, and another man took the point.

Almost at that instant he raised his hand.

The patrol's vanishing act was ragged, and before we had cleared the track there appeared at the end of it—materializing from the underbrush, itself, so it seemed—a young and powerful native. He stood in rigid salute, British-style, grinning broadly at us, as though he was both glad to see us and amused at our clumsy attempts to elude detection.

Easy and I regarded him and each other in amazement. The lieutenant motioned him forward. But the native remained at attention. He seemed to have a reason for not moving. He seemed to be guarding someone or something.

"Let me go up to him, Lieutenant," I asked. "Maybe he speaks pidgin."

"Okay," Easy said. "You talk to him."

His reluctance to move, his protective attitude—both became understandable when I had come up to him. Stretching away to the rear of him was the most sorry, the most suffering, the most carefree, and the most smiling procession I have ever seen. There were about fifty of them. Some were hobbling on rude crutches made from sugar cane, some—the ancients—were borne aloft on litters, some were supported by the more stalwart among them; all had been reduced by starvation to mere human sticks with every rib visible beneath hides stretched so taut that one feared they would burst through; and all were afflicted by yaws or bore the mark of them—yet every one of these dark faces came alight with beatific grins the moment they saw me come up to their leader.

He smiled, too, and it was a movement of such beauty and trust that I could have embraced him.

"You savvy pidgin?" I asked.

"Oh, yes, Massa—me all the same mission boy."

I motioned to the people strung out behind him, silently intent on our conversation.

"What name belong this fella?"

"This fella name belong 'em Waremo. This fella stop along Waremo." He pointed behind me toward the village by that name, which lay a mile or more to the north. "All the same good fella. No likem Jap."

"You talk true along me?"

"Oh, yes, Massa. Me talk true. Me mission boy." He looked at me solemnly. "Papa Mare he talk along us. He say we must talk true along God, talk true always."

He seemed bursting to tell me a story and I nodded to him to go on.

"Two fella Christmas ago, Jap he come. This fella Kanaka no likem Jap. Jap he kill. This fella Kanaka hidem long bush," he jerked his head in the direction of the inward-lying mountains. "Papa Mare he die finish. Jap he come. He catchem Papa Mare. He chopem head belong him. This fella Kanaka he hidem. You fella he come long water. Jap he run. This fella Kanaka he leavem bush, he stop long water. He likem stop along village Waremo belong him. Savvy?"

I nodded and motioned to him to accompany me back to the lieutenant. I explained what was happening. The natives wanted to return to their village. Was it safe to permit them? The lieutenant shrugged.

"Maybe we ought to bring them in with us."

"Yeah," I said, "but we've hardly got enough food for ourselves."

Easy took off his helmet and scratched his head. Then he said: "They can go up to the village and we'll keep this fellow here for a hostage. He can talk to Digger. After all, that's what the Digger's supposed to do—see to reorganizing the natives."

So that's the Digger's mission, I said to myself. Aloud, I said, "What about those Japs we were chasing? They might cut these people to hell and gone."

I turned to the native and asked about the Japs. He smiled. "Jap he run." I looked at the lieutenant. He laughed.

"Listen," I said to the native. "Number One Fella"—I pointed to the lieutenant—"he say this fella Kanaka stop along village Waremo, okay. You stop along us. Okay?"

He smiled easily. "Yes, Massa."

The native—his name was Kolo—returned to his people. Our men stood aside as they passed through us, and then, seeing them in their hardship, began to give them cigarettes and candy and rations, whatever their pockets contained. The natives accepted them gladly, and with dignity.

As they passed through, I saw the children among them—their tiny bellies distended with hunger. One of the ancients on a litter sucked on a bamboo shoot which he waved weakly.

Then they were gone, having vanished around a bend, and Kolo stood proudly beside me. At a mute command from the lieutenant, the patrol moved out again.

Once we came to a stream intersecting the trail as it swept to the sea. It was about ten feet wide and a foot or so deep. I rolled up my trouser cuffs preparatory to wading it, but as I did, strong arms clasped me from behind and lifted me, depositing me, dry, on the other side, where I turned to confront the smiling countenance of Kolo.

When we had regained our perimeter, Kolo was taken to the Digger's. Next day, a heavily armed patrol led the Digger and his police boys to Waremo, an event which marked the commencement of the Australian's real purpose with the marines, for the British, or their Australian cousins, must have had no intention of permitting this cheap labor resource to remain unexploited or unorganized, or, worse still, long exposed to the corrupting influence of American generosity.

But Kolo remained with us, or rather, with me.

He became my batman.

He slept beneath my jungle hammock. He even washed my clothes.

Two days after I had met him, standing so snappily at attention in the rain forest, I sat on the beach while he washed my dungarees. It was one of those rare times of sunlight.

The jungle steamed steadily and little clouds of vapor arose from our soaked clothing. At such times we would wash our clothes in the ocean by beating them against the waves, rubbing them against the abrasive sand and, at last, wringing them out. Then, half-dry, we would re-enter them, hoping that the heat of our bodies would complete the job before the rain returned.

The beach was crowded with naked marines flailing their clothes against the ocean, their bodies incredibly white, for the rains and that sunless, dehydrating jungle had long since drained all color off. Among them stood Kolo, his body brightly black against that background. They eyed him curiously. When he brought the clothes to me, I heard a whoop of derision and then the rough and unmistakable shout of the Chuckler.

"If that don't beat the hell outta me! Lookit him, will you? Lookit him—the lousy rear-echelon bastard. If he ain't gone and got himself a batman! I'm gonna write his old man and tell him it's okay to send that blue uniform now."

Kolo withdrew as they came up the beach and gathered around me, laughing.

I started to retort, but, at that moment, the sky darkened and the rains fell again. A general cry of rage and despair rose from the beach. We sat there in disgust. Finally the Hoosier got to his feet.

"Shoot me," he pleaded. "Why'nt somebody be a good guy and shoot me?" He looked despairingly at the ocean, turned steely gray again and dimpled by the raindrops, and then glanced down at his own half-dry clothing. "Hell's fire!" he swore, "what's the use of waitin' "—and ran like a madman straight into the ocean.

In the morning, I lost my batman. The officers came and took

Kolo away from me. They needed him to serve in the officers' mess that they had had contrived for themselves, erecting it almost the very day after the securing of our position. An officers' mess is one of the surest barometers of military success. So long as the officers continue to pig it with the men, there is danger of defeat. But once the officers' mess appears—raised almost on the bodies of the foe, contrived of sticks and pieces of canvas or perhaps only an imaginary line like a taboo—once this appears, and caste is restored, we know that victory is ours.

That same morning, our eighty-one-millimeter mortars ranged in on an eastward lying spot believed to be the position of the mysterious enemy artillery. Their guns never spoke again.

Our patrols were probing further and further in every direction.

To the east, in thickest jungle, Lieutenant Racehorse—the same who had placed Chuckler, Chicken and me in that tiny brig aboard the *Manoora*—killed one Jap while leading a patrol.

To the south, Lieutenant Commando ran into an enemy twenty-millimeter gun outpost and killed two of them.

Further south, to Laut, Lieutenant Liberal—a new officer—killed a Jap on patrol.

In the same direction, a fifty-man patrol of ours destroyed a three-man enemy ambush, blasting them with shotguns after the poor silly Japs had shouted out in their precise English, "Come here, please—Come here, please."

Again to the south, to Sag Sag, a patrol passed the plateau where I had had my own encounter, and we had to hold our noses passing the white moving mass of corruption which these bodies had become within a few days.

To the north a few days later, Lieutenant Racehorse contacted a friendly patrol from our main body at Cape Gloucester and conducted them to our perimeter.

Finally, far to the south, Lieutenant Commando was wounded by a Jap sniper in a jungle flare-up between his patrol and an enemy force composed of Nipponese soldiers, scout dogs and natives armed with bows and arrows. Because he was so big, he could not be carried the six or seven miles of rugged terrain lying between Laut and our position. A runner was sent back, and I was in the C.P. at the time of his arrival.

We went to rescue Commando in an amphibian tractor, sailing along the coast under a mackerel sky, a flight of scavenger birds accompanying us like ghoulish outriders over the bleak cliffs to our left. Commando lay in the forward part of the tractor on the return journey, his face ashen and his lips tightened against the pain. Commando might sit on his brains, but he fought with his heart.

Four days later, on the eleventh of January, we struck our lines and marched up the coastal track to Cape Gloucester, along the shore, past the wrecked barges, through the empty villages, through the ocean with rifles at high port, and up a beach of smooth white stones—and so to the airfield, back to the warmth and comfort of our division comrades.

4

I had spent the night beneath a native hut, protected from the pelting rain—damp, if not dry, but at least not drenched.

When I awoke I could hardly see. Something was wrong with my eyes. It was as though the lids were stuck together. I blundered out into the light and strained to see my comrades, in soiled ponchos arising from the wet earth like genies swirling into shape from the mists, and saw that they were laughing at me and pointing at me.

I felt my face and found that my lips had swelled like a Ubangi woman's and that my eyelids, too, had ballooned, as well as my nose. Someone took a mirror from his pack and handed it to me, and I saw myself a puffy gargoyle.

But my face subsided to normal proportions within a half hour. I ascribed the swelling to some obscure bug that dwelt beneath that unsavory hut—and forgot about it.

But now I remember, now I remember that here marked the midway point of the battle with the jungle. For the Japanese had been defeated during our solo mission down the coast, and even though the stiffest fight—the Seventh Regiment's conquest of Hill 660—would require another week for its consummation, it was the jungle and not the Jap that was now the adversary.

The puffing of my lips and eyes symbolized the mystery and poison of this terrible island. Mysterious—perhaps I mean to say New Britain was evil, darkly and secretly evil, a malefactor and enemy of humankind, an adversary, really, dissolving corroding, poisoning, chilling, sucking, drenching—coming at a man with its rolling mists and green mold and ceaseless downpour, tripping him with its numberless roots and vines, poisoning him with green insects and malodorous bugs and treacherous tree bark, turning the sun from his bones and cheer from his heart, dissolving him—the rain, the mold, the damp steadily plucking each cell apart like tiny hands tearing at the petals of a flower—dissolving him, I say, into a mindless, formless fluid like the sop of mud into which his feet forever fall in a monotonous *slop-suck, slop-suck* that is the sound of nothingness, the song of the jungle wherein everything falls apart in hollow harmony with the rain.

Nothing could stand against it: a letter from home had to be read and reread and memorized, for it fell apart in your pocket in less than a week; a pair of socks lasted no longer; a pack of cigarettes became sodden and worthless unless smoked that day; pocketknife blades rusted together; watches recorded the period of their own decay; rain made garbage of the food; pencils swelled and burst apart; fountain pens clogged and their points separated; rifle barrels turned blue with mold and had to be slung upside down to keep out the rain; bullets stuck together in the rifle magazines and machine gunners had to go over their belts daily, extracting and oiling and reinserting the bullets to prevent them from sticking to the cloth loops—and everything lay damp and sodden and squashy to the touch, exuding that steady musty reek that is the jungle's own, that individual odor of decay rising from vegetable life so luxuriant, growing so swifly, that it seems to hasten to decomposition from the moment of birth.

It was into this green hell that we were inserted a day or two after the march from Tauali-Sag Sag. And here was fought that battle with the rain forest, here the jungle and the men were locked in a conflict far more basic than our shooting war with the Japanese— for here the struggle was for existence itself.

The war was forgotten, Who could comprehend it? Who cared? The day was but twenty-four hours and the mind had but two or three things to command it, objects like dryness, food—oh, most of all, most unbelievably of all, a cup of hot coffee—a clean, dry pair of pants and a place out of the rain! Hours passed in precocious contemplation of that moment just before darkness, when—with cigarette wrappings and the wax-paper covers of the K-rations, with matches carefully wrapped in a contraceptive and kept within the liner of the helmet—a tiny fire was lighted and water heated in a canteen cup, and thus was the belly fortified to face the cold black night.

Once we had taken up these new positions, featureless in my memory except that a narrow but swift little stream swept through the Battalion C.P., I resigned myself to the dreary proposition that I would be wet so long as I stayed on New Britain. I would be wet not only from the rain—for sometimes it stopped, and at other times it did not fall so fast that a jungle hammock could not repel it—but because an affliction which had begun the moment I left Australia was now active again. It had begun during the discomforts of Guadalcanal, had disappeared in the civilized living of Melbourne, and had reappeared on Goodenough, New Guinea and now on New Britain. I learned later from doctors to call it enuresis. When one is asleep, the bladder empties—and that is that.

Our patrolling recommenced, for the Japanese had been put to flight, now, and our patrols were engaged in annihilating them, small unit by small unit, as they were encountered wandering in the rain forest.

Small, quick actions were common. Here a patrol would destroy a half-dozen Japanese, sometimes losing one or two of our own in killed or wounded, and here another would surprise a larger group of the demoralized tan men, or perhaps blunder into one of their ambushes. But running through this irregular rhythm of patrol action was the regular measure of attrition. The enemy, to use the Hoosier's phrase, was being whittled.

Days made uneasy with the anxiety of patrolling were capped by nights filled with the apprehension of infiltration by the foe. Not to say that the Japanese was a bloodthirsty human, alive only to the chances of killing. Rather the very disorganization of his forces made him more to be feared at night, for he would prowl within our lines, hungry for food—and, when detected, fight for his life.

The thought of a softly infiltrating enemy lay uppermost in our minds during the night watches, especially during a man's careful progress from jungle hammock to sentry post.

On the night of a heavy storm, it was on my mind when I had finished my sentry trick and climbed into my hammock, lying there half awake, half asleep, my knife held loosely in my hand—when suddenly I heard a scream not six feet away.

I turned to see—by the light of a lightning flash—turned to see two dark figures flailing against each other, before both fled and darkness reclaimed the field.

The C.P. was in a turmoil. Voices rose, inquiringly, querulously, and I could distinguish among them the cry of one of them from my section: "Japs in the C.P.!" Then another familiar voice: "A Jap just tried to get me!" I let myself down from my hammock, switching my knife to my left hand, groping for my machete lying against a tree, shouting: "Over here! Over here! I saw 'em!" In the quiet that followed, there rose the bellow of the major, commanding, "Don't shoot! Get 'em with your bayonets!" And then, in the ensuing silence, there was the distinct, the unmistakable, the lucid clicking of a hammer as the major cocked his pistol.

Ah, yes: get 'em with your bayonets, lads: don't shoot, lads, you may hit the major.

Click, click.

I went back to bed, and listened to the storm of wind and the storm of commands and countercommands raging around me, until one or the other or both subsided, or else I fell asleep.

In the morning, it became clear that the two men of my section who claimed to have encountered the Jap prowler had really run into each other. They had not been fond of each other before this incident, but thereafter they made a cult of their dislike.

At last we were withdrawn from this miserable morass, and we took up new positions. We slopped through a soup of mud that had once been a dirty road, and on our way we were joined by Eloquent, who had fetched Chicken and me from the brig, who now had come to Cape Gloucester from the battalion rear echelon on Goodenough.

He told us the first sergeant back there had killed himself. He grew despondent one night, Eloquent said, and shoved the muzzle of a Tommy gun into his mouth and pulled the trigger: a most messy end of himself. None of us could comprehend it.

We were now in reserve. We no longer had a front to defend. But we had a new enemy. The trees.

Our position lay in a blasted wood so grim, so stark, so scarred that it might have been the forest of the moon. The Japanese had defended here and a fierce artillery barrage had been laid in on them. Our shells ravaged that forest of giant trees. They lay uprooted, or stood broken and splintered, limbs dangling like broken arms, or decapitated, with their foliage tops lolling over like a poorly cut head, or they listed, weakened by cannon fire and watersoaked with rain.

Through the day and the night this grotesque forest resounded to the crash of falling trees.

And no less than twenty-five men were killed by them, crushed to death. An equal number were injured. And once, when we began to dynamite them, we killed another man, to prove that a bad cure can be as deadly as the cause. A great boulder fell on him as he sat beside his hammock.

We all mourned him, for he was the buffoon of the battalion. He was the nearest thing to a fat man I ever saw in the Marine Corps. He was not really fat, Loudmouth, but heavy-jowled and of pinkish complexion that always seems to bespeak obesity. Without age, without gifts, without authority—a fat man has no chance. Poor Loudmouth had none, even though he was intelligent and sensitive. So they were always at him, and when he sought to retaliate by assuming a superior air, the gibes and taunts turned his foolish vanity against him.

He liked to strut and to pretend that he was above the humdrum or the hazards of our daily life. He was fond of saying things that would enforce that pose: "Me, I'm gonna be in B Company. I'm gonna be here when you leave and be here when you don't come back"—"Next war, boys, there's gonna be two persons missing. Me and the MP they send after me."

So a boulder crushed the life and the pitiful boasting out of him. We felt sad, because Loudmouth had always seemed so much a waif, so forlorn. The others might die beneath the falling trees—the "widow-makers" as we called them—and no one would feel melancholy. But with Loudmouth, it did not seem fair. Loudmouth never seemed really to be involved in the war, he seemed more spectator than participant. And that was how he died, as though a foul ball had risen from behind home plate and brained him. He sat beside his hammock and a boulder blotted him out.

The last patrol was a prolonged one of several days. We were taken by landing boat down the east coast to a place called Old Natamo, and there deposited.

The place had once been inhabited by the Japs, but all of their emplacements were now empty. Those of the enemy who were discovered were in the last extremities of ordeal. Some were overtaken crawling on their hands and knees, some so badly decomposed it was as though their feet were rotting off, some weighing perhaps no more than eighty pounds, some without weapons, all without food—and all possessed of that indomitable fighting spirit that was the Japanese Imperial Army's greatest asset, the one single factor that made a poorly equipped soldier a first-rate foe.

They all resisted, and they were all destroyed, bayoneted, for the most part, for it was folly to fire a rifle on patrol in unfriendly, unknown territory. One of these stragglers was strangled in cold blood by The Kid, a youngster who, although already a veteran of Guadalcanal, was hardly acquainted with a razor. He was to go mad two months later.

So we mopped up.

At night a fierce rainstorm blew, and we huddled beneath the lean-tos we had built along the shore.

In the morning, it was still raining, but the sea had deposited a gift on our doorstep. The rain had caused a flash flood to sweep the forest of the "widow-makers," where our comrades reposed, and all of their food had been carried away to the beach, where it was swallowed by the sea. But the sea had coughed it up again on our strip of sand.

We fell upon this donation of Neptune with whoops of delight.

Even though the food was of common fare—cans of dried eggs, dried milk, sugar, coffee, dehydrated vegetables, syrup—it appeared to us the makings of a banquet, for we could use it as we wished and in whatever quantities we wished. Had we known that this was the lost food of our buddies, I suspect it would have tasted even better. We ate pancakes (fried in our mess gear) and drank coffee all that day, for it was storming intermittently and we did not go patrolling.

Next day, on a short patrol inland, I found a Japanese chest and carried it back with the help of Playboy. Solidly built, it was just the thing to hold my clothes and my books, which my father had now begun to send me from the States. I had perhaps a dozen books, now, among them a dictionary and an almanac—two works which sufficed to establish me as the Sage of the Second Battalion, First Marines. Many disputes were referred to me and my books of wisdom, with a confidence as unwarranted as the conceit it produced. In combat, my books were kept in company property, but presently, since we had come off the lines, I had reclaimed them—and the chest would make a magnificent locker library.

The landing boats came for us the next day and we piled aboard, Playboy and I carrying the Japanese chest between us. On our return, we found the battalion busily picking up and bidding good-by to that blasted unhappy forest, and moving to a new area where we were provided pyramidal tents and began to live with some degree of comfort.

Our comfort invited visitors. One morning the Artist reached for his poncho under his cot and found a bushmaster coiled beneath it. He seized his carbine and shot the snake through its horribly beautiful head. It measured about ten feet.

A week after our arrival, Lieutenant Big-Picture came to our tent and commandeered my chest. He took it in my absence. I would like to say stole, but I have already said commandeer, which is the word for official stealing. Grinding my teeth, I went down to see Big-Picture in the section tent.

It would be an unequal contest, it would be no contest. I would reason, he would command—and I would lose my chest, from which he had removed my books and clothes, casting them contemptuously on my cot—but I would still like Big-Picture to see my face.

"The Artist says you have my chest," I began.

He looked at me coldly and said nothing. I ground my teeth and smiled.

"Are you just borrowing it, sir?"

"I'm taking it. We need it in headquarters to store the gear in." I followed his eyes and saw the chest. In one corner of it reposed our meager map-making gear; in the other, Lieutenant Big-Picture's clothing. An insane rage swelled within me. Ivy-League stealing cigars, Major Major-Share taking all the bacon out of the battalion ration, the officers kidnapping Kolo, and here, Big-Picture stealing my chest. He spoke again. "You know an enlisted man can't have a thing like that in his tent." What could I say? This thing within me was bursting to be free and to do violence, my insides were like a cavern in which a chained demon bellowed and clamored—and I dared not speak for fear the sound of my own voice would set it free. I could only look at Big-Picture and let my face tell him that I wanted to kill him. And then I left him.

Next day, the map-making gear was back on the ground and the chest was in Big-Picture's tent, filled with his clothing and personal articles. The chest became a fixation with me and the insult and injustice ballooned far beyond proportion. I talked stupidly about killing Big-Picture, being careful to say the most dire things in the presence of those closest to him, men who would be sure to repeat my words to him.

It was all talk, big, empty, windy talk—but it had the desired effect. In a few days Big-Picture sent an emissary to my tent. He chose well, for his spokesman was the Gambler, perhaps the best-liked man in the battalion. A tough man across the poker table, the Gambler was a soft-touch in his position as Battalion Quartermaster.

"What's eatin' ya, kid? What's all this crazy talk about killin' Big-Picture?" He laughed as though it were all a joke, and I laughed, too.

"Who told you?"

"Who told me? Don't make me laugh. You've practically got it written in neon on your back: 'I'm gonna get Big-Picture.'" His tone changed and he spoke earnestly. "C'mon, now, kid, you ought-n't to be talking like that. Somebody's liable to take you seriously. And you've got poor Big-Picture going nuts."

"I hope they do take me seriously—and I hope that lousy little shavetail blows his stack."

"What've you got against him?"

"He stole my foot locker."

Gambler grinned. "How d'ya mean—stole? Where'd you get it?"

"I know what you mean," I said. "But the Japs can come and take it back any time they want. I said he stole it, and that's what he did. He said he was taking it for the section property, but he's using it to keep his clothes in."

Though warned that Big-Picture might take reprisal, I remained stubborn. The Gambler's visit only made me apprehensive. I was relieved when, a few minutes later, Eloquent and the Playboy came into the tent and suggested a swim at the waterfall.

The waterfall lay upstream of the narrow river that ran behind our tents. It fell about fifteen feet into a deep and foaming pool. About a third of the way down it, and behind it, was a hollow space in the rock. You could climb down to it, and then, standing on a smooth stone platform, dive into the waterfall.

The moment you entered that downpour of water, it took hold of you, forcing you to fall like a stone into the cold pool, down, down, down, into the blackness and the thrill of fear when the lungs begin to strain and the legs start kicking, braking your descent, thrusting frantically, now, for the surface and the good sweet air and the roar of the falls and the sound of voices.

But this day, on my first dive, I felt a sudden pain in my lower regions. Perhaps it was a minor rupture, or the sign of an incipient one. On Guadalcanal, I had felt similar pains while burying the heavy crates of ammunition. But there had been no hope of treatment there, and I had ignored it. Here it was again, though, and it worried me.

It was difficult to walk. There was a heavy sensation. Playboy helped me back to the tent. Still, I did not want to turn in to the hospital, hoping that the affliction would disappear. But when I got there, I changed my mind.

"Big-Picture wants to see you," said the Artist. "He's going to put you into the galley. What happened to you?"

I said, "I think I got myself a big fat rupture."

"What's so funny about that?"

"It means I won't be going to the galley, and I can't wait to tell Big-Picture."

I hobbled down to sick bay. The doctor examined me and began writing on a blue ticket.

"What's that, sir?" I asked.

"Evacuation order. They can't do anything for you here. I'm evacuating you to New Guinea. Report here in the morning with your toilet gear."

What a pretty blue ticket! What a lovely way to run a war! I eyed it like a prisoner receiving his pardon, and set off for Big-Picture's tent.

"Did you want to see me, sir?" I could not have been more respectful.

His face was bleak, his tone resentful. "Yes. Get your gear and report to the mess sergeant. You're going into the galley."

"But, sir," I said, with plaintive respect. "I thought that Intelligence personnel were exempt from galley duty. That's one of the benefits you talked about when you asked me to join the section."

He avoided my eyes, but his voice was filled with the determination of revenge.

"Not anymore. From now on, we have to provide a man. And you're it for the month of March."

"Gee, sir, that's too bad."

"What's too bad?" he repeated angrily, looking at me fiercely.

"I can't go. I have to go to the hospital."

He was so plainly frustrated and consumed with rage that it was embarrassing. I had come to gloat, but I could only hope that he would terminate the interview and let me free.

"What the hell d'ya mean, go to the hospital? Who the hell says so? I'm your commanding officer!"

"The doctor down at sick bay says I have a rupture," I said, withholding the part about evacuation to New Guinea. No sense risking things. I would tell the battalion sergeant major in the morning before I left. "It may have to be operated on," I added, just to fortify my position.

Now it was Lieutenant Big-Picture who did the staring. He gazed at me with unconcealed hatred, but with far too much sullenness for a person accustomed to the upper hand.

"All right," he said. "I'll take care of you when you come back. You may think you've beaten me this time, but you're still going into the galley."

"Yes, sir," I said. "May I go now?"

The big transport plane rose with a roar from the airstrip at Cape Gloucester, and I settled with relief into my bucket seat while the plane leveled out to fly low over the Dampier Strait and then gained altitude over New Guinea, where the jungle had the appearance of row upon tightly packed row of Brussels sprouts.

Our airplane came down with a rush at Cape Sudest. There was a khaki-colored ambulance waiting for us. We were in the hands of the army now. We were being taken to one of their station hospitals.

The ward was in a Quonset building. A nurse—the first woman I had seen in nearly six months—gave me pajamas and assigned me to a cot. Two or three days passed like an idyll, reading, eating three fine meals a day, going to movies at night—and then came my examination. The doctors decided that they did not want to undertake such an operation in the tropics, nor did they consider the affliction serious enough to send me farther back to a general hospital in Australia or the States, even if they had had the authority to do so.

I was dejected. Back to Cape Gloucester and Big-Picture's revenge, and good-by to the hospital library. But with nightfall the future changed again. I came down with malaria.

Never again may I have recourse to such a malignant savior! I was delivered from mess duty and the persecuting revenge of Big-Picture, but the fires that racked me and made of my body an oven were such as to make me wish for a year in the galley and a dozen Big-Pictures to command me. But of course I wished for no such thing. I wished only for release from this fiery vise, and if death were the only release, then I wished for death.

To lie on my back was torture, to lie on my stomach a torment. I tried to lie on my side, but even here my bones ached as though they were being cracked in the grip of giant pliers. I could not eat, I could not drink—not even water. They fed me through the veins, intravenously, for I do not know how long—ten days, two weeks. All the time I lay baking—not burning or flaming, understand, but baking, as though I were in an oven—feeling the will to live shrivel within me, yearning only for a tiny trickle of sweat to burst from my desiccated flesh, hearing people alive and talking around me, the touch of the nurse, the momentary cool of the alcohol being rubbed upon my back like a blissful reminder of the world I had left, but comprehending nothing, lying there, only a rag of aching bones slowly shrinking in the glowing oven of malaria.

Then the fever broke. Sweat poured from my pores like a balm. It bathed my body in a blessed cool, and I could laugh, sing, shout, if only I had the strength. It seemed ungrateful to lie there as the liberating fluid flowed from my body, not to make some sign of thanks. But I was too weak to move, like an atheist who has no God to thank for present favors; and because I had so far forgotten my own religion, I felt no impulse of mental thanksgiving.

The sweat soaked my bedclothing, and the nurse, happy to see my ordeal ended, moved me with smiles to another cot. I soaked this one, too—and then came the chills. I kept on shivering and they piled the blankets higher over me. It was well over one hundred degrees outside, but they covered me with blankets as though it were only a quarter of that. And I still shook. But this I did not mind. I could even smile—like the Runner grinning with quivering lips, "It feels so good, it feels so good."

It was over, but several more days were required before I could sit up or take food. The smell of food nauseated me; tea and a slice of toast were all that I could bear. Finally, I ate with the rest of the patients, and I can remember the extreme effort needed to insert the first forkful of food into my mouth.

But in a week, I was leaving the hospital. Back to an evacuation point on the beach, and thence to Cape Gloucester via a nocturnal crossing of the Dampier Strait in a converted fishing schooner. A storm broke upon our heads. Black water came over the sides, flooding the deck where we slept, and we retreated to a cabin where we spent the night, half of these "ambulatory patients" seasick by the dizzy rise and fall of our puny craft.

Fate chided me gently upon my return to Cape Gloucester. Most of the battalion was away on an extended patrol—Lieutenant Big-Picture among them—and the battalion sergeant major, seeing that I was still weak, kindly gave me light duty in the Senior N.C.O.'s Mess. So my flight to New Guinea was almost futile; the threat of rupture was still with me; I had gained a delay only by being felled by that filthy bout of malaria, and here I was, on mess duty, to prove how presumptuous can be the private who believes he can accomplish anything by himself.

But there was nothing to this assignment, merely a matter of keeping the tent clean, brushing the crumbs from the rough wooden table and setting out the places for the handful of men who had not gone on patrol. They helped themselves, eating in a sort of buffet from the pewter containers of food sent over from the main galley.

In a few days, the battalion returned, with only a few wounded, and I was overjoyed to hear that Big-Picture had been transferred and that our new section commander was Liberal, the young second lieutenant who had distinguished himself by killing a Jap on his first patrol.

Two or three more weeks passed in lolling about our tent area. We began to play bridge. We played obsessively, pausing only for meals or sleep so as to gain sustenance or refreshment for playing more bridge. Some of us even began to think in bridge terms—of finessing or reneging or crossruffs—and the breaking point of our mania was reached one night when the Gambler, exasperated by the play of a poor partner, rose up wrathfully to tear up the only deck of cards we possessed and to overturn the candles.

But no one minded, for we were leaving the next day—as the Gambler well knew when he made his disgust so flamboyant.

An Army unit was arriving as we were departing. There were hoots and mock falsettos from our raggedy ranks when we perceived the first equipment to be deposited on the beach—stoves and suitcases—and then we were marching aboard the L.S.T.'s, the now-familiar Trojan seahorses, and leaving that accursed island forever.

We were going: As they say in the song, we don't know where we're going—but we're going.

SEVEN

VICTIM

1

All the way from New Britain there had been foolish, hopeful talk of "going home." All the way we had indulged in silly speculation on the impossibility of sending our diseased, decimated divison into action again without a rest in Australia, or New Zealand, if not back in the States. All the way we had pointed to our emaciated frames and rotting legs and festering armpits, and then, arguing out of jaundiced lips and prejudiced hearts, had pronounced ourselves unfit. All the way there had been the erection of castles in air upon the cobweb of the government's new troop rotation plan and the single fact of our having served the required two years overseas.

All the way high hearts and foolish hopes—and now, Pavuvu.

"What is it?" asked Eloquent, when first we heard the island's name from Lieutenant Liberal. "What in the name of heaven is Pavuvu? A tropical disease, like the mumu?"

"It's Pavuvu with a capital P," said Lieutenant Liberal reprovingly.

"So?"

"It's a place. It's where we're going. Pavuvu Island in the Russells. Part of the Solomons."

"Sounds poetic," said Playboy dreamily.

"Oh, I'll bet it is," said Eloquent, with heavy sarcasm. "The wind sighing gently in the palm fronds, white beaches kissing the blue sea, undulating island beauties coming down to meet us with songs and leis—"

"Leis? Who's gettin' leis?"

"...Songs and leis," Eloquent continued, loftily ignoring the interruption. "Oh, it'll be peachy dandy. When do we get to this wretched place, Lieutenant?"

"Tomorrow," said Liberal.

We marched ashore in the rain and inched up a mud-slicked slope into a coconut grove, and there sat down to contemplate our misery. This was our new home. Pavuvu was to be our rest area. Here we were to make ready for our next campaign.

Instead of a machete we were given shovels and buckets. There was no underbrush to be cleared, but there was ubiquitous mud to be conquered by quarrying uncounted tons of coral from an open cut in a hill opposite us.

We shared Pavuvu with multitudes of rats, and these, too, we set to conquering with our busy American ways. But soon our supplies of poison ran out and the piles of little carcasses became more obnoxious in their state of stinking corruption than the live rats had been in pelting flight across our tent tops.

When dusk set a limit to our assault upon mud or rat, a soft rustling in the palm fronds suggested a more exotic foe, for then we would see the darkly beautiful bat stretching its silent wings upon the winds of evening.

In the end, it was only the mud we conquered. We left the rats alone, and never bothered the bats, only wondering, sometimes, where the rats came from; and, if it were the palm fronds, as many believed, how did they get along with their laconic neighbors, the bats.

The food was bad, too, and our tents were rotten and punctured with holes. There was no water except what was caught in our helmets during the night. We bathed by dashing naked into the rain, soaping ourselves madly in a race against the probability of the rain's ceasing and being left streaked with sticky soap, and we washed our clothes by boiling them in cans of rain water. Our jungle rot had become so bad, so persistent, that there was an appointed time each afternoon for the men to take off shoes and socks and to lie on their sacks with corrosive feet thrust out into the sun.

But we had borne all this before and we could bear it again, nor could mere bad food or leaky tents press upon the ardor of my comrades. It was the death of hope that bore us down.

There had always been hope; hope of relief, hope of the sun, hope of victory, hope of survival. But when they came and told us that none of us were going home on rotation, we strangled hope and turned into wooden soldiers. The future looked to innumerable enemy-held islands and innumerable assaults, and we had already noticed how the ranks of the New River originals were dwindling with every action. There were even a few suicides to suggest how despairing some could find the situation.

We lay on our sacks and listened to the rain or the rats and contemplated some drab substance the color of gray.

Then the thing changed.

They came and said half of the originals could go home.

There was joy, and then, once the method of selection for the Stateside bound became known, there was anger. There would be a drawing, a "Stateside Lottery," in which men's names would be pulled from a hat, but only the names of those who had never been in trouble.

I was among those whose name did not go into the hat, and so were Runner and Hoosier and Chicken and Souvenirs and a host of others. It seemed that the originals of the Second Battalion, First Marines, had been neatly divided into good guys and bad guys.

Among us there raged a profane anger. I know now how a convict must feel upon being turned down at job after job because of his past. That was what disqualified us—our past. It made no difference that we had been punished—yes, punished again and again, for it had become customary to solve all problems of selection this way— by marking brig-rats for dirty duty and excluding them from special benefits. Nor did it matter that we had good war records.

It must have been even harder for a third group, a few men, like the Artist, whose skills were so rare they could not be spared whether they had been good or bad. Without the Artist, we had no map-making section. I suspect that if the Artist had had a violation against him, they would have barred him under that pretext, just as I suspect that someone high in command was a believer in Smedley Butler's axiom about brig-rats.

In retrospect, it is easy to forgive my commanders this. But then, it was hard; it was too much like being unfairly condemned to death. The injustice of it overwhelmed me, and I burned with a resentment that was dangerous to carry around. When the departure of the lucky ones was succeeded by a period of the most rigid discipline, I resolved to get away from Pavuvu to a place of solace and rest where I might recover my equilibrium.

What better place than the hospital across the bay on Banika?

The episode with Lieutenant Big-Picture had shown me how a flight to the hospital—like a retreat to the wilderness—could solve my problems. Why not try it again? Because of the rain, falling daily even though the rainy season was supposed to have ended, my enuresis was more noticeable than before. Perhaps, too, the agitation of the moment aggravated it. I know that the men in my tent had been urging me to report it to sick bay. I did.

The doctor, who knew of my case, ordered me to Banika. I was to leave in the morning.

I walked back from sick bay with a sense of grim satisfaction, and strode into my tent to find Rutherford sitting on my cot. Suddenly the palms and the tropic night had vanished and I was standing in front of the bank on Station Square at home. Many a Saturday night, Rutherford and I and the others had stood there, rehashing the high school football game. He had joined the Marines the same month I did, and had been assigned to the Fifth Regiment. I had not seen him since New River.

He grinned cheerfully, and I said, "You no-good—how come you didn't go home on rotation?"

Rutherford chuckled. "I wasn't a good boy, I guess."

"Same here," I said, and then, as he drew a huge Japanese pistol from beneath his coat—"What the hell've you got there?"

He looked around furtively and thrust it beneath the blanket. "Keep it for me, will you?" he said. "I clipped it from the company commander this morning, and he's raising hell about it. They're gonna have a shakedown tomorrow." His round sallow face darkened. "It's mine, anyway. That lousy captain pulled rank and took it from me. I got it from a Jap major at Talasea. He killed himself with it."

"Give it to me," I said. "I'm going to the hospital on Banika tomorrow and I'll take it with me."

His eyes glowed. "Good! They can shake down the whole damn island tomorrow—and they'll never find it."

Rutherford left, immensely relieved.

In the morning, I hung Rutherford's machine pistol underneath my armpit, by means of a length of white cord, put my coat over it, picked up my bag of toilet gear and went down to the division hospital. From there a landing boat took me to Banika.

———

Banika was a fleshpot, Banika was the big town, Banika was Broadway. Banika had women, it had buildings of steel and wood, it had roads, it had thousands of sailors as sleek as capons, it had movie amphitheaters, it had electric lights, it had canteens overflowing with candy and comforts. And Banika had beer.

Walking with the others from the beach to the Navy Hospital I felt like a hick on his first visit to New York. Jeeps and trucks and staff cars swept over the island's roads, raising a busy cloud of dust. Cranes croaked and cranked on the beach, loading and unloading the boats. MP's patrolled a stockade of pointed sticks behind which dwelt the women—the Navy nurses and Red Cross workers. Everyone was well fed and unworried, the seat of every pair of pants was well filled and happy. Banika was a bovine buttocks.

We lean ones who wore our discontent on our faces and carried our nervous impatience in our hands must have been a disturbing presence in that purring island incubator. Yet, as I walked along, I was filled with the uneasy suspicion that it would be the image of Banika and not Pavuvu that would be presented to America as the Pacific War. I thought of a U.S.O. singer whom I had known before the war, who had entertained us at New River. She had asked to see me, and when I was fetched, we walked about our barren base. "What do you think of it?" I asked. And she—perhaps thinking of other bases she had visited, shiny with brass and gay with military balls—she had looked down her nose at our poor tents and huts, and said, "Not very glamorous." Pavuvu was like New River, like every place we had been: not very glamorous. But, ah Banika! There was glamor for you. This was war in the Pacific. This was what America would hear.

A Navy corpsman led me into a ward and off into a side room—a little cell.

"Take off your clothes," he said, coldly, throwing pajamas and robe at me. Clearly, the duty was distasteful to him.

I started to comply.

"Give me your belt and your razor blades," he said.

It was an odd command, but I obeyed. I was still undressing, and my eyes traveled to the window. It was barred. Belt? Blades? Bars? Where was I? The corpsman intercepted my gaze and said, "This is just the overflow ward. There isn't any room right now in the ward you're supposed to go to."

I nodded, but I did not believe him. I examined him. His face was still white with the pallor of civilization. He could not have been long out of the States. He was young, too. Above all, he had the sneering look of the sailor who finds it painful to associate with foot sloggers. I remembered Rutherford's pistol under my arm. I had not yet taken off my coat, and I delayed it till last, waiting until the corpsman had gathered up my belt and shaving gear and had started to leave the cell for the "overflow ward." I drew the pistol, shucked the coat, and then, standing naked, pointed the pistol at him, and said, "Hey."

He turned, exasperated, saw the huge pistol pointed at him, and stood transfixed. I remained silent and motionless. It was pleasant to see the look of superiority fade from his face, to see the tongue flick out nervously, like a lizard's. If I was in the Nut Ward (as I was), if they thought me crazy (as they thought all marines), I would play the part to the hilt, and enjoy it. A nude nut brandishing a blunderbuss.

At last I said, "What shall I do with this?"

He was too weak to reply, so I went on, "Here, you'd better take it and store it in the hospital property for me, or something." He took it gingerly and left. Poor, superior fool, he had not the sense to determine if it was loaded or not—which it wasn't.

In faded pajamas and red robe I went out in the ward. The first man I encountered stopped me and said, "I'm going to a party tonight and I've got to get my brain polished up. Would you mind holding it until I get a cloth?"

I knew where I was, now. Overflow ward!

"Sure," I said, humoring him. "Hand it over."

He placed his hands to his head, cupped them, affected to deposit something in my hands, scurried off, returned with a handkerchief, retrieved his "brains," mumbled, "Thanks a lot," and betook himself outdoors, to a little caged enclosure where he fluttered his handkerchief busily while murmuring nonsense to himself.

I watched him for a few moments, hoping that he would raise his head and burst into laughter. But he did not. He was really insane.

At the end of the brightly sunlit ward were tables on which the inmates could read, write or play games. Two men sat there now, playing cards. I came up and sat down.

After a time, I jerked my head in the direction of the brain-polisher and asked, "What the hell's the matter with him?"

"He's nuts," they said in scornful unison, neither looking up from his cards.

Silence.

I spoke again, timidly, "What ward is this?"

"P-38 Ward," they said, irritably.

I gathered that "P-38 Ward" was the lingo for mental ward, perhaps because many of its patients were certain that they could fly. The card players had stopped their game and were examining me attentively, as though waiting for me to expostulate, "But what am I doing here?" Rather than gratify them, I arose and wandered down to the other end of the room.

There, in a glass-enclosed cubicle, sat the Navy nurse. Hygienic, unfriendly—she would never lift a finger to nurse a man. The corpsmen would do the nursing. The nurse would keep the records. So far from being angels of mercy in the Pacific, Navy nurses were recording angels, they were accountants. They surveyed us from the eminence of their rank, for they were not nurses and we patients—they were lieutenants and we enlisted men, dirty-mouthed, half-crazy marines, to boot. We wished the Navy nurses to hell and gone, to anywhere but in the hospitals, where they got in the corpsmen's way, and infuriated the patients.

At the moment, a chubby patient was pestering her to look at a choice piece of pornography smuggled in to him by some well-meaning nitwit. I was to learn later that sex was this man's problem, as it was for many of them. She pretended to admire it and got rid of him. Then she saw me, and her frosty look made me determined to play my part again.

"Nurse," I said, looking at her fixedly, "I'd like to have my razor blades back."

"Why?" she countered, concerned.

"I want to settle a grudge."

She gazed at me in astonishment and I returned her stare. She wrote the request down as though she were recording a mortal sin in the Book of Judgment, and I walked away satisfied. To hell with them all! If they thought I was a nut, all right, I'll be a nut—at least until I see the psychiatrist.

I saw him the next day.

He regarded me good-humoredly as I came into his office and took the seat opposite him.

"What's this about razor blades?"

"What? Oh, I was just kidding, sir."

"I know you were," he said, looking at me reprovingly. "But don't do it again, eh? You got the nurse all upset."

"Yes, sir." It was difficult not to vent my vexation at having been placed in the P-38 Ward, rather than in some place which seemed more likely to cure my weak kidneys, as I called it. But I stayed silent, watching Doctor Gentle as he bent, grunting, to give me the "hammer test." This was to strike a patient's crossed leg just below the knee to measure the speed of his reflexes.

He was intent upon it, and I could study him. Square. Powerful. Squareness in body, hands and head, with power throughout. He was bald, a man of about fifty. Gentleness of manner and speech seemed to approach the effeminate, an impression fortified by a certain oversupple softness of face and body. But it was a bad impression to act upon, although it might have been deliberately cultivated by Doctor Gentle for just that purpose—to beguile the patient off his guard in order to learn more about his character.

He began the routine psychiatric examination, and from it I deduced that he was a Freudian. The majority of his questions, and all of his preliminary queries, were based upon sex. He sought abnormality. Then he asked of my childhood. Finally, after fifteen minutes, he concluded his interview, and since I seemed to be regarding him with the intentness of the accused awaiting the judge's verdict, he said:

"Just take it easy. You're going to be here for a month at least and we're probably going to see a lot of each other. So relax. As far as I can see, you seem to be all right. A bit hot-tempered, but—"

"What do you mean, hot-tempered!" I blazed out at him.

He smiled, and I might have felt foolish had I not seen the humor in it—that I was like the man running about in a frenzy, exclaiming, "Who's excited, who's excited?" After a lifetime spent in denial of my hot temper, it was a relief to acknowledge it.

He began to question me about my experiences in the war, and, as I told them to him, he shook his head from side to side, as though to indicate that my whole division, not only myself, ought to be psychoanalyzed. Then we talked of books, for he was well read, and philosophy.

Suddenly he broke it off and said, "What did you say you were?"

"A scout," I said, proudly. "I used to be a machine gunner."

"But that's no place for a man of your caliber."

Now I was shocked! The old shibboleth, intelligence! Had not our government been culpable enough in pampering the high-IQ draftees as though they were too intelligent to fight for their country? Could not Doctor Gentle see that I was proud to be a scout, and before that a machine gunner? Intelligence, intelligence, intelligence. Keep it up, America, keep telling your youth that mud and danger are fit only for intellectual pigs. Keep on saying that only the stupid are fit to sacrifice, that America must be defended by the low-brow and enjoyed by the high-brow. Keep vaunting head over heart, and soon the head will arrive at the complete folly of any kind of fight and meekly surrender the treasure to the first bandit with enough heart to demand it.

But Doctor Gentle seemed not to perceive the pride behind my words, and so I stammered and made some weak joke about it and hoped he would change the subject.

"Oh, by the way," he said. "I have that gun of yours. How would you like to sell it to me? I'd like to send it home as a souvenir."

"Sorry, sir, but I can't. It's not mine."

"Too bad," he said, rising, "but if you should change your mind, let me know. The folks back in Atlanta'd get a kick out of it."

He looked at me thoughtfully. "There isn't very much to be done about that enuresis of yours. A corpsman will wake you at intervals during the night. You aren't restricted to the ward, like the other patients. You can go to the movies and eat at the regular hospital mess. Oh, and remember—no more of that razor blades kind of thing."

That night a corpsman awakened me each hour, the next night he did the same, and the following night. But the fourth night there was no call, and the enuresis claimed me again. So the awakenings were resumed, then, without warning, stopped. Active still. It was obvious what they were doing. They were only trying to establish the legitimacy of my complaint, for this affliction is a common dodge of fakers and malingerers anxious to gain a medical discharge.

Because it was a general suspicion, I did not resent it, and soon I even forgot about it. Life was much too pleasant in the P-38 Ward, and there were too many interesting things happening. Perhaps I should have said odd things.

Among the oddest was Captain Midnight, and it may have been from him that the ward gained its fancy name. During the day he was an avid reader of comic books, especially the strips about the adventurer Captain Midnight.

At night, he *was* Captain Midnight.

He would rise from his cot, stretch out his arms as though they were wings, hunch up his shoulders, and race on tiptoe about the ward, lifting and dipping his "wings" and canting his body like an airplane, all the while emitting a droning buzz.

"Cap'n Midnight callin' the airfield," he would call. "Cap'n Midnight callin' the airfield."

Immediately, the ward took up the cry.

"Hey, Cap'n, watch out there! There's a Zero on your tail!"

"Ack, ack ahead. Careful of the flak, Cap'n!"

"Nice going, Cap—you shot that Zero clear to hell!"

The Kid was confined behind the bars which kept the violent patients separated from us. I saw him there, to my surprise. He looked at me sheepishly and asked me for some candy, which I gave him. I could not refrain from gazing at his hands, for it was the Kid who had strangled the Jap. They were the short, square hands of the painter—powerful. How much, I mused, had that deed to do with his insanity? How much was retribution, how much remorse? Or was there a difference?

I asked a corpsman about the Kid.

"He blew his stack," he said simply. The corpsman had been on Pavuvu and knew the terrain.

"You know that road around the island? And the little airplane that they park on the road? Well, this kid went down to the road one day and climbed into the plane. They grabbed him when he started the motor. Somebody asked him where he thought he was going. 'Home,' he said, 'I'm gettin' the hell out of here.' So they brought him here instead."

They had brought him to Banika instead. Not as long a trip as the Kid's insanely conceived flight home, but it would get him there eventually. The Kid's war was over. He would go home, and, probably, regain his sanity when he got there. The unbearable pressure would be off. How much pressure will it take for me, I wondered; how much longer will I hold out?

Insanity had been my foremost fear since the moment I had vaulted over the side of the Higgins Boat on Guadalcanal and seen those spiky fronds swinging overhead. To be killed—even to be taken prisoner by a cruel and vindictive foe—seemed preferable to madness. And I had always thought madness possible, not so much from within, from the pressure of events upon the mind, but from without, from a bullet, a piece of shrapnel, concussion. I had thought it physical rather than psychical.

Here, in the mental ward, I saw that I was wrong. I saw what a man's own mind, what despair, could do to him.

I am thinking of the pitiful beings they call manic depressives. These are the sons of despair. I saw them, I felt the dejection of their spirit, and I wondered sadly what could have happened to a man to turn him into a ghost walking the ward with silent lips and blank eyes.

If Banika was an island paradise, it had, for enlisted men, its forbidden fruit: the nurses.

"It isn't personal," explained the corpsman who had told me about the Kid. "It's just that they're women, and women out here are just no good. They cause too much trouble." He reflected a moment. "You know, we didn't have nurses when we first got to Banika. There was just the doctors and ourselves." He sighed wistfully. "It was wonderful. The doctors shared their liquor rations with us and everything. It was like one big happy family. We ate good, too, as good as the doctors. You never heard of a doctor pulling his rank. We got along wonderfully together." His face darkened. "Then the nurses came, and everything changed overnight. We weren't good enough anymore. No more liquor, no more top chow, no more friendliness. The nurses talked only to doctors and the doctors talked only to God. And the trouble is, our work hasn't gotten one bit easier. If anything, it's harder, what with the tension." His face got gloomier. "And look what the nurses did to the whole base. Look at the fancy stockade they had to build for them and get a whole MP battalion to stand guard over them. Look at how the men eat their heart out every time they see an officer riding around in a jeep with a nurse beside him. And how do you think they feel when they see the officer has a pistol on his hip? What the hell does that mean, eh? It means he's supposed to defend this pure woman's honor against an attack by us crummy enlisted men. We're the only ones that'd do it, y'know. The lieutenant's glands have been to Officers' Candidate School." His voice was bitter, now. "It's crazy. It's unfair. Women have no place out here. Not just a few of 'em, anyway. If they can't send a woman for every man, they'd better keep 'em all the hell home!"

The hospital had a good library, and reading became an obsession with me. I read two or three books a day, scorning the nightly movies, often reading in the head after lights out.

But at last I did go to the movies, when even my seemingly insatiable appetite for reading had been sated, and when there had begun to stir within me a vague sense of shame. The softness of my life in the hospital had begun to mortify me, and occasionally I would surprise myself comparing it with contempt to the Spartan regimen of my comrades on Pavuvu. My resentment of the "Stateside Lottery" had vanished, and I had forgotten even the reason for my flight to Banika.

Bored now with the books, and with everything around me, I decided to go to the movies. I accompanied a detachment of the men from the P-38 Ward, who were escorted there by corpsmen. There were the usual searching looks and rippling titter when we nuts took our seats in the amphitheater of coconut logs curving around the hillside. Then the island commander entered, and everyone stood at attention. When he sat down, the movie began.

There was an interruption.

Over a public address system, a voice announced: "Allied troops have just invaded Northern France. The Second Front has been opened."

Cheers and exultant shouts rose into the soft night, to be followed by a buzz of excitement, but then the film began again and silence was restored.

I arose and left the amphitheater, my heart throbbing in excitement. It was difficult to comprehend, this excitement. In it was mixed a thrill of pride, but predominating was the heartbeat of anxiety, for suddenly it had been borne in upon me that great events were happening, that the war was now rushing downhill to victory—and here was I, clad in pallid pajamas and robe, lounging around a hospital. Yearning came upon me in a rush and I wept, hurrying along the dark road back to the hospital. I wanted to rejoin my comrades.

The doctors sent me back to them soon after.

I was summoned to Doctor Gentle's office. Seated with him at his desk was the hospital commander. I noticed Rutherford's pistol on the desk, and realized that I was not long for Banika.

"There's not much that we can do for this trouble of yours," the hospital commander told me. "There's no curing it out here. What you need is a change of climate and a less nerve-racking assignment."

"You mean shipment back to the States, sir?" I asked.

He smiled wanly. "Ordinarily, yes. Unfortunately, you marines can't go home unless you're carried home. So we are sending you back to duty with the suggestion that your commanding officer have the sentry wake you during the night."

I laughed and he laughed and Doctor Gentle laughed. There was no bitterness or reproach, for they knew as well as I how impossible that suggestion was. Pity the poor sentry who should have the temerity to blunder about the lines solicitous for his comrade's full bladder. There would be no trigger fingers so solicitous for him. But I suppose the doctors had to say something.

"Don't forget your gun," said Doctor Gentle. "Sure you haven't changed your mind about selling it?"

"Sorry, sir. No, sir. Thanks again for your help."

He nodded, and I left. I picked up my toilet gear and departed the P-38 Ward and caught the next boat back to Pavuvu.

2

Pavuvu throbbed with renewed spirit. I felt it the moment I came ashore, and saw the hundreds of men bathing in the bay. They were carefree again, laughing, shouting, frolicking in the bright water like porpoises, their strong bodies glistening in the sun, the bronze of their flesh accentuated by the white midriff. I could discern it in the tidiness of the tents lying in rows among the palms, the neatness of the company streets bordered by coconuts stuck into the earth, and of the busy vehicular commerce sweeping around the single road that girdled the island. There were screen-enclosed heads, there were showers, there were basketball courts blocked out on the dried clay, there was an open-air movie, there was even a laundry battalion! But best of all was this rebirth of spirit—the old sardonic sureness of the raggedy-assed.

Such change is as sudden and inexplicable as a shift in the wind. The silent men take to cursing, and then they take to joking, and before the first sound of laughter has died in their throats, the change has been worked.

They begin to be careful of their clothes, they shave more frequently, someone finds a broom and sweeps out the tent, another takes a packing box and makes a locker of it and begins a fashion that has the whole division roaming the island for boxes or spare lumber, and, finally, a basketball or a volleyball arrives from division and teams form, by platoon, by company, or by battalion;

challenges are laid down and accepted, rivalries grow, the old designations are hurled back and forth like howitzer shells, and the great thing is abroad again, the fighting spirit is unfurling like a banner on the winds of pride, and all that remains is to draw up the plan of battle.

So I met the old spirit when I came back, and I found a thing as good or better—a new friend.

The Scholar was among a shipload of replacements who had just arrived. They were being marched to their new units as my boat pulled up on the beach. As soon as they came to the company tents, they took off their shiny Stateside khaki to exchange it for the sun-bleached uniforms of the veteran, the "salty" clothing prized for its aura of experience. An insecure replacement would feel more confident clothed in the faded ensigns of "the old breed," while the veterans, having no psychological problem of "belonging" to distort their sense of value, were quick to sense a sucker. Within a few days, the change was so complete that the veteran who could formerly be recognized by his lusterless garb was now identified by its shiny newness.

I sat in our tent, watching in amusement, when my view became blocked by a bulging sea bag being pushed through the entrance. Behind it was a sweating replacement.

"This the Intelligence Section tent?" he asked, half timidly. "Sure, c'mon in," I replied, eyeing that sea bag and unwrapping a bar of chocolate I had brought from Banika. "Put it down anywhere you want. Here," I said, breaking the bar in two, "have some candy." He took his half and shoved it hungrily into his mouth. "Thanks. We haven't eaten since we got off the ship this morning."

"Whatcha got in that bag, huh? Got any shoes?" I needed shoes badly. But in dismay my eyes fell upon his feet.

"What the hell size shoe d'ya wear?"

"Five, five and a half. Pretty small, eh?" He snickered and I lost interest in his sea bag, and somehow he did not look like a man who would trade new khaki for old. He surveyed our tent and saw my bookcase made of a packing case. "Hey—where did you get the books?"

"My father sends them to me."

"That's great," he said with quick enthusiasm. "I've got a load of books in the bottom of my bag. How would it be if I whipped them out and stuck them in with yours?"

"Fine," I said, making room for his books on my shelf, and his friendship in my heart. It was not only the books—I recall only Romain Rolland's *Jean Christophe* and something of Calderón, in Spanish—but it was the steel that I felt in him and perhaps most of all for the expression of stubbornness on that half scornful face. So we became friends and remain so still.

After the Scholar came four more replacements for our section, who were quartered in our tent. Two of them were hardly more than high-school boys, each about eighteen—the one quarrelsome, the other tractable; the first a midwesterner, the second a southerner; the quarreler aggressive and intelligent and often offensive, the mild lad shy and slow and likeable. Though dissimilar, they stuck together and became the Twins.

White-Man was the third replacement. From the hills of Virginia, White-Man was a bigot from the tip of his blunt-toed feet to the top of his high and narrow and brindle-haired head. "Lucky," he said to me once, "know whut weah gonna do after the war? Weah gonna clean up them niggahs. And when weah finished with the niggahs— weah gonna staht on the Catholics!" The tent roared with laughter, for only a humorless bigot would resent White-Man's amiable animus. White-Man was also the first drafted marine of my experience. The Corps had begun to accept draftees from the general pool—not many—but enough to weaken our own proud position as an elite. This was the only time White-Man rubbed us the wrong way, when he spoke scathingly of volunteers—"You damn fools asked for it.

Russ Davis ("The Scholar") on Pavuvu, 1944

Ah didn't. They had to come and get me." Only our silence could express our contempt.

Filthy Fred—the fourth new man—was a rawboned, eagle-beaked, easygoing farm lad from Kansas, full of the lore of the barnyard and with something of a rooster's approach to life. He was fond of applying the standards of barnyard crises to those of human life, and was not only boring but disgusting—often provoking cries of outrage from these less-than-squeamish marines.

With these replacements, life on Pavuvu now turned to training designed to integrate the new men into the division. But many of the Old Salts disdained to go through that dull dispiriting routine again, and did as I did—secured a sinecure that kept them back in the battalion area. Others, like the Artist, simply stayed aloof.

Like Achilles, the Artist sulked in his tent. Many a morning at ten o'clock, after I had finished my duties with Lieutenant Liberal, the battalion censor, duties which consisted in licking envelope flaps and sealing them closed, I came to the Artist's tent bringing a few slices of bread begged from the galley. The Artist would break out the little cans of caponata which his mother sent him regularly, and I would boil coffee and we would have a feast.

Coffee made the evenings, too. After the movies, the men would drop in to drink from the pot I had prepared. Warmed by this black liquid, they would talk and argue and jokingly discuss the comparative merits of my coffee-making and the rival beverage of the quartermaster sergeant. They would flatter me on my cooking—"best damn cuppa joe on Pavuvu"—but I think it was the conversation and not the coffee that drew them to my tent. My kitchen was not equal to the QM sergeant's. He cooked his coffee over an acetylene torch, while I was reduced to boiling it in an old can over a tomato can filled with gasoline. But if he had the cuisine, my place had the atmosphere.

The books belonging to the Scholar and me—most especially, the almanac and the dictionary—made our tent a meeting place for the battalion literati. Then there was always an argument to be had with Eloquent, who was most obliging in opposing anyone. Then, too, there was the attraction of taking coffee from the hand of an "Asiatic." This last is a term expressing the mixed reverence and fear for a man who has been in the tropics too long. I learned from Eloquent to embrace such a designation, for it made one an untouchable, almost, and automatically excluded one from dirty duty and the more prosaic forms such as falling out for calisthenics at reveille.

My having spent four weeks in the P-38 Ward on Banika made me the Asiatic par excellence. In my case, it was official. So none of the officers objected when I took to sealing the envelopes every morning for Lieutenant Liberal, avoiding all other duty, or when I clothed myself in a pair of moccasins and a khaki towel wrapped around my waist like a Melanesian's lap lap. They shrugged and tapped their heads and called me Asiatic.

Now, a person thought to be different can exercise a peculiar attraction among men, and one result of my reputation was that every night, when I had finished writing letters on the rickety old typewriter I had bought for ten dollars, I could expect the tent to fill up with the men returning from the movie, eager for a cuppa joe and perhaps a full-scale argument between the two Asiatics—Eloquent and me.

Sometimes a bottle of whiskey would find its way to our tent, either purchased for some outrageous price, or, on one occasion, blackmailed from Lieutenant Liberal, when he, deciding that the men of the Intelligence Section should stand guard with the others, let fall the fatal remark, "I am an egalitarian myself," and was immediately requested to extend his principles to his liquor ration. If the whiskey ran out too soon, I would coax a canteen of jungle juice from the Chuckler's tent, or else we would drink our shaving lotion or hair tonic. Once I drank a horrible green concoction called Dupre, and awoke with a tongue that seemed to have been shaved and shampooed.

Milton Fogelman ("Eloquent"), Robert Leckie,
Russ Davis ("The Scholar")

With alcohol rather than coffee, our voices rose from talk to song. Once again it was the ribaldries and the songs of World War One, and we even sank to a pitiful low when we began to hum classical symphonies in unison—a depth from which we were rescued by a macabre composition of our own inspired by the news that the division was ready to go again. To the tune of "Funiculi, Funicula" we sang a ghoulish serenade. We would form a circle around a man and sing:

Ya-mo, ya mo Playboy's gonna die
Ya-mo, ya mo Playboy's gonna die
He's gonna die, he's gonna die, he's gonna DIE
So what the hell's the use
You're gonna die, you're gonna die.

We sang it to all, to everyone—except Liberal, the Artist and White-Man.

Word began to spread that the next one would be quick. It would not be like Guadalcanal or New Britain. It would be rough, real rough, while it lasted. But then, home for the Old Salts. We rejoiced. That was the best way—short and sweet.

Rutherford recovered his pistol. He came one night when all were at the movies and I was alone in the tent, typing a letter by the light of a piece of rope dipped in a can of gasoline. He and a friend came in out of the darkness, like conspirators. I was glad to be relieved of it, for I had been afraid someone would steal it from me.

"See you in the old home town," Rutherford said, and slipped back into the dark with his comrade.

We left Pavuvu. Victors of Guadalcanal and New Britain, we went out to fight again; marching into the open-jawed landing craft driven up on the beach. Never before were we so confident of victory, never again would its price be so high.

3

Peleliu was already a holocaust.

The island—flat and almost featureless—was an altar being prepared for the immolation of seventeen thousand men.

Army and Navy planes had pounded her. A vast naval armada of heavy cruisers and battleships had been lobbing their punishing missiles onto that coral fortress for days before our arrival. The little atoll—only five miles long, perhaps two wide at its broadest—was obscured beneath a pall of smoke. It was a cloud made pinkish by the light of the flames, and at times it would quiver and flicker like a neon sign, while the rumble of an especially heavy detonation came rolling out to us.

Our landing craft had disgorged our amtracks about a half mile from shore. We had come rolling out of their bowels like the ugly offspring of a monster Martian, and had felt the impact of a vast roaring and exploding and hissing and crackling—the sound of the bombardment, and, so it seemed to us, the sound of the utter destruction of that little island.

Our great warships lay behind us, and before us lay the foe. Overhead all of the airplanes were ours. It was a moment of supreme confidence. A fierce joy gripped me, banishing that silly conviction of death, and I ran my eye over all that bristling scene of conquest.

Naval shells hissed shoreward in the air above us. Those of us who had been on Guadalcanal, remembering our own ordeal with naval bombardment, could spare a pang of pity for the foe—thankful nevertheless for the new direction the war had taken. Slender rocket ships and destroyers were running close in to shore, as graceful as thoroughbred horses. When the rocket ships discharged their dread salvos there came a terrible roaring noise, like the introduction of hot steel into water, and the air above them would be darkened by flights of missiles.

Now, the great furor was dying down. The curtain of fire was lifting. In my exhilaration, I turned for a last look at our landing craft, and saw the prow black with sailors waving us on, shaking clenched fists in the direction of Peleliu as though they were spectators come to see the gladiators perform.

Now, at once, silence.

The motors of our tractors roared, and we churned toward that cloud of smoke.

I had my head above the gunwales because I had chosen to man the machine gun. So had the Hoosier in a nearby amtrack. He caught sight of me, nodded toward the island and grinned. I read his meaning and lifted my hand in the gesture of perfection.

"Duck soup," I shouted into the wind and noise.

Hoosier grinned again and returned the salute, and at that moment, there came an odd bump against the steel side of our craft and then a strangled sound. The water began to erupt in little geysers and the air became populated with exploding steel.

The enemy was saluting us. They were receiving us with mortar and artillery fire. Ten thousand Japanese awaited us on the island of Peleliu, ten thousand men as brave and determined and skillful as ever a garrison was since the art of warfare began. Skillful, yes: it was a terrible rain and it did terrible work among us before we reached the beach.

At that first detonation, Hoosier and I had ducked below the gunwales, and I had not dared raise my head again until we were a hundred feet offshore.

Our amtrack was among the first assault waves, yet the beach was already a litter of burning, blackened amphibian tractors, of dead and wounded, a mortal garden of exploding mortar shells. Holes had been scooped in the white sand or had been blasted out by the shells, the beach was pocked with holes—all filled with green-clad helmeted marines.

We were pinned down.

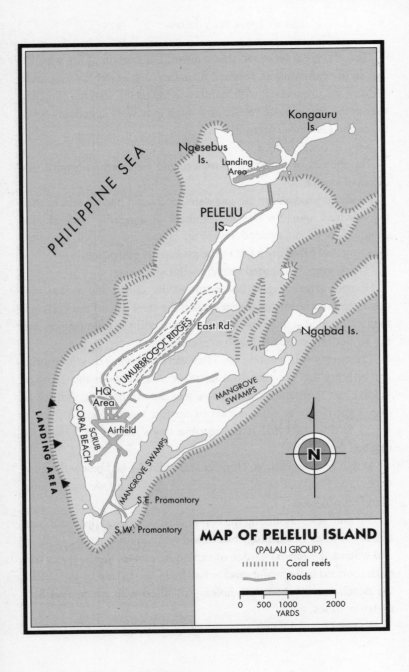

PHILIPPINE SEA

Kongauru Is.

Ngesebus Is.

Landing Area

PELELIU IS.

Ngabad Is.

UMURBROGOL RIDGES

East Rd.

HQ Area

SCRUB CORAL BEACH

Airfield

MANGROVE SWAMPS

LANDING AREA

MANGROVE SWAMPS

S.E. Promontory

S.W. Promontory

N

MAP OF PELELIU ISLAND

(PALAU GROUP)

|||||||||| Coral reefs

Roads

0   500 1000   2000
YARDS

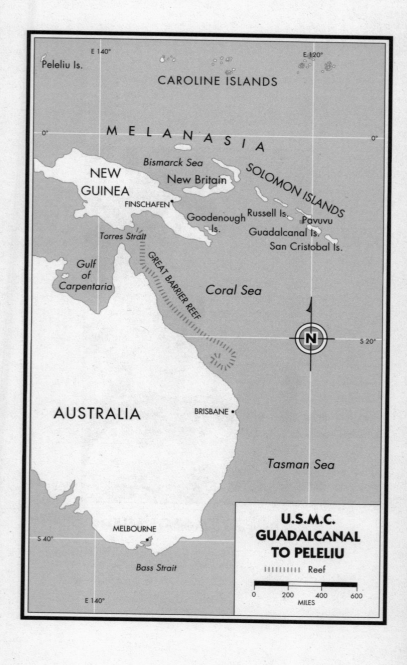

Peleliu Is.

E 140°   E 120°

CAROLINE ISLANDS

M E L A N A S I A   0°

Bismarck Sea
NEW   New Britain   SOLOMON ISLANDS
GUINEA
FINSCHAFEN•
                    Goodenough   Russell Is.   Pavuvu
                         Is.   Guadalcanal Is.
Torres Strait   San Cristobal Is.

Gulf
of   Coral Sea
Carpentaria

                                                 S 20°

AUSTRALIA   BRISBANE •

                                    Tasman Sea

S 40°
        MELBOURNE
                •
        Bass Strait

U.S.M.C.
GUADALCANAL
TO PELELIU
||||||||||| Reef

0   200   400   600
         MILES

Russ Davis and Bill Smith ("Hoosier")

With Lieutenant Deepchest of F Company, to whom Filthy Fred and the mild Twin and I had been assigned, I leapt over the side of our amtrack and scraped a hole of my own. Behind me a shell landed, blowing a man clear out of his high-laced jungle boots. He was the fellow who had been with me on New Britain when the Japs had come up behind me, the one who had fired over my head. He lived, but the war was over for him.

Lieutenant Deepchest tried to say something but I could not hear, motioning to him to write it down. He shrugged: it was not important. Just then, a marine came dashing over a sand dune in front of me, his face contorted with fear, one hand clutching the other, on which the tip of the index finger had been shot away—the stump spouting carmine like a roman candle. It was the corporal who had earned Chuckler's enmity the night of the Tenaru fight on Guadalcanal, when our machine gun, which he had set up, had slumped into the mud. Now, behind that fearful face, I thought I detected amazement and relief.

We were pinned down, but not by mortars alone. Machine gun fire came from an invincible outpost which the Japanese had blasted out of a coral promontory jutting into the bay. We had found an opening in it, and even then were filling it with all manner of small arms fire: grenades, sticks of dynamite hurled by men who had crept up to it, or billowing fire from the flame throwers who also had gained the hole—but the answering fire continued to rake our deadly picnic ground.

Examining our position, now, I saw that the beach lay before a line of scrub. Beyond this were the coveted airfield and the main enemy fortifications, which we were to call Bloody Nose Ridge. In the scrub I saw a yellow butterfly darting among the foliage and the waving pennant of a moving thing that turned out to be a tank—a Marine tank. There came a lull, and I could hear the shout that rose when the tank rumbled into position opposite the fortress that had pinned us down. It fired shell after shell down the hole, its machine gunner discharged a belt into it—but still that outpost's guns worked against us.

Then began an odd procession. The hole suddenly was filled with the figure of a Japanese soldier. He jumped out of sight. Then another. Another. Each appearance set off a mad crackle of small arms fire. We might have been shooting at rabbits, for they appeared with the quick furtiveness of rodents, disappearing just as swiftly, as though their fortress were a warren—which is what it was, for the Japanese had possessed Peleliu for two decades and had blasted into the coral a network of mutually supporting caves. When a Jap jumped, he was making his exit to another position—perhaps even scurrying away beneath us.

One, only one, of these departing defenders died. He was fat and ponderous, with his blouse and trousers stuffed with rice like the poor chow hound consumed by the crocodiles on Guadalcanal, and because he moved so slowly the bullets struck him in a sheet and disintegrated him in a shower of flesh and rice.

It was hot. The white sand burned through our clothing. It was the enervating heat of the steam room. The sweat slid into one's mouth to aggravate thirst. The water in our canteens was hot, and when I had drunk it all, I filled it with dirty rain water lying in shell craters. Peleliu has no water. The Japanese caught theirs in cisterns open to the sky, and ours had been floated in to us in gasoline drums, from which some fool supply officer had neglected to cleanse the residuary oil. Smelling and tasting of gasoline, it was undrinkable. A brazen sun beat upon us when, freed by the silence of the fortress, we rose and marched through the scrub to the airfield.

Just before the airstrip, on the edge of the scrub, lay an enormous shell crater. In this we took up positions. I met the Artist.

"Liberal's dead," he told me. "A mortar shell got him and the Soldier."

"How about the Soldier? How's he?"

"Tore his leg up pretty bad. But he's okay." The Artist laughed. "Better'n us, anyway—he's out of it."

"Yeah, too bad about Liberal, though. He was a nice guy."

"He got it in the stomach. I saw him sitting up against a tree when I got off the beach. He was laughing. I asked him, and he said he was fine. But he died while he was sitting there."

The Artist shook his head and walked away. Too bad about Liberal: all the fine education, all the good humor on that blond, blunt face, all the good will in his socialist schemes for humanity—all and everything gone, trickled away through some unknown fissure in this frail vessel of life, while the man leaned against the tree and smiled and smoked and contemplated a future made safe by an Allied victory and sure by this temporarily incapacitating wound. And so he perished, may he rest in peace.

We stayed in the crater. Our advance had halted. There had been many casualties. The defenders were resolute and resourceful. The marines began to chip foxholes in the airfield coral.

At noon I tried to eat, but I could not swallow even a mouthful of beans from the ration in my pack. I never ate on Peleliu.

Their tanks swooped suddenly upon us. They came tearing across that airfield, a dozen or so of them. It was startling. They came out of nowhere, and here were only riflemen and machine gunners to oppose them.

There was a violent outburst of gunfire. I poked my head above the crater. Through the lacy branchwork of the scrub trees I saw an enemy tank streaking along, with snipers in camouflage hanging onto the rear. It was but a moment's glance, but at the same time, my eye caught sight of a marine from F Company, a veteran, running bowlegged to the rear, his face writhing, shouting, "Tanks! Tanks!"

An officer grabbed him and spun him around and kicked him and propelled him back to his post. In the crater, we prepared for defense, like a caravan attacked by Indians. The enemy tanks whizzed past, their little wheels whirling within their tracks. Machine guns clattered, bazookas whammed—our airplanes came screeching down from heaven, and there rose the detonation of their bombs and the roar of exploding tanks.

Once a torpedo plane flashed by, so low its belly might have scraped the coral. To my right, I saw a line of our tanks advancing, firing as they came, seeming to stop each time their guns stuttered. Then it was over.

The Jap tanks had been destroyed.

I got up and made for the airfield. About twenty yards away was a burning tank. Some of the enemy dead were inside. The snipers hung in their nets like dolls stuffed in a Christmas stocking. I turned to go, and as I did, nearly stepped on someone's hand. "Excuse me," I began to say, but then I saw that it was an unattached hand, or rather a detached one. It lay there alone—open, palm upwards, clean, capable, solitary. I could not tear my eyes from it. The hand is the artisan of the soul. It is the second member of the human trinity of head and hand and heart. A man has no faculty more human than his hand, none more beautiful nor expressive nor productive. To see this hand lying alone, as though contemptuously cast aside, no longer a part of a man, no longer his help, was to see war in all its wantonness; it was to see the especially brutal savagery of our own technique of rending, and it was to see men at their eternal worst, turning upon one another, tearing one another, clawing at their own innards with the maniacal fury of the pride-possessed.

The hand saddened me and I offered it a respectful inclination of the head while recovering my balance and making a careful circle around it.

I gained the edge of the airfield and saw the other tanks and the scattered piles of corpses. Among them prowled Souvenirs, busy with flashlight and pliers. His curled mustache bristled in anticipation. But this was Souvenirs' last plundering excursion among the mouths of the dead. He was killed an hour later in an assault on an enemy position. So was Lieutenant Commando, whose epitaph Souvenirs himself had spoken. May they rest in peace.

Our casualties were extremely heavy. Before the day was done they would total five hundred in the First Regiment, something like twenty percent. This, on the first day.

We were advancing again. Our objective was Bloody Nose Ridge. This was the high ground visible from across the airfield. It gave the enemy perfect observation. Advancing across the flat table of crushed coral on which there was hardly a single depression, we were as easily sighted as clay ducks in a shooting gallery. But there was no other route and we had to take it. Grass-cutting machine gun fire swept the airfield. Mortar shells fell with the calm regularity of automation. It was as though they had determined at what rate they could kill the most of us and were satisfied with it, unhurried in its application. Marines fell. They crumpled, they staggered, they pitched forward, they sank to their knees, they fell backward. They kept advancing.

Now the day was dying amid hoarse cries for water or help for the wounded. An empty amtrack from another unit had strayed into our sector, and Lieutenant Racehorse, seeing it, bounded alongside, sprang aboard and ordered the driver to our front. Racehorse wanted to bring back the wounded.

But the driver was not eager to obey. He was from another outfit, he was tired, he saw no reason in risking his flesh for a strange officer. He said he could not obey. Racehorse told him he had better. The driver refused openly.

Racehorse drew his pistol and laid it against the driver's head and said, "Get youah ass moving," and the driver quickly shifted gears and drove frontward with a roar. Racehorse had won a Navy Cross for his bravery on Guadalcanal. He won another on Peleliu, but it was awarded posthumously. He perished attacking a pillbox, may he rest in peace.

Now it was growing dark but it was still the first day of battle. We had drawn back to consolidate, and I, with Filthy Fred, lay inside the big crater again. I had tried to eat another mouthful of beans but I could not. Tension made my stomach a vibrating intestinal harp. Finding the water in the crater exhausted, I scrambled out and headed toward the beach, hoping to find some there. Perhaps they had gotten rid of the gasoline-filthy stuff—which had already sickened many men—and had brought clean water ashore. I made my way cautiously through the brush.

Runner came out of the brush.

"Chicken got it," he said. "Damn fool kept pulling out the plasma needle the corpsman stuck in his arm. You know how Chicken was. Stubborn. I don't know," he said, shaking his head gloomily, "I don't know. Maybe he would have died anyway. It was a nasty wound. But he didn't help himself any, poor kid." Runner peered at me through the dusk. I got the feeling that he had distinguished himself that day and was struggling with his modesty to tell me. "Boy, it was rough!" he burst out. "Ask Chuckler—he'll tell you Guadalcanal was a pink tea compared to today. I mean for the fighting. And this one was supposed to be easy! You should've seen it when they threw those tanks at us! We knocked them out with machine guns and hand grenades!" he proclaimed triumphantly.

"How's everybody else?"

"Okay. Chuck and Hoosier are all right. The Gentleman got hit, though—but he's okay. Lucky bastard—he's had it." He peered at me again. "How about you? How'd you guys make out?" I told him about Liberal and the others, and he shook his head. "There won't be too many left after this one. And did you notice who's getting it?" I nodded. "All the veterans."

I asked him if he had found any water, but he turned his canteen upside down in reply. We walked back together, sadly, each to himself alone, wondering if this were to be the end.

"Remember the guys who got it back on Guadalcanal?" Runner asked. "We used to think they were poor slobs—getting it so soon.

Maybe they were the lucky ones. They didn't have to go through all of this crap and wind up getting it anyway."

"Maybe," I said. "But they never got to Melbourne, either."

"That's true. But right now I'm thinking about anything but Melbourne. I've been doing plenty of praying. And it isn't any of that no-atheists-in-a-foxhole crap, either."

Runner's dark oval face had never been so serious. I remembered that he had been baptized by Father Straight on Pavuvu. How different he was! How different everything was! Gone the camaraderie. Gone Guadalcanal. Gone the pagan naïveté of the first battle. How much easier to be a pagan again and to refuse to take the thing seriously.

We parted at the lip of the shell crater. I had never missed him and Chuckler and Hoosier more.

It was dark now but the noises of battle were resuming. Mortars were crashing again. From point to point on our lines rose the angry chatter of machine guns and rifles, sometimes sounding indignant, as though the marines resented these nocturnal intrusions in the manner of a farmer chasing poachers. Even the dark retreated, for we began to use flares. They were of the kind that had illuminated our second night of warfare, when they were dropped above the jungle roof on Guadalcanal: persistent, greenish, eerie.

Then our rockets roared overhead in a dreadful hissing barrage that must have been terrible to receive. Someone within the crater muttered that the Japs had carved a gap in our lines and that the rockets were being used to plug the hole with steel. I tried to snatch moments of sleep, lying against the crater rim with my helmet over my eyes. But it was impossible. The night passed like an interminable waking nightmare.

We met the heat of morning with dried mouths, and lips that were beginning to crack, and stomachs grumbling with unrequited hunger. The heat began to rise again refracted off the coral surface of Peleliu, baking the atmosphere, encompassing us in an oven.

"Let's go," said Lieutenant Deepchest. "Right," I said, and told Filthy Fred and the Twin to get their gear on. We left the hole and made for an opening in the scrub to the left, through which the airfield was visible. It was early morning.

We passed two marines lying in their foxholes, asleep. I bent to wake them. "Hey," I said, shaking one of them. "Wake up. We're moving out." He did not answer. He lay inert. I rolled him over. There was a bullet hole in his head. He was dead. So was his comrade.

Through the gap in the scrub I could see F Company attacking again. The Artist was standing there, watching them.

The mortars had stopped. The first F Company wave was advancing across the airstrip, running low with ranks scattered, breasting a withering machine gun fire that had begun to rake the runway. They were falling. It seemed unreal, it seemed a tableau, phantasmagorical, like a scene from a motion picture. It required an effort of mind to recall that these were flesh-and-blood marines, men whom I knew, whose lives were linked with mine. Still more was required in facing up to the fact that my turn was next. And here is the point in battle where one needs the rallying cry. Here where the banner must be unfurled or the song sung or the name of the cause flung at the enemy like a challenge. Here is mounted the charge, the thing as old as warfare itself, that either overwhelms the defense and wins the battle, or is broken and brings on defeat. How much less forbidding might have been that avenue of death that I was about to cross had there been some wholly irrational shout—like "Vive l'Empereur," or "The Marine Corps Forever!"—rather than that educated voice which said in a sangfroid that was all at odds with the event, "Well, it's our turn, now."

I bade good-by to the Artist. He looked at me sadly from beneath his helmet, his face made darker and more angular by its shadow. He cast a rueful glance in the direction of the airstrip and the still-falling men. "Good luck, kid," he said, and turned away.

I began to run.... The heat rose in stifling waves.... The bullets whispered at times, at other times they were not audible.... I ran with my head low, my helmet bumping crazily to obscure my view, like waves rising around a small ship.... In a moment I could not see Lieutenant Deepchest or Filthy Fred.... I was alone and running.... There were men to my left, still falling.... I ran and threw myself down, caught my breath, rose, and ran again.... Suddenly I ran into a shell crater full of men and I stopped running.

The crater was like an oasis. I had imagined there was no cover available on the airport, and suddenly, this. It was not nearly as large as the one in the scrub where I had spent the night. But it was large enough to contain about ten men.

Four of these were men from the Fifth Marines, among whom was a wounded lieutenant, and the rest were men from my battalion, including the commander of F Company—Captain Dreadnought! They made room for me without a word, and suddenly, with the sound of enemy shells crashing around the hole, I realized that I had found cover indeed, but also the only feature on that entire airport which enemy gunners could see and shoot at.

A heavy machine gun mounted at the lip of our crater, facing toward what we called the enemy "built-up" area—a cement-and-steel blockhouse and some barracks, the only above-ground structures on the island—had also drawn those red and roaring missiles down on us.

So far, one thing seemed to have saved us from destruction. The Japanese gunners (it was a land-mounted naval rifle, as I discovered later) could not get their shells into our pit. They could neither lower nor raise, nor shift their sights to the exact point which would land a missile among us.

Regularly, with stomach-squeezing accuracy, those shells landed before, behind and to the sides of our hole. Sometimes the shell came closer—whereupon we cringed while the fragments hummed nastily overhead—or sometimes they drew further away.

"That one was close," someone murmured, when an especially loud crash rocked us.

"Yeah," another whispered. "I sure hope they don't come up with any short shells. That might do it, y'know."

"Shut up!" Captain Dreadnought commanded fiercely. "Here," he said to his walkie-talkie man, "see if you can get that thing going. I want to talk to Battalion."

Walkie-Talkie sat below me on the crater floor. He hunched his shoulders toward me and asked me to twirl certain dials. I did, but he could not seem to get through. There came the screech of a shell. I braced my back for it, even though I knew that the ones you hear are not to be feared. But how fear the one that gets you, the one you do not hear?

Another voice was audible now. The Fifth Marines lieutenant who was wounded—who was, in fact, dying, as I learned later—was speaking by his walkie-talkie to his regimental commander.

"The glorious Fifth Marines have gone through, suh," he was saying, "and have achieved theah objective. We ah now in contact with the First Regiment."

I looked at the lieutenant. He was young and possessed of those clean-cut athletic good looks characteristic of West Point or Annapolis men. He was in pain, now, and the ordeal was beginning to wear upon the discipline of his facial muscles.

A shell screamed in and we ducked. It exploded with a shattering squeezing roar. It was the closest yet. Captain Dreadnought shouted, "Where is that fire coming from?" The men looked dumbly at one another, shrugged, and contemplated the atmosphere, through which a fine dust was falling. "Here, there—let me up there," Captain Dreadnought shouted at the man on the machine gun. He crawled up to the crater lip and raised his head. He studied the built-up area and Bloody Nose Ridge rising to the left of it. Then he crawled back to his former position, drew forth his map, examined it, and made a random mark with his pencil.

"Try Battalion again." This time contact was made. "Hello, Battalion, this is Fox Company. Enemy artillery fire sighted at 128 George. Request fire mission on same. Over."

Incredible! Captain Dreadnought had no more idea of the location of that enemy gun than he had of the shape of the enemy commander's nose! When he raised his head and took this hurried glance he saw only the blasted face of Bloody Nose Ridge. Had he seen so much as a puff of smoke, which he did not, it would have been impossible still to gauge its exact position, still more to relate it to a map. The coordinates he gave Battalion were based on hope and the law of averages. But he could expect more from the former, for the chances of his having hit upon the right spot were as great as his having called for fire upon the tip of the Japanese general's nose.

In a moment I heard the sound of our own shells roaring out toward "128 George." I looked at his tense sunburned face and wondered if he was not too disturbed by the enemy shells still falling around the pit. But then he spoke and I realized that his stupidity was matched at least by his courage.

"How many men here from the First Marines?" he asked.

We raised our hands.

"Six, eh? That ought to be enough. We'd better take that blockhouse over there. That's where all that machine gun fire seems to be coming from. As soon as this shellfire stops, we'll move out against it."

Just like that. The blockhouse had resisted even naval gunfire. It had taken bombs point-blank, and remained standing. It was obviously covered by a maze of pillboxes. We—six of us—were to take it.

Captain Dreadnought might be stupid, but no one could say that he was not gallant. I felt disgusted and resigned myself to an unprofitable death. I looked at the men from the Fifth, who were regarding us with wonder, and envied them for having retained diplomatic relations with the state of sanity. Their commander was hardly conscious, now, but he had heard. He waved a hand weakly in our direction and grinned, as though to say: "You'll never make it, but there's no harm trying." And, of course, to a dying man, I suppose there was no harm.

It had been quiet for some minutes. The enemy bombardment had stopped, as though to confirm Captain Dreadnought in his miraculous powers. From behind came a rumbling noise, and peering out, I saw one of our Sherman tanks approaching, firing at the blockhouse. Captain Dreadnought was overjoyed. A tank! With a tank to aid us, we hardly needed anybody! Six was overwhelming. Captain Dreadnought might almost do it alone!

We scrambled out of the crater and deployed behind the tank, which lumbered in the direction of the blockhouse. But the tank was now the object of the enemy gunners, and shells began to land around us again. The air buzzed and hummed again with vicious and invisible fragments of steel. It was not wise to stay close to this clanking behemoth. At that moment, the tank commander decided that it was not wise to remain such an obvious target, and shied his metal mount farther off to our right flank.

The shells drove us back to the crater. Once again Walkie-Talkie had difficulty with his apparatus. He could receive, but not send. Battalion was asking for positions. "You'd better report back to the Command Post," Captain Dreadnought said to me. "But come back out."

I scrambled out and darted back to the scrub. As I reached the C.P., the artillery fire increased. It grew furious for a minute or so, then ceased. I found Major Major-Share leaning against his pack with an expression of extreme disgust on his heavy-jowled features. A few feet away were his walkie-talkie man and Eloquent, who had inherited my old job of keeping the battalion diary. I gave him our position and sat down to smoke. I was terribly thirsty but still I smoked.

"How is it out there, Lucky?" the Major asked.

"Bad, sir," I said, adding nothing, for my notion of this battle was still a confused jumble of men and movement and explosions, in which a blistering hot airfield was somehow involved. I sat and smoked, enjoying the small shade of the scrubs. Then I arose, and said, "I'd better get back out." The Major nodded and waved "Good luck."

I struck out more to our right flank, because the artillery had begun again. As I walked, I came upon a Japanese rifle which had been thrust into the ground by its bayonet. Odd. I approached it to examine it. Perhaps it was booby-trapped. I came up to it and looked it over curiously, and there came the sharp crack of a rifle and the ping of a bullet passing me.

Another report! A puff of dust behind me. Get out of here, you fool! It's a sniper's trap. The rifle is his aiming stake! The cool brass of him—operating right inside our C.P.

I came to an ammunition dump, which had been set up on the edge of the airstrip. Stretcher-bearers were bringing in a wounded man. A bullet had pierced his shoulder and blood oozed thickly from a ragged hole. He was in a gay mood, laughing, looking up at the men who had brought him back, as though to say: "I've got mine, boys, how'd you make out?"

I took firm hold of my Tommy gun and adjusted my pack, secured my map case, and circled the pile of shell casings to return to the shell crater. It was my last warlike act. For the last time, I set my face toward the enemy.

About a hundred yards out, a shell exploded in front of me.

I veered to the right.

Another shell exploded in front of me.

I veered more.

Another shell. Another. But closer. Four more. Another, closer still. I halted. A horrifying fact became clear. I had inserted myself between the enemy artillery and their target! They were hunting something, perhaps the ammunition dump behind me, and were "walking" their fire in its direction.

There was no cover. To go forward was to die. I could only run away from this approaching death, hoping to get out of the target area before it caught me.

I turned and ran.

I ran with the heat shimmering in waves from the coral, with the sweat oiling my joints and the fear drying my mouth, with the shells exploding behind me, closer, ever closer—and the air filled with the angry voices of the shrapnel demanding my life. I ran with an image in my mind of the Japanese gunner atop his ridge, bringing each burst carefully closer to my flying rear, chasing me across that baking table in a monstrous game of cat-and-mouse, gleeful at each greater burst of speed called forth by a closer explosion—and then, tiring of the sport, lifting the gun and dropping one before me.

A shell landed alongside me, perhaps five feet away, but it did not explode, or at least I do not think it did. One cannot be certain at such times: there is a different space and time with fear. But there was the shell—a two-foot blob of burning red which struck the coral with a thunderclap and then seemed to glance off into the air to go wailing away into the bay.

With that, I called upon my remaining strength, and also then, the Japanese gunner hit his target. The ammunition dump was hit.

The war ended for me. I had been shattered. No good, a dry husk. Modern war had had me. A giant lemon squeezer had crushed me dry. Concussion, heat, thirst, tension—all had had their way with me. I must have stumbled about, unable to speak, until at last I sank to my knees beside two men scratching a foxhole in the sand. They were startled. As though from afar, I could hear them discussing me.

"He can't talk. What d'ya think's the matter with him?"

"Search me. He don't look wounded. Maybe he got a near miss. Hey, fella, what's wrong with ya? Can't ya say something?"

(Useless. I had felt like this when I was a kid playing football and had had the wind knocked out of me.)

"What d'ya think we ought to do with him?"

"I don't know. You notice he has a Tommy gun?"

"Yeah. That'd sure come in handy around here at night. I wonder where the hell them Japs came from last night? I thought the beach was secured."

"Underground. They got a whole setup underneath. Boy, we sure could use a Tommy gun. Rifle's no damned good. D'ya think maybe we ought to take him down to the aid station?"

"Might be a good idea. Poor guy looks really beat-up."

They arose and pulled me erect, got a shoulder apiece beneath my armpits and dragged me like a dummy through the sand. Like a life-sized doll in whom the spring has been broken, they dragged me to the doctor.

A corpsman laid me on a blanket and tied a ticket to me. He thrust a needle into my arm to which was attached a hose running back to a bottle of liquid suspended upside down on a wire frame. The pair who had brought me crouched beside me.

"What's wrong with him, Doc?" one of them asked.

"I don't know," the corpsman answered. "He's pretty beat-up, though. Blast concussion. I'm sending him back to the hospital ship."

One of the pair looked longingly at the Tommy gun beside me. His glance seemed to say: you won't need that anymore. I told him with my eyes to take it, and he slung it over his shoulder with immense satisfaction. Then they left. They had had their reward.

Mortars were falling as they carried me onto the beach with about half a dozen other casualties. We lay there and I wondered dully if the Jap gunners were to catch me after all. At last a landing boat took us aboard and roared off for the ship.

I began to feel shame. The others were badly wounded, some put out of pain by morphine, and here lay I in a corner, quietly retching like a frightened kitten, intact, my face unblemished, my bones un-broken. The war was ending in ignominy. I was ashamed.

My spirit crept away from the staring eyes that fastened upon us as the boat was drawn up out of the water to the deck. People in white coats thronged the rail, and two of these at the center gazed with authority into the boat, searching for the wounded most in need of aid. I shrank from that expert stare, when suddenly one of them pointed at me, and said: "Him. Get him downstairs right away."

They grasped me, stripping me naked as they did, and hurried me down a ladder, laying me on a table and again thrusting a needle into my arm. With the liquid flowing into my body came the warming flood of returning self-respect. The dull, dispiriting shame had dis-appeared the moment that pointing finger singled me out. I had been hurt. I was in need of aid. With a healing power of which he had no inkling, the doctor had restored my spirit to me.

So the war ended for me.

From the operating room I was taken to the cots below, and in the space of three days my power of speech returned and I was able to walk.

Each day for a week I ascended the ladder to the deck and gazed in morbid fascination at Peleliu a mile or so away. They were still fighting. One could hear the sound of firing. Bloody Nose Ridge rose like a blasted lunar mountain from that pock-marked coral plain.

Each day the news was bad. We were winning, but at a fearful price.

Rutherford was killed. I heard it from his friend, the short sleek fellow who had come in out of the darkness with him that night to reclaim the pistol. He had been wounded, the friend. His arm was in a sling. He told me that Rutherford had been hit by a mortar shell and been blown to bits.

Rutherford had said, "See you in the old home town." But now I would go home alone. May he rest in peace.

White-Man had been killed. He perished outside our lines during that fierce first-night rocket barrage. White-Man, born and bred to bigotry; but he died with his face to the enemy. May he rest in peace.

And the Artist. Killed by a cowardly hand. Returning alone from a night patrol, he had leapt the barbed wire guarding the C.P. and been shot in the chest by the major's batman, a coward who had not the courage to issue the challenge before he shot. The Artist was dead, a brave man, may he rest in peace.

Three in our Section to whom we had not sung that macabre serenade of Pavuvu—Liberal, White-Man, the Artist. All dead.

It had become holocaust in the fullest sense. Scores of others in the battalion perished. Captain Dreadnought fell, dead of a sniper's bullet (it had at last taken a direct bombardment from the battleship *Mississippi,* to reduce the blockhouse), his F Company but a remnant. There were those who have not been mentioned in this book, friends who did not fit the narrative, men whose faces I have not forgotten and whose bravery and sacrifice have deposited a vast spiritual credit for our nation to draw upon. These, too, fell—wrestling that island rock from the grasp of its most tenacious defender. May they rest in peace.

We were leaving. The battle had been won. Extermination had come to the Japanese ten thousand on Peleliu and my regiment—the First—was licking its wounds on the beach. Of my battalion—a force of some fifteen hundred men—there remained but twenty-eight effectives when the command came for the last assault on that honeycomb of caves and pillboxes which the Japanese had carved into Bloody Nose Ridge—in men and blood and agony the most costly spit of land in the wide Pacific. When the command came, they rose from their holes like shades from sepulchers . . . and advanced. They could not run, they could barely walk—and they dragged their weapons. But they obeyed, and they attacked. They were taken from the line on the brink of collapse.

We were leaving. The more badly wounded were to be transferred from our attack hospital ship to a splendidly equipped one that would sail directly for the States. Among those leaving was the Soldier, whom I had found on the third or fourth level below decks, lying on his bunk in an agony of suffering from a terrible hole in his thigh.

It had been stifling and I had found a helmet which I filled with water to bathe his forehead. I had found a doctor, too, who relieved him of his pain and ordered the dressings changed. I was sorry to say good-by to the Soldier, but my spirits rose as though rocketed when I saw Runner among the minor casualties transferred to our ship in exchange.

Runner still had a Japanese bullet in his arm. He was proud of it, quick to pull back the bandage and show it to me when I hailed him.

"That'll get me plenty of free drinks back in Buffalo," he giggled.

His good spirits were reassuring, almost a guarantee that the others were safe. But, of course, I asked the question, "How're Chuck and Hoosier? How'd they make out?"

"Okay, I guess—but Chuck sure got a nasty wound. Hoosier got hit, too, but not bad. He didn't get it until the sixth day. Chuck and I got hit on the fourth."

"Together?"

"Not exactly, but almost. I'll tell you." His face saddened and his dark eyes shone with compassion. "You know that replacement from Texas? The good-looking kid, nice-mannered? Well, maybe you didn't know, but he'd already had two brothers killed in the war. He was scared of dying, not for himself, you know, but for his mother. He was afraid of what it'd do to her if a third son was killed. Well, on the fourth day, they began to hit us with mortars. And this poor kid gets hit." Runner looked closely at me. "Honest, Luck, I'll never forget it. The corpsman gave him morphine right away, but it was no use. 'I'm dyin',' he said to Chuckler. 'Chuck, I'm dyin'.' Chuckler tried to joke with him. 'No, you're not, kid. It's just a bad wound, that's all. You'll be all right.' 'I'm goin', Chuck, I'm goin',' the kid said. 'I don't want to go.' And he died right there." Runner paused, and then resumed his tale. "Then the mortars came in again. Chuckler got a big hunk in his left thigh, close up to the crotch." Runner laughed in retrospect. "It was funny. He was so scared he'd lost the family jewels. 'Are they all right?' he asked the corpsman. 'Quick, tell me—are they all right?' 'Take it easy,' the corpsman tells him—'it wasn't even close. You got plenty of sack time ahead of you.' So the Chuckler lies back smiling. He was so relieved you'd think he'd only cut his finger or something. I swear he'd have begged the corpsman to shoot him if it had been the other way."

The ship's engines throbbed. We were moving. Runner and I crowded to the rail with the others, bumping against Rutherford's friend with the slung arm. In silence we studied Peleliu, tan and blasted, a few scrubs standing starkly on Bloody Nose Ridge, their ragged branches raised to heaven in supplication, like the gaunt cross I had seen in the Ozarks.

We were going to a naval hospital on Manus Island in the Admiralty group. There we would find Hoosier, and poor Smoothface, his fine white skin drawn like parchment across his small-boned face, lying in bed with a hole in his kidney, hiccuping to aggravate the pain, yet smiling at the sight of us, and there we would find many others like Amish and Oakstump until Manus would become a reunion for the remnant of the originals.

There would be a bigger reunion in San Diego, when all of us would have arrived home at last—even Chuckler would be there, leaning on a cane with the laughter rumbling from his deep chest— and once more we would be as carefree as the early days in New River, the ordeal behind us and the prospect of home before us.

But now we, the preserved, were leaving Peleliu, departing the holocaust. The ship was gaining speed. We gazed upon that diminishing dot of rock.

"So long, boys," Runner said, as we reached the open sea.

EPILOGUE

I lay in the hospital ward and the Sign of the Mushroom rose over the world.

I lay in a hospital for the tenth time since I had chosen to enter the Marines. My comrades and I had suffered in our persons as the world had suffered in her peoples since the Nazi swastika had clasped the Japanese rising sun in spidery embrace—the whole world, racked for six years like a giant organism; and now the Sign of the Mushroom was rising over it.

The ward in Newton D. Baker Army Hospital in Martinsburg, West Virginia, was quiet—shocked, still. The impersonal radio voice said, "America has just dropped the first atomic bomb in history on the major Japanese city of Hiroshima. The city has been destroyed."

Monster cloud rising over Hiroshima, over the world—monstrous, mushrooming thing, sign of our age, symbol of our sin: growth; bigness, speed: grow, grow, grow—grow in a cancer, enlarge a factory, swell a city, balloon our bellies, speed life, fly to the moon, burst a bomb, shatter a people—explode the world.

So it rose and I shrank in my cot, I who had cringed before the body-squeezing blast of a five-hundred-pound bomb, hearing now this strange cold incomprehensible jargon of the megaton. Someone had sinned against life, and I felt it in my very person.

But then I, too, sinned. Suddenly, secretly, covertly—I rejoiced. For as I lay in that hospital, I had faced the bleak prospect of returning to the Pacific and the war and the law of averages. But now, I knew, the Japanese would have to lay down their arms. The war was over. I had survived. Like a man wielding a submachine gun to defend himself against an unarmed boy, I had survived. So I rejoiced.

A few days later, the war did end, and there was a victory celebration in Martinsburg. The townspeople walked and rode around the square twice and then everyone went home. A slender Chinese gentleman, noticing my green uniform among the khaki, my ribbons and my shoulder patch, perhaps concluding from these that I had fought the Japanese, came up to me out of the crowd as I stood before the beer hall, and said, "Thank you." Then he walked away. That was victory, that was jubilation—under the Sign of the Mushroom. I returned to the hospital, stark sober. In a few weeks, I was a civilian.

A woman made heavy with the girth of affluence said to me: "What did you get out of it? What were you fighting for?" I thought to reply, "Your privilege to buy black-market meat," but I did not, for flippancy would only anger her and insult my comrades. Nor did I answer, "To preserve the status quo—to defend what I now have," for this would have pandered to her materialism, which is always a lie. Most of all I could not tell the truth: "To destroy the Nazi beast, to restrain imperialist Japan," for this she would not have understood. This we had done, and done it without a song to sing, with no deep sense of dedication.

But I could not answer the first question, for I did not know what I had gotten out of it, or even that I was supposed to profit.

Now I know. For myself, a memory and the strength of ordeal sustained; for my son, a priceless heritage; for my country, sacrifice.

The last is enough for all, for it is sacrifice—the suffering of those who lived, the immolation of those who died—that must now be placed in the scales of God's justice that began to tip so awkwardly against us when the mushroom rose over the world. It is to sacrifice that men go to war. They do not go to kill, they go to be killed, to risk their flesh, to insert their precious persons in the path of destruction.

It is sacrifice that answers the interminable argument about peace and war; whether the meek Jesus is not betrayed by the man of Mars. We have the answers of the philosophers and theologians, that a man may fight in a just war. We have, too, the ancient wisdom of the Church pointing to the impossibility of any man's ever ascertaining the justness of his cause, bidding him, if he believes his leaders to be honest, to obey them and shoulder arms.

But we have the men who say: "This is too weak. I cannot kill upon a casuistry. I must know my cause to be just. I will always fight to defend my country against an invader or to suppress an aggressor or chastise a tyrant. But I must know that this is so, and, turning to my account your own demonstration of the impossibility of ever knowing—I say with a logic as compelling as yours, a logic that does not require the blood of my brothers—I will not go."

But sacrifice says: "Not the blood of your brother, my friend—your blood."

That is why women weep when their men go off to war. They do not weep for their victims, they weep for them as Victim. That is why, with the immemorial insight of mankind, there are gay songs and colorful bands to send them off—to fortify their failing hearts, not to quicken their lust for blood. That is why there are no glorious living, but only glorious dead. Heroes turn traitor, warriors age and grow soft—but a victim is changeless, sacrifice is eternal.

And now to that Victim whose Sign rose above the world two thousand years ago, to be menaced now by that other sign now rising, I say a prayer of contrition. I, whom you have seen as irreverent and irreligious, now pray in the name of Chuckler and Hoosier and Runner, in the name of Smoothface, Gentleman, Amish and Oakstump, Ivy-League and Big-Picture, in the name of all those who suffered in the jungles and on the beaches, from Anzio to Normandy—and in the name of the immolated: of Texan, Rutherford, Chicken, Loudmouth, of the Artist and White-Man, Souvenirs and Racehorse, Dreadnought and Commando—of all these and the others, dear Father, forgive us for that awful cloud.

Robert Leckie, finally in his dress blues, 1945

Robert Leckie, office of the
Associated Press, Buffalo, New York, 1947

Robert Leckie receiving the Marine Corps Combat Correspondents Association award for Helmet for My Pillow, *1958*

ABOUT THE AUTHOR

ROBERT LECKIE was the author of more than thirty works of military history as well as *Marines,* a collection of short stories, and *Lord, What a Family!,* a memoir. Raised in Rutherford, New Jersey, he started writing professionally at age sixteen, covering sports for *The Bergen Evening Record* of Hackensack. He enlisted in the United States Marine Corps on the day following the attack on Pearl Harbor, going on to serve as a machine gunner and as an intelligence scout and particpating in all First Marine Divison campaigns except Okinawa. Leckie was awarded five battle stars, the Naval Commendation Medal with Combat V, and the Purple Heart. *Helmet for My Pillow* (Random House, 1957) was his first book; it received the Marine Corps Combat Correspondents Association award upon publication.

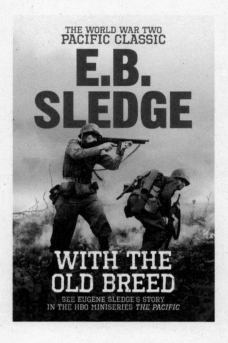

THE WORLD WAR TWO
PACIFIC CLASSIC

E.B.
SLEDGE

WITH THE
OLD BREED

SEE EUGENE SLEDGE'S STORY
IN THE HBO MINISERIES *THE PACIFIC*

You can also read the true story of EB Sledge's experiences
in some of the bloodiest battles of World War Two in *With the
Old Breed* – this too is part of the inspiration behind the
HBO series *The Pacific*.

'Eugene Sledge became more than a legend with his memoir,
With The Old Breed. He became a chronicler, a historian, a
storyteller who turns the extremes of the war in the Pacific –
the terror, the camaraderie, the banal and the extraordinary
– into terms we mortals can grasp' — Tom Hanks